The 761st "Black Panther" Tank Battalion in World War II

The 761st "Black Panther" Tank Battalion in World War II

An Illustrated History of the First
African American Armored Unit to See Combat

by JOE WILSON, JR.

FOREWORD BY *Julius W. Becton, Jr., Lt. Gen., USA (Ret.)*
AFTERWORD BY *Joseph E. Wilson, Sr., 1st Sgt., USA (Ret.)*

McFarland & Company, Inc., Publishers
Jefferson, North Carolina, and London

Cover photograph: Tank gunner Carlton Chapman manning the .50 caliber anti-aircraft machine gun, November 8, 1944 (courtesy National Archives)

Frontispiece: The author's father, Joseph E. Wilson, Sr., Co. B, 761st Tank Battalion, Siegsdorf, Germany, 1945.

Library of Congress Cataloguing in Publication Data

Wilson, Joe, Jr. 1955–
The 761st "Black Panther" Tank Battalion in World War II:
an illustrated history of the first African American armored unit
to see combat / by Joe Wilson, Jr.
p.   cm.
Includes bibliographical references and index.
ISBN 0-7864-0667-4 (illustrated case binding : 50# alkaline paper) ∞
1. United States. Army. "Black Panther" Tank Battalion, 761st — History.
2. World War, 1939–1945 — Afro–Americans.   3. World War, 1939–1945 —
Regimental histories — United States.   4. World War, 1939–1945 — Tank
warfare.   I. Title: Seven hundred and sixty-first "Black Panther" Tank
Battalion in World War II.
D769.306 761st.W55   1999
940.54'03 — dc21   99-26868 CIP

British Library Cataloguing in Publication data are available

Manufactured in the United States of America

*McFarland & Company, Inc., Publishers
Box 611, Jefferson, North Carolina 28640
www.mcfarlandpub.com*

IN MEMORY OF THOSE WHO
MADE THE SUPREME SACRIFICE

Private Clifford C. Adams (Nov. 8, 1944) of Waco, Texas.

Staff Sergeant Harvey Woodard (Nov. 8, 1944) of Howard, Georgia.

Technician Claude Mann (Nov. 8, 1944) of Chicago, Illinois.

Corporal Carlton Chapman (Nov. 8, 1944) of Pembroke, Virginia.

Private Nathaniel Simmons (Nov. 8, 1944) of Beaufort, South Carolina.

Private L.C. Byrd (Nov. 8, 1944) of Tuscaloosa, Alabama.

Private Emile I. Armstrong (Nov. 9, 1944) of Cincinnati, Ohio.

Sergeant Roy King (Nov 9, 1944) of Rouge, Michigan.

First Sergeant Samuel J. Turley (Nov. 9, 1944) of the Bronx, New York.

Private Robert W. Briscoe (Nov. 9, 1944) of Baltimore, Maryland.

Second Lieutenant Kenneth W. Coleman (Nov. 9, 1944) of Washington, D.C.

Private Willie C. Lofton (Nov. 9, 1944) of Corsicana, Texas.

Sergeant James W. Harrison (Nov. 9, 1944) of Brooklyn, New York.

Private Theodore R. Cooper (Nov. 9, 1944) of Camden, South Carolina.

Private Alexander S. Anderson (Nov. 9, 1944) of Washington, Pennsylvania.

Technician Horatio Scott (Nov 10, 1944) of Lynn, Massachusetts.

Technician Walter J. Campbell (Nov. 11, 1944) of Hempstead, New York.

Sergeant George Shivers (Nov. 11, 1944) of Bainbridge, Georgia.

Staff Sergeant Ruben Rivers (Nov. 19, 1944) of Holtulka, Oklahoma.

Technician Roderick Ewing (Nov. 19, 1944) of Oklahoma City, Oklahoma.

Second Lieutenant Robert C. Hammond (Nov. 19, 1944) of Cleveland, Ohio.

Private First Class Ivory Hilliard (Nov. 19, 1944) of Houston, Texas.

Corporal Ardis E. Graham (Nov. 25, 1944) of Raeford, North Carolina.

Technician Lane Dunn (Nov. 25, 1944) of Scottsville, Kentucky.

Private Coleman Simmons, Jr. (Nov. 25, 1944) of Detroit, Michigan.

Private James Welborn, Jr. (Nov. 25, 1944) of Jonesville, North Carolina.

Technician Horace G. Johnson (Dec. 19, 1944) of Tabor City, North Carolina.

Sergeant Robert A. Johnson (Jan. 3, 1945) of Washington, D.C.

Staff Sergeant James W. Nelson (Jan. 4, 1945) of Detroit, Michigan.

Private Thomas S. Bragg (January 4, 1945) of Elizabeth, New Jersey.

Technician Jessie J. Bond (Jan. 5, 1945) of Gates, North Carolina.

Technician Willie J. Devore (Jan. 9, 1945) of Greenwood, South Carolina.

First Lieutenant Maxwell Huffman (Mar. 20, 1945) of Newell, South Dakota.

Corporal Fred L. Brown (April 14, 1945) of the Bronx, New York.

MAY THEIR SACRIFICES NOT BE IN VAIN

The author with his father in Munich, Germany, 1960 (courtesy Joseph E. Wilson, Sr.).

Acknowledgments

This book would not have been possible without the cooperation and efforts of many dedicated people who have contributed their hard-earned knowledge, precious photographs and rare documents. Many have departed this world, leaving their stories and photographs behind. To those who contributed to this effort, I wish to express my sincere gratitude and acknowledge with great honor and respect their endowment to future generations.

To everyone who sent in memoirs, photographs, or gave interviews: I thank you. Almost everyone in the unit participated.

I make absolutely no apologies for any seeming inaccuracies in the combat stories! They are as the eyewitnesses told them and in the confusion and danger of battle, things happen for which there is no obvious explanation — the fog of war.

As I reflect with pride on the research, planning and actual writing of this book, my gratitude goes out to all who so willingly gave encouragement and inspiration. This will be a memory I'll forever cherish. I therefore hope that when you pick up this phenomenal book (because you made it this way) you know that I'm saying a warm personal thanks to you all. Over the years the notes for special mention grew and grew. I wanted to mention you all personally but I would still be writing. Please know that your kindness is etched in my heart and mind forever. Thank you.

Contents

Contents

Foreword

by Julius W. Becton, Jr.
Lieutenant General,
United States Army (Retired)

On 1 October 1944, Headquarters, Army Service Forces published ADF Manual, M5, **LEADERSHIP AND THE NEGRO SOLDIER**, some 23 days after the 761st Tank Battalion arrived at the Port of Avonmouth, England. If the Army brass had only been able to foresee the performance of this experimental battalion in combat, the Army wouldn't have wasted lots of money in the manual's publication, and almost another decade ignoring the black man's competence on the battlefield.

The 761st "Black Panther" Tank Battalion in World War II is a detailed history written by the son of a tanker in the battalion. It describes the many battles the battalion had to face — including battles far beyond most combat duties. They fought the stigma of being branded "Eleanor Roosevelt's Niggers," one of three experimental tank battalions activated to placate the First Lady, with no intended replacements to be trained. They faced widespread disapproval as the battalion which refused to court-martial Lt. Jackie Robinson when he wouldn't get off a post bus in Camp Hood, Texas, to make more room for whites; they struggled against other manifestations of racism in all forms, including questionable and even horrible utilization of the troops by some commanders of the 761st tanks in combat. Finally, they fought on the battlefield, where they were considered "the unstoppable brown tankers" by the SS troopers.

The Army leadership by and large was opposed to this experiment, relying on World War I commanders' assessments: "As a fighting troop, the Negro must be rated as second class material, this primarily to his inferior intelligence and lack of mental and moral qualities," and, "In a future war, the main use of the Negro should be in labor organizations." Even "Blood and Guts" Lt. General George S. Patton, Jr., stated that "a colored soldier cannot think fast enough to fight in armor." (It is rather ironic that the last Cold War European assignment of his son, Major

General George S. Patton, was as Deputy Commander to the black VII Corps Commander.) Lt. General Leslie J. McNair, Chief of the U.S. Army Ground Forces, was one of the few senior officers who believed that the United States could ill afford to exclude such a potentially important source of strength. In contrast to McNair's attitude, Patton persisted in his denunciations of the African American soldier. Even after the battalion's first bitter battle on November 8, 1944, at Bezange La Petite, Patton said that they gave a very good first impression, "but I have no faith in the inherent fighting ability of the race."

While some senior Army commanders retained their doubts, even to the extent that they were reluctant to accept the battalion's record, Lt. Colonel Paul L. Bates never doubted the indomitable courage of his black troopers. Division commander after division commander ended up with high praise for the Panthers. It is interesting to note that the German Army quickly learned to respect and fear the Panthers.

Major General William M. Miley, CG, 17th Airborne, wrote, "During the Ardennes operation we had very little armor unit support, but of that we had, the 761st was by far the most effective and helpful." General Miley went on to say that he would "prefer to have five tanks from the 761st than to have any larger comparable number from any other armored unit."

On March 23, 1945, the Panthers finally were permitted to fight as a cohesive unit, which is the dream of any proven combat commander. Task Force Rhine, composed of the 761st (minus its Charlie Company), the 2nd Battalion of the 409th Infantry Regiment, a reconnaissance platoon from the 614th Tank Destroyer Battalion, the 103rd Signal Company, and a detachment of combat engineers, under the command of Lt. Colonel Paul L. Bates, spearheaded the assault through the Siegfried Line. Three days later the entire 14th Armored Division passed through the breech created by the Task Force. During this period the 761st amply displayed its tenacity and heroism, capturing or destroying 7 towns, more than 400 vehicles and 200 horses, more than 80 heavy weapons, and many hundreds of small arms. At the hands of this battalion, the German Army suffered more than 4,000 casualties. Afterwards, an examination of those casualties showed that 14 German divisions had been involved in this battle, unleashing their combined fury against the 761st. Additionally, no one will ever know how many casualties were inflicted from the reconnaissance by fire. The TF covered 15 miles of death and destruction.

At the completion of TF Rhine, Major General Anthony C. McAuliffe (who, as the Assistant Division Commander of the 101st Airborne Division, told the German commander "Nuts" when surrender was demanded) sent a congratulatory message to the participants of the Task Force: "The first stage of our operation has been brilliantly completed. You broke through the famous Siegfried defenses and then boldly exploited your success. You have taken more than 4,700 prisoners. You have fought gallantly and intelligently, and you have led all the way. I congratulate you."

The 761st had 183 days of continuous combat, participated in four major Allied campaigns in six countries, and was attached or assigned to three different American armies and seven divisions. Yet it took almost 33 years and considerable political clout for the battalion to be properly recognized with the award of the Presidential Unit Citation, the highest honor a unit can receive. And over a half of a century was needed for the final approval of the Medal of Honor for Staff Sergeant Ruben Rivers. Clearly, the 761st laid the groundwork for those of us armor-types who followed.

1

The Fight for
the Right to Fight

By December 1941, Hitler had conquered and held control of more than 330 million people, from the Mediterranean to the outskirts of Moscow. The Nazis had murdered Jews routinely since 1933, but in July 1941, Reichsmarschall Hermann Göring called for the "final solution." Special killing units called *Einsatzgruppen* began rounding up Jews for extermination. In September, some 34,000 died in the ghastly pits of Babi Yar (Old Woman's Ravine) near Kiev, Ukraine. In December, Jews in Latvia were taken into the Rumbuli Forest, stripped naked, and shot. Many were only wounded and then buried alive. Some dug themselves out of their graves only to be shot again. Approximately 36,000 died in less than two weeks. This was only the beginning. Millions of people that the Nazis deemed politically and socially undesirable would die under Hitler's crushing power.

In North Africa, forces of Italian Fascist dictator Benito Mussolini invaded Ethiopia and indiscriminately used poisonous gas. Ethiopian Emperor Haile Selassie called the attack a "refinement of barbarism." In Libya, an army of British, Australian, and Indian soldiers defeated the Italians and took more than 40,000 prisoners. Several months later the desert winds shifted as Germany's Afrika Korps, commanded by General Erwin Rommel (the Desert Fox), came to Mussolini's aid.

In the North Atlantic Ocean, packs of German U-boats prowled the depths, hoping to cut England's vital supply artery with North America. In May 1941, President Franklin D. Roosevelt declared an "unlimited national emergency" and thereafter waged an undeclared war against German submarines. Destroyers from the U.S. Navy joined the British Royal Navy's convoy network in September. In October, the USS *Reuben James* became the first American warship to be sunk. By the end of 1941, nearly 200 Allied ships had been torpedoed and sent to the bottom.

In Asia, the Japanese Army swept through China, bringing millions of people under its brutal rule. The Chinese, ravaged by a 15-year civil war between Mao Tse

Tung's Communists and Chaing Kai Shek's Nationalists, could not defend against the Japanese onslaught.

In America, the daily newspapers reported death and destruction around the world. These reports touched many Americans who nevertheless felt safe and isolated from the world's problems. Military preparedness and the building of Roosevelt's "Arsenal of Democracy" created a national prosperity on an unprecedented scale that ended the Great Depression. This brought steady paychecks to more Americans than in the pre–Depression era. Life became good for many Americans who had never known anything other than poverty. The military ranks increased with enlistees and draftees during the nation's first peacetime draft, and the government encouraged the public to invest in America's security by purchasing defense bonds.

During this national prosperity, a wave of bitterness, disillusionment, and desperation swept through America's black communities. African Americans wanted their slice of the national pie of prosperity. Unfortunately, 75 percent of defense contractors refused to hire African Americans in any capacity, 15 percent offered only menial labor positions, and skilled labor was institutionally excluded. Many craft unions under the jurisdiction of the American Federation of Labor barred African Americans from admission to their local chapters. W. B. Sanders wrote the following letter to President Roosevelt: "Dear President, I am writing you in regard of the job in the Pollack Shipyard and for colored people. The boilermakers union A F of L have the contract for all skilled labor. A Negro can't go to work unless they belong to the union & the union won't accept a colored man. All welders & burners that came out of school can't get a job, so you know how a colored man feels. So in your speech you said bring your troubles to you. They are crying for help, but won't let a Negro work unless he's just a common laborer."[1]

A. Philip Randolph, head of the Brotherhood of Sleeping Car Porters, along with other African American leaders, called for an exercise of First Amendment rights by marching on Washington. The march, scheduled for July 1, 1941, was against employment discrimination and segregation in the national defense program. Randolph pledged that 100,000 Negroes would participate.

On June 25, FDR called Randolph and other African American leaders to the White House for an urgent meeting. The president urged the civil rights leaders to call off the march, characterizing it as a "bad and unintelligent" tactic. Randolph urged FDR to issue an executive order with enough teeth to compel the defense industry to give all citizens equal employment opportunities. Later that day the president issued Executive Order #8802 forbidding racial and religious discrimination in defense industries and government training programs. Randolph called off the march.

On July 19, FDR established the Fair Employment Practices Committee to monitor discrimination in defense industries. This committee, along with Executive Order #8802, was initially hailed as the most significant executive action since the Emancipation Proclamation. But disappointment followed when discrimination continued due to the committee's bureaucratic inefficiencies and stiff opposition from southern states.

Despite treatment as second-class citizens, segregation in the armed services, and being shut out of most munitions jobs, African Americans embraced World War II with the same patriotic fervor as the rest of the nation. Women knitted socks and sweaters for the troops. Victory gardens sprang up in every vacant lot. Volunteers collected metal and worked as air-raid wardens. World-renowned entertainers put on benefits to raise money. And young and middle-aged men unhesitatingly enlisted in the armed services.

With the American economy on the rise for the first time in 12 years, the debate over isolation versus intervention in the war intensified. On December 7, 1941, the debate ended when Japan attacked United States forces in the Pacific.

Early Sunday morning on December 7, Pearl Harbor on the Hawaiian Island of Oahu came under attack without warning by Japanese Naval and Air Forces. Mess Attendant Dorie Miller, from Waco, Texas, was aboard the battleship USS *West Virginia* when the general alarm sounded.

Miller, age 22, a former high school halfback and current heavyweight boxing champion of his ship, went immediately to his battle station. He found it destroyed. Despite intense strafings, bombings, and fire-swept decks, he aided in the removal of the ship's gravely wounded captain from the bridge to a safer location.

Although Miller had no weapons training, he manned a machine gun and fired back on Japanese aircraft. He blasted a confirmed two Japanese planes out of the sky.

Public pressure forced the Navy to recognize Miller's heroic achievement. The Navy reluctantly issued Miller a letter of commendation, one of the lowest forms of recognition. After more public pressure, FDR ordered Miller's commendation upgraded to the Navy Cross, second only to the Medal of Honor. African Americans had their first war hero.

Dorie Miller's mother, Henrietta Miller, proudly penned:

> Uncle Sam, I give my son to you.
> A tall young lad, whom you'll find loyal, true.
> He joins brave men who've come from far and wide
> To keep aloft our heritage and pride.
> These 18 years, my boy laughed and played.
> Grew to young manhood eager, unafraid.
> A way of life blessed by the one above,
> That he will guard with all his strength and love.
> Uncle Sam, my son belongs to you,

Admiral Chester W. Nimitz pins the Navy Cross on Dorie Miller at Pearl Harbor on May 27, 1942 (National Archives photo 08-NP-8PP-2).

Now proudly clad in uniform of blue.
When victory is won, and men again are free,
God willing, you will give him back to me.[2]

Taken by complete surprise at Pearl Harbor, the United States suffered the loss of 18 ships sunk or seriously damaged; 347 aircraft destroyed or disabled; Hickam, Wheeler, Ford Island, Kaneohe, and Ewa in flames; 2,403 Americans dead and another 1,178 wounded. To inflict this lethal pain, the Japanese had to sacrifice fewer than 100 men, 29 planes and five midget submarines. On December 8, 1941, FDR asked and received from Congress a declaration of war against the Imperial Japanese Empire. Two days later, Hitler and Mussolini declared war on the United States of America. A stunned America found itself in World War II.

With the hope of the world resting with America, FDR challenged the nation with these words: "We are now in this war. We are in it all the way. Every single man, woman and child is a partner in the most tremendous undertaking of our American history. We must share together the bad news, the good news, the defeats, the victories, the changing fortunes of war."

The fear of a Japanese attack on the West Coast coupled with the built in prejudices of wartime America started a deplorable search for scapegoats. This led to the forced removal of Japanese Americans to relocation centers in the nation's interior. The government claimed it was forced by public hysteria, agitation by the press and radio, and finally, military pressure to establish a War Relocation Authority mandated by Executive Order #9066 and signed by the president. Under the jurisdiction of the Western Defense Command, approximately 110,000 Japanese-born Issei and American-born Nisei were relocated in the spring of 1942.

During this period Dorie Miller and his mother went on a national tour for the War Department. They went mainly to the black communities, where they encouraged enlistments, sold war bonds, and supported the war effort. Two years later Miller found himself still a messman, this time aboard the escort carrier USS *Liscome Bay*. Early Thanksgiving morning of 1943, Miller's new ship rolled over and sank in about six minutes after being struck by two Japanese torpedoes near the Gilbert Islands. Mrs. Henrietta Miller was heartbroken from the news that her son had been trapped inside the burning ship as it went down. Dorie Miller was reported missing in action and never heard from again.

Filled with a patriotic zeal, African Americans sought to be a part of the crusade to crush the oppression imposed on the world by the Axis Powers of Japan, Germany, and Italy. Allowed to participate only under the same humiliating discrimination that was their plight since the Reconstruction period following the Civil War, black soldiers found their assignments menial and unglamorous: digging ditches, driving garbage trucks, sweeping out warehouses, and slinging bedpans in hospitals.

Before and during this period of mobilization for war, the Office of the U.S. Army Ground Forces in Washington debated whether or not to use African American soldiers in armored units. The power structure in Washington fostered the attitude that African Americans did not have the brains, the quickness, or the moral stamina to fight in a war. Referring to their experiences from World War I, the commander of the 367th Infantry Regiment, 92nd Division, stated: "As fighting troops, the Negro must be rated as second class material, this primarily due to his inferior intelligence and lack of mental and moral qualities."[3] The commander of the 371st Infantry Regiment, 93rd Division, stated: "In a future war, the main use of the Negro should be in labor organizations."[4] George S. Patton, Jr., in his book *War As I Knew It*, stated his opinion: "A colored soldier cannot think fast enough to fight in armor." The armed forces embraced these beliefs and recommendations, overlooking the documented fact that African Americans fought with courage and distinction in every war and conflict ever waged by this nation from the Revolutionary War through World War I. They especially overlooked the fact that the four separate regiments of the 93rd Division served with the French in World War I and that the French government awarded the coveted Croix-De-Guerre to three of the four regiments and to a company of the fourth, and also to the 1st Battalion, 367th Infantry Regiment, 92nd Division.

Against this mindset, Lt. General Leslie J. McNair, Chief of the U.S. Army Ground Forces and main proponent on the side to allow African Americans into armor, had to fight. He never accepted the vehement denial of the fighting qualities of the African American soldier. He believed this nation could not afford to exclude such a potentially important source of strength.

The Negro Press, the National Association for the Advancement of Colored People (NAACP), and the Congress of Racial Equality (CORE) put increasing pressure on the War Department and the Roosevelt Administration to allow African American soldiers to serve on equal footing with white soldiers. Ira Lewis of the Pittsburgh Courier inspired the "Double V Campaign" that called for victory at home and victory abroad. Labor leader A. Philip Randolph, NAACP activist Walter White, educator Dr. Mary McLeod Bethune,

Lt. General Leslie J. McNair, Chief of the U.S. Army Ground Forces, never accepted the vehement denial of the fighting qualities of the African American soldier (National Archives photograph 111 SC-251475).

and other civil rights leaders fought with the Negro press for this victory at home that would mean full civil rights for future generations.

The president's wife was ahead of her time regarding the equality of the races, and stood up front with the civil rights leaders and the Negro press. Eleanor Roosevelt began her anti-racist struggle in the 1930s. It was she who chastised the Daughters of the American Revolution for their refusal to allow black opera singer Marian Anderson to perform at Constitution Hall. She then arranged for Marian Anderson to sing at the Lincoln Memorial. In 1934, she assisted Walter White in the struggle to place into law the Costigan-Wagner Anti Lynching Bill. She invited African American citizens to the White House as guests and friends. The treatment of African American servicemen was one of her chief concerns, and she was determined that they would receive a chance to fight in this war. She stated her views clearly: "A wind is rising throughout the world of free men everywhere, and they will not be kept in bondage."[5]

Tuskegee Airman Celes King III recalls how Eleanor Roosevelt helped to disprove the myth that African Americans did not have the intelligence to fly or the courage and discipline it took to fight in a war:

> Of the few people that had an impact on opening up the U.S. Army Air Forces for blacks in the air, you certainly could not overlook Eleanor Roosevelt. She had a mind of her own and sat in on many instances with the President in crucial meetings. She had no reservations to raising issues she felt were in the interest of this country. There were two separate instances where she had a major impact.
>
> One would be when she went to Tuskegee and went to Moton Field where blacks were beginning to train. There she got into one of the aircraft and went around the field for a spin. And of course, needless to say, the secret service people just about had a fit. They were on the phone calling Washington to see what to do. There was no controlling her. The next day's news across the country addressed the issue of her riding in a plane being flown by a Negro. It certainly did give impetus to our position.
>
> The other time was when she was sitting in the White House, probably the Oval Office. At that time the President and members of his military staff were discussing the situation of what they were going to do about all these white lads who were being shot out of the sky. At that time Eleanor Roosevelt stepped in and said: "There is no reason not to let the Negroes go over and have an opportunity to fight." That was all it took.
>
> We were eminently qualified to fly because we had been spending a lot of time practicing. That was one of our hold cards, this is, we had more of an opportunity to practice.[6]

Secretary of War Henry L. Stimson had little patience with Eleanor Roosevelt's

Tuskegee Airman Celes King III in his B-25 bomber receiving flight instructions from George Matthews (courtesy General Celes King III).

liberal views and her desire to advance civil rights while there was a war going on. To pull the thorn from his side he appointed Judge William Hastie, an African American, to handle the sticky issue of race relations for the War Department. Judge Hastie lobbied for integration in training centers and combat operations. Secretary Stimson, influenced by the strident traditional racism of the South, resisted change. At times notations with the force of "not to be shown to Judge Hastie" were attached to papers dealing with phases of Negro troop utilization. Hastie often replied: "I wish again to emphasize the fact that the principal usefulness of this office is destroyed if we are not consulted with reference to such matters." After two years of frustration, Judge Hastie resigned in disgust. He was succeeded by Truman K. Gibson, Jr., who was described by *Time* magazine as "a less insistent Negro."[7]

Along with the appointment of Judge Hastie, Colonel Benjamin O. Davis, Sr., was nominated for promotion to brigadier general. The War Department committed itself to these appointments in answer to the promises of the 1940 political campaign. However, African Americans still remained in segregated units.

The contrast between Hastie and Davis could not have been clearer. The 36-year-old judge was an activist by nature. The 64-year-old general, who had served over 40 years in the U.S. Army, had embraced early in his career the philosophy that the best way for an African American soldier to survive in the military was to accept his second-class citizenship. Although Davis became the first African American to achieve the star rank, the message he sent to the black soldier was: "You are my color, but not my kind!" This floated through the ranks, causing black soldiers to feel that the general considered himself better than they.

For a number of years the judge and the general urged the War Department to assign black troops to combat units. In 1942 the War Department appointed an advisory committee for policies on "Race Troops"—a euphemism for black troops.

One of the committee's recommendations was that an all-Negro parachute battalion be formed. Army Chief of Staff General George C. Marshall directed that a parachute company be organized, and designated the 555th Parachute Infantry Company.

Twenty hand-picked enlisted men were selected to undergo airborne training to form a test platoon. As word of this experiment reached their white counterparts, bets were wagered. Many believed that black men lacked the courage to become paratroopers. Sixteen of the original 20 earned their airborne wings and formed the foundation of what became the 555th Parachute Infantry Company and ultimately the 555th Parachute Infantry Battalion, the "Triple Nickels."

In 1943, Japan began the launch of high-altitude balloons carrying incendiary bombs across the Pacific Ocean. A few landed in Washington, Oregon, Idaho, and Northern California. These bombs caused intense forest fires that were not revealed to the American public. The "Triple Nickels" fought these fires as smoke-jumpers in the highly classified "Operation Firefly," their only deployment of the war.

In March 1941, 98 African American enlisted men reported to Fort Knox, Kentucky, from Fort Custer, Michigan, for armored warfare training with the 78th Tank Battalion. The pioneer tankers trained steadily as more enlisted men from other U.S. Army installations joined their ranks. In June of the same year, the Army designated the 758th Tank Battalion (light), "light" indicating light tanks. The battalion continued to train in tank operations, mechanics, and related phases of mechanized warfare.

The M-5 Stuart light tank had a crew of four. Powered by twin, 220-horsepower Cadillac V-8 engines, it had a maximum speed of nearly 40 mph and an open-road cruising range of 172 miles. After modifications it could move faster. It was armed with a .30 caliber machine gun mounted to fire along the same axis as the main armament, a 37 millimeter cannon. When the tracer bullets from the .30 caliber showed they were on the mark, the cannon could be fired for a direct hit. The M-5 also was armed with two more .30 caliber machine guns, one on the turret and one in the bow. The light tank was employed to provide stinging firepower, mobility, and crew protection in screening and reconnaissance missions.

E. G. McConnell, 16 years old at the time, remembers his rail journey from Camp Upton, New York, to Fort Knox, Kentucky, for basic training in the armored specialty: "The cars were not integrated at all, and they put all of the black cars at the front part of the train where all of the soot and ashes were. As it was slowly climbing the hills in Kentucky, they came through our cars and ordered us to pull our shades down. I couldn't understand this. My curiosity got the best of me, so I went between the cars to see exactly what was happening, why we had to pull our shades down. I saw a bunch of hillbillies out there, this was real hillbilly, redneck country. And they were waiting alongside the tracks with rifles. I later found out that several troop trains were fired on. So they were ordering us to pull the shades down for our own safety. Yeah, and we were going to fight for the whole United States, not just Harlem."[8]

Franklin Garrido describes his first trip to the South and how segregation struck him:

Sixteen-year-old E.G. McConnell in 1942. "Moms went back talking to the recruiting sergeant, 'Take care of my boy.' Good God! Was I embarrassed!" (courtesy E.G. McConnell).

761st Tank Bn.

26th Inf. Div.

87th Inf. Div.

17th Abn. Div.

79th Inf. Div.

95th Inf. Div.

103rd Inf. Div.

71st Inf. Div.

Patches representing each division that the 761st Tank Battalion fought with during their 183 days of unrelieved Front Line Duty.

Segregation affected me hard. I was born and raised in California and I never knew de facto segregation. I was happy go lucky and I didn't know I was segregated. I was shocked as I got off the train in Louisville. I was warned in advance by my parents. When I got off the train again at Fort Knox, the first thing that hit me in the face was the "white" and "colored" signs. I was shocked, it was really traumatic. I was prepared for it, but I wasn't prepared enough.

At Fort Knox everything was segregated, including the training barracks. They had "colored" and "white" drinking fountains. They had "colored" and "white" latrines. In some of the barracks they had three toilets, one for the officers, one for the white enlisted men and one for the black enlisted men. With all that plumbing and everything the War Department could have built more tanks. That's how I felt about segregation"[9]

Christopher P. Navarre recalls segregation at home and his days in the Army before he came to the 761st Tank Battalion later in the war:

I was born in LaFayette, Louisiana, on January 20, 1920. I attended a segregated Catholic high school and a segregated Catholic seminary for the priesthood. I recall during my school years we were not permitted to drink at any public water fountain, eat in any white restaurant, or go into any white tavern. We were allowed to be buried in the same graveyard, but only in a small plot in the rear section. We were allowed to go to the Catholic church but had to remain in the rear and only sit in the rear seats if they were not occupied by whites. We were allowed to attend the movie but we had to enter through a side door leading to a small balcony in the rear.

In 1940 I entered the United States Army under segregated conditions and was assigned to the 25th Infantry Regiment (Buffalo Soldiers) at Fort Huachuca, Arizona. It was composed of white officers, real Indian Scouts, and all colored enlisted men. We also had dogs, mules, and horses with military ranks.

During my assignment with the 25th Infantry Regiment, Pearl Harbor was bombed and the entire United States Army began mobilizing. One unit of my battalion was dispatched to Fort Polk, Louisiana, by motor convoy. We were scheduled for a two-night bivouac in Brown Woods, Texas. Upon arriving we were welcomed by a hostile demonstration. On the first night of our bivouac some of the colored soldiers were attacked and beaten, which resulted in a riot, my first riot. The stay was cut short and we departed the next day for Fort Polk, Louisiana.

Upon arriving at Fort Polk, part of my unit was assigned cadre mission to Van Dorn, Mississippi. Within two months of our arrival, friction between the colored and white soldiers was such that a riot erupted, my second riot. We managed to complete our training assignment and began maneuvers in preparation for overseas move-ment.[10]

The War Department activated five tank groups made up of three tank bat-talions each. The 5th Tank Group, commanded by Colonel LeRoy Nichols, was to be made up of black enlisted personnel and white officers. With the 758th Tank Battalion in place, two more tank battalions were needed to complete the 5th Tank Group.

On March 15, 1942, the War Department ordered the activation of the 761st Tank Battalion (light). The actual activation came on April 1 with Major Edward E. Cruise as the first commanding officer. A cadre of enlisted men from the 758th, along with officers and enlisted men from the Armored Force Replacement Train-ing Center at Fort Knox, formed the 761st Tank Battalion (light) at Camp Clai-borne, Louisiana. The authorized strength at activation was 36 officers and 593 enlisted men.

2

Camp Claiborne

Two months prior to the activation of the 761st Tank Battalion, Alexandria, Louisiana, experienced a bloody race riot. On Saturday night, January 10, 1942, a number of black soldiers from northern states who were unfamiliar with the implications of "Jim Crow" reacted to the violent arrest of a black soldier by white MPs. Hostilities flared in front of the Ritz Theater when city and state police engaged the black troops. As word spread, additional MPs from Camp Livingston and a mob of white civilians swarmed in and started busting heads. Many black civilians were trapped in the melee along the four block corridor of Lee Street, a bustling thoroughfare through the isolated black section of town where brothels and bars were hosts to nightly fistfights and stabbings.

The MPs were mainly from the 32nd Military Police Company. The black troops were from the 367th Infantry Regiment and the 758th Tank Battalion stationed at Camp Claiborne, and the 350th Field Artillery Regiment quartered at Camp Livingston. Although clubbed, tear-gassed, and fired on by shotguns and pistols, the black troops fought back using bricks, rocks, and sticks. By 2200 hours the battle was over. Lee Street resembled a war zone. The beaten soldiers left standing awaited transfer back to camp to be confined to quarters. The bodies of others lay where they had fallen.

The sector of Lee Street where the deadly clash occurred was immediately cordoned off and cleaned up. The Army refused to divulge any information other than prepared general statements, and denied the press interviews with the soldiers who had been involved. The coverup was perhaps perpetrated to avert further divisiveness on the home front.

Despite the Army's attempt to restrict coverage and the conservative newspapers printing, "DON'T BELIEVE THE WORST," word got out that many black soldiers had been killed. The city's police force was described as "The Famous Alexandria Nigger Killing Squad." The riot, it was said, "gave them the opportunity that they wanted, a slight excuse to shoot and beat Negro soldiers, as well as a chance to remind Negro civilians that this is still the South."[1]

James LaFourche, NAACP public relations council and president of the New Orleans Press Club, submitted a report to Walter White, the executive secretary of the NAACP. LaFourche reported that from his "closest informants" he had learned of the deaths of ten black soldiers in the Lee Street riot. He made numerous references to indiscriminate shootings of black civilians as well as soldiers. He made it clear that in gathering this information he had placed himself in great peril, expounding: "I beg to inform you after a very dangerous undertaking by me, the facts as they happened, and told to me, by persons who miraculously escaped...."[2]

Two weeks after the Lee Street riot, Cleo Wright was savagely murdered by a white mob in Sikeston, Missouri, in one of the most brutal lynchings ever recorded. These events became a harbinger of what would magnify the plight of African Americans during the war.

David J. Williams II recalls his arrival to Camp Claiborne: "When I got to camp, driving through the nice white barracks, this guy named Chico from Detroit was driving me. I asked, 'Where are we going?' He said, 'Lieutenant, you'll see.' I looked down in a valley and it looked like a Civil War lithograph, weather-beaten tents. He said, 'You're in the tent at the top of the row.' I thought that being an officer I would at least have something."[3]

Williams went on to describe the welcome he received from the commanding officer:

> The next day I reported in to Captain Barnes, 758th Tank Battalion. Captain Barnes sat me down and said, "Boy, I'm gonna teach you about Nigras." I didn't know what to say. Then he said, "You're down here with Eleanor Roosevelt's niggers, boy! These people you've got to handle different. You're young and you're from up East." My Dad's friend, Ira Lewis, put my face on the front page of the Pittsburgh Courier with the headline: "Pittsburgh Industrialist's Son And Politician Goes With Race Troops." Captain Barnes had this and said, "Your old man has influence. These Nigras ain't gonna fight. Your old man put you in a safe place." Imagine, telling me this. This was the greatest war in history, everyone wanted to fight. We had two enemies to fight, Hitler and Hirohito. Who needed better enemies? So I'm sitting there and Captain Barnes is saying "You're not going nowhere, we're just marking time down here." Then 1st Sergeant Sam Turley came in. He said, "Turley, I want you to meet our new 2nd Lieutenant from up East, from the uppity college, Yale University." So I shook hands with Sam Turley. Captain Barnes said, "Turley, get out of here!" He stuck his finger out at me and said, "Boy, don't you ever put yourself on the same level with a Nigra!" Well, my 1st Sergeant from the 70th Tank Battalion, where I went to OCS, our Captain and Colonel had us both for dinner. I said 1st Sergeants run the Army, they command respect. He said: "Boy, you don't know nothing! You're up in that college and the only Nigras you see up

there are sheltered." So two weeks later he called me in and said, "I'm getting rid of you. April Fool's Day they created another Nigra tank battalion, the 761st." So he kicks me and Turley out and said, "Boy, you done ruined my best 1st Sergeant."[4]

The War Department designated Camp Claiborne on October 28, 1940, from what was formerly Camp Evangeline in the early 1800s and later Camp Beauregard. It was located in Rapides Parish on the west side of U.S. Highway 165 about 17 miles southwest of Alexandria, Louisiana. In the snake infested swamplands within the Evangeline section of the Kisatchie National Forest, the camp consisted of tents, hutments, and only a few permanent structures.

The nearby communities harbored an unyielding tradition of intolerance, segregation, and a doctrine of black inferiority and white supremacy that they and their ancestors had cherished for over a century. The sight of proud black men roaming the area with their heads held high was an outrage that would not be tolerated. The exasperated white community defended their traditions through intimidation and Ku Klux Klan-inspired violence. The African American who ventured off camp risked harassment, humiliation, and physical harm.

The "Panthers" from the North had to learn in a hurry that they must step off the sidewalk when approaching a white person. They found out the hard way that a "Negro" could be beaten and tortured to death and that a "Negress" could be violated by white men without any protection and recourse from the law. Voting and other basic rights were unheard of.

L. Z. Anderson recalls how this mistreatment often ended up: "They would always find one or two dead right out from the post. These guys would leave the post and go to the little old towns right out of the camp. There were a lot of other black soldiers down there. There was an engineer outfit down there. Most of the time it was some of their boys. I don't remember us ever having one of our boys found dead, but they found black soldiers dead down there all the time."[5]

Anderson went on to describe how he, on few occasions, went into town: "We stopped going into town on weekends, we went on Mondays to avoid trouble. The bus depot down on Lee Street is where a lot of the problems would start. When I got off the bus, I caught a cab and went directly to our USO or to 3rd Street. I didn't spend much time there, I would always go down to lower 3rd Street where it was real quiet. I met a few nice people there and never got caught up in any of the madness. However, I knew what went on. I never came in contact with any whites from there. I remember we had some white soldiers who would go around with us in Alexandria. They would associate with us because they couldn't associate with the other white boys because they were Yankees. They caught hell too."[6]

Franklin Garrido will never forget the hostility there: "I didn't take any chances by putting myself in a position where I could get into trouble. It was in the air. We knew that at Camp Claiborne and Camp Hood that the bus drivers wore pistols. We knew that if they told you to go to the rear and you didn't they would stop at the nearest sheriff or MP station. I personally did not try them. I just went along with the program. It was a hostile environment."[7]

Training for the 761st Tank Battalion intensified at Camp Claiborne with Major Edward E. Cruise at the helm as the first commanding officer. With an initial strength of 313 black enlisted men and 27 white officers, the battalion enjoyed high morale. On May 28, 1942, 216 enlisted men from the Armored Force Replacement Training Center at Fort Knox, Kentucky, joined the battalion as fillers.

The battalion's morale remained high despite substandard living conditions, limited recreation, and mistreatment aimed at its black members. The hostile treatment received from white soldiers was condoned by the camp's leadership. German prisoners of war roamed the camp and enjoyed rights and privileges that the black soldiers were deemed unworthy of. The Army's official policy was nondiscriminatory, but Camp Claiborne and all Southern Army camps operated under the Jim Crow laws of "separate but equal."

The War Department had a long-standing policy that decreed white Southerners, by virtue of their life experiences, best knew how to handle Negro troops. These officers cleverly played upon factors such as skin color, age, and geographic origin of their men. They used artful and insidious means to instill fear, envy, and distrust for control purposes. They took the biggest, nastiest, loudest, and most brutal black soldiers and made them sergeants. This was practiced during slavery and passed down through the generations. Captain Charles Wingo, the commanding officer of Charlie Company, 761st Tank Battalion, gave David J. Williams II, a Northern white officer, some advice: "You gonna learn, lieutenant, you got to have a mean coon ... to keep these boys in line."[8]

With service clubs, movie theaters, and post exchange (PX) facilities under strict segregation, movement around camp was limited. Soldiers of the 761st often found themselves confined to their barracks to prevent civil disturbances. Most of the Panthers stayed in the clear and concentrated on mastering the intricacies of the light tank.

Franklin Garrido describes the barracks he stayed in: "Camp Claiborne was a miserable camp! We had miserable barracks, one story with coal heating stoves on each end of the barracks. I think maybe 12 bunks each. In the summer they had screens and mosquito nets."[9]

On July 26, morale received a boost and racial tensions were lowered with the arrival of the battalion's first black officers. The new 90-day wonders came from the Officer Candidate School (OCS) of the Armored Force Replacement Center. The 2nd lieutenants were Charles H. Barbour of Junction City, Kansas; Samuel Brown of Charleston, South Carolina; and Ivan Harrison of Detroit, Michigan. First assigned as platoon leaders, they later became staff officers and unit

July 4 —
1942

Leonard Keyes and his wife, Dorothy. Camp Claiborne, Louisiana (courtesy E. G. McConnell).

commanders. Other officers joined the battalion at various intervals, some from the Cavalry Replacement Center at Fort Riley, Kansas.

Three months before this assignment of black officers, Brig. General R. W. Crawford of the War Department's general staff submitted a discouraging memorandum to General Dwight D. Eisenhower: "Probably the most important consideration that confronts the War Department in the employment of the colored officer is that of leadership qualifications. Although in certain instances, colored officers have been excellent leaders, enlisted men generally function more effectively under white officers. Officers experienced with colored troops lay this to the lack of confidence on the part of the colored enlisted men in the colored officer."[10]

On August 23, the 761st Tank Battalion, with a strength of 34 officers and 545 enlisted men, departed Camp Claiborne for a one-week training exercise with the 78th Infantry Division. The maneuvers consisted of a mounted field march with full combat gear to Camp Livingston for a field exercise in the Kisatchie National Forest. Armored field operations conducted there pressed into service fire and movement tactics against fixed fortifications set up by the 78th Infantry Division. The weather was warm, humid, and clear; the battalion's morale, high.

Johnny Holmes recalls the area around Camp Claiborne: "They trained us in the back country, and it's like a jungle in there. You can see moccasins 16 feet long. This is the truth. And some of the biggest rattlesnakes I ever saw in my life was out there. There were seven, eight foot long rattlers. Heads as big as tarantula spiders. Good God! They were as big as your fist."[11]

The 761st returned to Camp Claiborne with a new sense of confidence. The maneuvers acclimated the Panthers to armored field operations in a far more useful manner than could have been achieved through routine training at Camp Claiborne. On September 7, the battalion received more enlisted men from Fort Knox, bringing its strength up to 34 officers and 603 enlisted men.

Leonard "Smitty" Smith recalls training at the camp: "It was very intensive. We had so many seconds to get in and out of a tank. You had to learn each man's position ... how to drive, how to be a bow gunner, how to load, how to shoot. We had to learn each other's position so well that in case anything happened, the bow gunner could drive or the driver could be a gunner or a loader. We had to learn how to take weapons apart almost blindfolded. We shot .45's, machine guns, all types of weapons. We went to the range practically every week. We kept our tanks clean. They shone almost like they were Simonized. When we came back from any trip, you better believe we cleaned those tanks before we ate. On maneuvers, we had combat simulations. We were shooting live ammunition. We stayed out in the rain, we bivouacked, we ate out as though we were in actual combat."[12]

Franklin Garrido recalls certain individuals in the training program who had a knack for tank driving: "The Mississippi contingent, the ones from Camp Shelby, made excellent drivers. My best friend, Dewey McFarland, said that was from plowing with mules. He said, 'If you can control a mule you can control a tank.' He was probably the best tank driver in the 784th. In addition to being a good driver he could also maintain a tank. His engine compartment was always like a refrigerator inside. His tanks were always clean, spotless."[13]

On September 10, 23 officers and 191 enlisted men from the battalion received the American Service Medal, also known as the "Pre Pearl Harbor Medal." Again on October 28, 41 more enlisted men received this award.

On September 25, five more black 2nd lieutenants joined the 761st Tank Battalion. They were Carl Bowman from Los Angeles, California; Spencer Hardy from Chicago, Illinois; John D. Long from Detroit, Michigan; Irvin McHenry from Leavenworth, Kansas; and Warren F. Taylor from Philadelphia, Pennsylvania. Initially assigned as platoon leaders, they later became staff officers and unit commanders.

Later, Charles Gates, a former Buffalo Soldier, came to the 761st as a 2nd lieutenant. He recalls his journey:

> I was 29 when I joined the service on April 10, 1941. I was sent to Fort Riley, Kansas. You had the Ninth and Tenth Cavalries there, who established a heck of a record. I might attribute my success to the training I received from old soldiers who had no more than a fifth-grade education. Regular army men. I had noticed that every new white officer who came there was told to observe the old black sergeants.
>
> They asked if I'd be interested in goin' to OCS. I said no, I wanted to do my 12 months and get out. The regimental commander said, "Do you know any question about the Field Manual, FM105-dash-one?" I said yes. He said, "What are you supposed to do when a commanding officer requests you to do something?" I said, request in that particular case is considered an order. He said, "Well, I'm requesting that you just sign these papers." So that's how I got stuck and ended up goin' to Officer's Training School. I did that in July of '42. Fort Knox, Kentucky.
>
> I had been strictly an outdoors man. To be inside a building and listen to a monotone all day long, I couldn't take it. I did nothing but sleep those first days. The instructor said, "You sleep in my classes, you'll not get anything but a bunch of demerits." I said I didn't want to come here anyway. After six weeks, we had our first examinations. Fifty percent of every OCS class lost in the first examination. I ended up with an average of 96 point-something. So the last six weeks, they just said, let him sleep. My success came as a result of the training I had gotten at Fort Riley.[14]

On November 22, Lt. Colonel Edward E. Cruise transferred out of the battalion and Major John R. Wright, Jr., assumed command. The battalion continued to train.

2nd Lieutenant Gates became the assault gun platoon leader. He recalls the prejudice he experienced at Camp Claiborne:

> The nearest town was Alexandria. Our placement in camp was down in the sewage area. All black. When you went to town, you were faced with nothing but white MPs. We had to change that. They required the Negro officer not to carry a sidearm. Yet the others carried sidearms. So I went in town with a sidearm. They questioned me: "You don't need a sidearm." I said, is everybody gonna be without sidearms? "Oh, no, no, but you don't need 'em." I said, I'm performing the same type of duty you're performing. I'm gonna be equally as well prepared as you. They knew I was right. I was very foolish, maybe.
>
> They threatened me with charges. I told 'em my parents would be just as proud of me as a dishonorably discharged private as they would if I were a general. It don't matter to them and it won't matter to me. But since I'm in this thing, I intend to do my best according to rules and regulations. And I do study rules and regulations. After that, we carried sidearms. I had experienced so much prejudice in Louisiana that when I got to Europe, it was a joke.[15]

Boxing became a popular extracurricular activity for the Panthers, who participated as hard-hitting pugilists and enthusiastic fans. The *Camp Claiborne News* of January 20, 1943, reported:

> COLORED TANK MEN HAVE GO AT LIVINGSTON BOXERS HERE TONIGHT. SEEK TO REPEAT 5–4 WIN: WORLD'S MOST ENTHUSIASTIC ROOTERS WILL PACK ARENA.
>
> Seeking revenge tonight, Camp Livingston's 351st Field Artillery boxers will appear in our Sports Arena to avenge a 5–4 trouncing by those West End Fifth Group Tankers.
>
> Since that meeting, the cannoneers, with a revamped line up have developed three 46th Field Artillery Brigade Champions: Art Cureton, at 160 pounds, Lee Harvey, at 175 pounds, and Jimmy Campbell, the heavyweight king. To add to this spearhead, their coach, Lieutenant George Felton, stated modestly that his whole team is sharp and the team to a man asserts that those "Tin-Can-Riders" won't even show up.
>
> Reports from the Armored Force prides on the other hand says the Fifth Group will humbly and bravely back their schoolboy fighters to the limit with Sam Brown, Georgie Riley, and Tony Kelly meeting Cureton, Harvey and Campbell, respectively.
>
> At any rate, rivalry and sportsmanship is "high" between these two outfits and Wednesday night is certain to further the value of a well-organized boxing show, as the Fifth Tank Group and the 68th Tank Destroyer Battalion displayed in two previous cards.

"Bloody Wednesday" at Camp Claiborne as the "Tin Can Riders" root their fighter on. The winner received a three-day pass (National Archives photograph).

L. Z. Anderson remembers fight night: "The black MPs from Camp Polk gave us hell when we went into town. We had to fight like cats and dogs. I remember the boxing matches we had against them. Every time our boys hollered MP, they lowered the boom on them. That is when we really took it out on them. Lieutenant Warren Taylor was our boxing coach. We had a good team."[16]

Several weeks before the 761st Tank Battalion celebrated its first anniversary, a near mutiny occurred. Several members of the 761st and some from adjoining outfits, infuriated over the persistent bludgeoning of their comrades, decided to fight back. L. Z. Anderson recalls:

> It was a Sunday night, I believe. I was in the theater and it was still light, about 6 or 7 o'clock. When they got word back to us at the post that they were beating up on our boys, everyone took off from the movie and went to the motor pool. When we got to the motor pool they had already cranked up those tanks. Captain Wingo was there, up on the hood of his car, begging the guys not to go into town. They had the tanks cranked up at the gate ready to come out. From what I heard they had ammunition. They had broken into our armory where we had live ammunition. They were really going into town to shoot up the place. What distracted their attention, was one of them damned old buses that came by. These bus drivers were the ones who

Left to right: Jay Johnson, Frank Jackson, Waldo Kinch, L. Z. Anderson, and Dexter Fuller at the Camp Claiborne Post Exchange (PX), 1943 (courtesy L. Z. Anderson).

caused most of the problems. When the bus came through everybody left the gate and rushed this bus and tried to turn it over. They started throwing bottles and everything they could at the bus. How they stopped this I really don't know. The boys calmed down and everything came under control. I don't remember any charges being filed.[17]

On April 1, 1943, the Panthers celebrated their first anniversary of existence with an "Activation Day Ceremony." The activities consisted of a gala-field day highlighted and addressed by the battalion commander. He emphasized that the unit must pull together, train harder, and justify the faith that Lt. General McNair had in them. Afterwards, an elegant dance party was held and young ladies from the surrounding communities came as dance partners for the evening.

The saxophones wailed tunes like "Don't Get Around Much Anymore" and "After Hours." The sounds were "reet" for dancing or just listening: "The jivin' sax rhythm section of the Fifth Tank Group Ork Cats, hepped by Sergeant George Ruffin (The Mad Ruffin) and PFC James 'Jeep Blues' Ellison, these 'cats' promise to 'jamb-up' that 'ain't nowhere feelin.' When Charlie McCullough taps those tubs, and Sam White slaps that bass, with weenie wise boogie-woogying the 'box,' synchronized with hot saxes and a Jim Ellis, Jim McCarter guitar combo, you're 'Reet.'"[18]

Also on April 1, the 5th Tank Group (light) finally rounded out with its third and final tank battalion, the 784th. The 761st provided much of the personnel. On April 8, the 761st Tank Battalion departed Camp Claiborne for the second phase of the Third Army maneuvers. The Panthers operated with the 85th Infantry Division, the 93rd Infantry Division, and the 100th Infantry Battalion of the 442nd Regimental Combat Team composed of Japanese-American Troops. Maj. General Willis D. Crittenberger, Sr., commander of the III Armored Corps, directed the exercise.

The field exercise started out with a mounted field march of approximately 45 miles. In the Kisatchie National Forest, the Panthers performed a vital role as part of a team in simulated battlefield conditions. Many aspects of mechanized warfare surfaced under varying field conditions. This served to acclimate the 761st Tank Battalion to armored field operations.

High-ranking officers observed the Third Army maneuvers. Lt. General Ben Lear, the commanding general of the Army Ground Force Reinforcement System of the European Theater of Operations and Lt. General Leslie J. McNair, the Chief of the Army Ground Forces, visited on several occasions. The 761st received high marks and returned to Camp Claiborne by way of an 83 mile mounted field march. The Panthers distinguished themselves by not losing a tank, a half-track, a truck, or a jeep to terrain difficulties or mechanical failure. On June 6, the battalion made it back with a renewed sense of esprit-de-corps.

During this period race riots continued to erupt throughout the nation as African Americans migrated in increasing numbers to urban areas. They came seeking the American Dream but met overt hostilities.

On June 20, 1943, Detroit, Michigan, erupted in the most serious race riot of World War II. This industrial complex crucial to the war effort was temporarily paralyzed. More than 600 people lay injured and over 1,800 were jailed. Twenty-five blacks and nine whites were dead or dying. Nineteen of the dead blacks had been slain by the police. None of the dead whites had been killed by the police. Federal troops had to be called in to bring the situation under control.

Brig. General William E. Gunther, the commander of the federal troops stated: "They've been very handy with their guns and clubs and have been very harsh and brutal.... They have treated the Negroes terrible up here and I think they have gone altogether too far.... If they want everybody else to get back to normal, then the police will have to get back to normal themselves."[19]

On the 4th of July, Major Paul L. Bates, the battalion's XO (Executive Officer), assumed command of the 761st as Lt. Colonel Wright transferred out. Paul Bates held the position of battalion commander longer than any other commander, leaving only for a brief period between 1944 and 1945 due to wounds received in action:

> When people heard I'd been assigned to this new all black battalion, they went around saying what bad luck I had. I honestly didn't have any idea what they were talking about. The town I lived in near Los Angeles didn't have a Negro in it, nor did my high school or my college. I had no idea about Negroes one way or another.... I found out that when the first Negroes were to arrive they had a heritage of undeserved attributes that were all on the down side. I never looked at them like that. I never had reason to because I make up my own mind! There is something that exists between men and men and men and women and this is empathy. You can feel towards a person when you first meet them. It has nothing to do with words, you get a feeling between the two of you where you know you are on the same playing field. That happened because of my lack of knowledge and that we made it out together."[20]

Commanding an all black unit was considered a hardship assignment and white officers were eligible for reassignment after 18 months. At the Officer's Club, the white officers would often sing, "I'm Dreaming of a White Battalion" to the tune of "White Christmas" in the presence of Bates and the "colored" servants. Bates pointed out: "My being an athlete helped, too. The men used to run obstacle courses, and I'd run them with every company. As you run, you talk, and get to know one another.... My 18 months came up, we were still in the States. And did I want to go? Hell no! I didn't want to go."[21]

Bates has a motto: "Never leave to chance anything that hard work and intelligent application can reduce to a certainty."[22] He applied this to his leadership of the 761st Tank Battalion:

> I've always lived with the point of view that the rest of my life is the most important thing in the world. I don't give a damn about what happened before. Let's go from here. And if you're gonna go from here, and you're gonna make it, we got to do it together. So I made a point of being with them as much as I could, for better or for worse. I always lived on the post where we were. And we just sort of came together, where if I told them to do something, they would do it. There were a lot of little things. One was: "Hey, you guys are not supposed to be as clean as other people," and there's a very simple answer to that: Make damn sure that you're cleaner than anybody else you ever saw in your life, particularly all of those white bastards out there. I want your uniforms to look better, cleaner, than theirs do. I want your shoes and boots to shine better. So they would set up their own tailor shops and everything, and man, we were the best looking outfit you've ever seen."[23]

Training continued at Camp Claiborne and on September 14, 1943, the battalion packed up and moved to Camp Hood, Texas, for advanced armored training. The 761st Tank Battalion arrived at its new duty station the following day with a strength of 42 officers and 601 enlisted men.

Opposite top: Service Company, 761st Tank Bn. Camp Claiborne, Louisiana, 1943 (courtesy of the family of the late MSG Ernest D. Hill, Sr.). *Opposite bottom:* Headquarters Co., 761st Tank Bn. Notice the "Go to hell" tilt of the overseas caps worn by the tankers. Camp Claiborne, Louisiana, 1943 (courtesy E. G. McConnell).

3

Camp Hood

The 761st Tank Battalion arrived at Camp Hood, Texas, on September 15, 1943. They were delighted to be leaving Camp Claiborne, and hoped their new duty station would be nothing like the one in Louisiana. It was a relief to leave a place where they were clearly not welcome on and off camp. They had received a taste of Southern hospitality at Camp Claiborne, but during their stay at Camp Hood they would have the main course, seasoned with humiliation.

Major Paul L. Bates, the commanding officer of the 761st, recalls the transition and continued training:

> Camp Hood, for us it was the best of times and the worst of times. The best of times was coming from Claiborne where the land was swampy, flat, and densely vegetated. We were masters at getting tanks out of mud spots where they couldn't move.
>
> When we got here in the marvelous terrain, hills, valleys, woods, open grounds, closed grounds, that was great. Another thing is we were here about a month and we were converted from a light tank battalion to a medium tank battalion. That was from a 37 millimeter to a 75 millimeter cannon. That's like going from the second team to the first.
>
> When we trained here as school troops we were on constant maneuvers. We tested our skills against everybody else. The tank destroyers were taking their tests that were called Army Ground Forces Tests to see if they are ready for combat. Our men defeated them so many times and enjoyed it thoroughly.
>
> During those times we learned not to depend on anyone else. Anything we ever were going to accomplish would be related to our own abilities. We learned to respect ourselves and to respect our buddies, that we can't exist unless we support each other. They learned that so clearly here. Even on a maneuver against the tank destroyers, if the tank wasn't properly maintained and fell out, it was ruled against you and you got a bad mark. All you had to say is, man, if it's in combat, you're dead. So do it right!

They had their own tailor shops and they were the best looking outfit on the post. That's pride! They had pressed uniforms, they had shined boots and when they came to an officer they would salute and they would say to themselves, "I am a man and you've got to return my salute." When we left here, there was so much pride in ourselves.

Now to go to the other side. This was a segregated post. We had separate officers clubs, separate special services clubs. If they wanted to do an exchange, they got their supplies, went over to the cashier, maybe two or three of them. If a white man came up, they were pushed aside. This was required of them. We learned to stuff it, there was no choice, and we were going to make our name for how well we trained, how well we outmaneuvered those tank destroyers. I knew they had the spirit when one day I went over to the tank area where they were maintaining their equipment. There was a lot of laughter going on over around one of the tanks and I went over to find out what it was about and I asked one of the men. He said, "You know what those tank destroyers call themselves? They have the logo; seek, strike and destroy. Man, seek, strike and destroy? When we appear it is Sneak, Peek and Retreat!"[1]

On October 29, a change in the battalion's organization occurred. This reorganization involved the 761st's designation and equipment. The designation changed from the 761st Tank Battalion (light) to the 761st Tank Battalion. The equipment changed from the M-5 Stuart light tanks to the M-4 Sherman medium tanks.

During this period of reorganization, a company was added and designated Company D (Dog Company). They operated with the old M-5 light tanks for screening and reconnaissance missions.

Also during the reorganization, the black officers from the newly formed 784th Tank Battalion shifted over to the 761st. The Panthers gained the services of Captain Garland "Doc" Adamson, 1st Lieutenant Wendell P. Earling, 1st Lieutenant John D. Long, 2nd Lieutenant Richard A. Williams, 2nd Lieutenant Kenneth W. Coleman, 2nd Lieutenant Jay E. Johnson, and Warrant Officer James E. Williams.

On October 30, 1st Lieutenant Ivan H. Harrison assumed command of Headquarters Company. He became the second African American to take command of a company in the 761st. The first was 2nd Lieutenant Irvin McHenry who took over Charlie Company when Captain Charles M. Wingo moved up to executive officer back in June.

1st Lieutenant Harrison believed early on that one day this company would be his to command. He remembers sitting in as commanding officer of Headquarters Company back at Camp Claiborne during a group photo session in the motor pool:

Ivery Fox during the first snowfall to hit Camp Hood in decades. February 1944 (courtesy Margaret Crecy).

Charles P. Ashby and Herman Taylor at the U.S.O. Service Club in Austin, Texas, 1944 (courtesy Charles P. Ashby).

In the photograph I was commanding the company because we had a few white officers who didn't want their pictures taken with Negroes. In this case one was Geist. When he came to the battalion, Lt. Colonel Bates briefed him and then asked if he had any questions. Geist told him that he wanted out of this outfit because he didn't want to serve with Negroes. Lt. Colonel Bates told him, "Go down to this company and you are company commander. You will serve here!" Geist in his heart didn't want to but he went ahead and did it. There were men in the company like Thomas Ashly from Washington. He was brilliant with radios and Geist was interested in radios. Geist would stand around and watch him. We also had this thing called a gyro-stabilizer which was new then and classified. It was that thing on the big gun and while you were riding, where you pointed that gun, the gyro-stabilizer would keep it on target. It was sealed and only people with top secret clearances could break one of those seals. But this colored soldier would break that damn seal when something went wrong and fixed it. Geist was amazed that a Negro

35

Harry K. Tyree and Fred L. Brown on reconnaissance motorcycles. Tyree transferred to the 761st from the 828th Tank Destroyer Battalion Camp Hood, Texas, 1944 (courtesy Margaret Crecy).

knew that much and that son-of-a-gun fell in love with those men and did a complete about face. And during the war when other white officers would not go to the front, he would go forward with those men. He just completely reversed! Russell C. Geist from Germantown, Pennsylvania. So in the photo I was actually a platoon leader but since the two or three white officers refused to have their pictures taken with Negroes, they made me the company commander.[2]

One month later a third African American officer assumed command of a company, when 1st Lieutenant Sam Brown took command of Able Company. Twenty-five-year-old Sam Brown had been a star football player at Buck High School in Charleston, South Carolina, where he was class valedictorian.

In November, the Panthers received their first 93 Good Conduct medals. Their training intensified and they performed exceptionally well. The assault gun platoon made a sparkling fire record for itself.

During this intense training the Assault Gun Platoon was singled out for its ability to zero in on a target with one shot and destroy it with the second. This platoon was an element of Headquarters Company. Captain Ivan Harrison remembers: "At Camp Hood, Gates was the commander of the Assault Gun Platoon. There was this white colonel who had been fighting in North Africa who came to Camp Hood. He was an artillery man and he took a special interest in Gates and that platoon. They would stay for days on a hillside shooting indirect fire, which is an art. They were out there for three, four or five weeks firing all types of ammunition. They were getting additional ammunition so they were able to fire much more ammunition than any other group firing. That platoon, they were all good men. They were terrific!"[3]

A white native Texan named Philip W. Latimer was about to become a Panther. He graduated from Detroit High School as class valedictorian in 1934. In 1938 he graduated from Paris Junior College, again as class valedictorian. He went on to earn a Bachelor of Arts degree in mathematics from Baylor University in 1940. Latimer recalls:

> I was a white high school teacher of mathematics from rural east Texas when I was drafted into the Army in June 1941. I served as a private in the 3rd Armored Division and a sergeant in the 7th Armored Division before enrolling in Armor Officer's Candidate School and becoming a 2nd Lieutenant in October 1942. I became a mortar platoon leader in the 12th Armored Division.
>
> In January 1943, all 2nd lieutenants in the 12th Armored Division were asked if they would be willing to serve with black tankers. I had grown up in an area where there had been many blacks and with parents who were not prejudiced. I also was a very patriotic person, and so I said yes because I felt that perhaps I was extremely well

Phillip W. Latimer. On the back of this photograph is written, "To my good friend Joseph Wilson in appreciation of all he is doing to help publicize the 761st Tank Battalion. — Phil Latimer." Camp Hood, Texas, 1944.

qualified to do this. It was July 1943 before I was finally transferred to the 761st Tank Battalion, and by then I was a 1st Lieutenant. It was not long before the 761st was transferred to Camp Hood, the home of the Tank Destroyer Center. We had been designated as the "enemy" for the center. Lt. Colonel Paul L. Bates, our commanding officer, took great delight in showing tank destroyers that the Panthers were indeed a formidable opponent. Time after time, the tank destroyers were outmaneuvered and defeated. By this time, I was a captain and the battalion supply officer. I began to realize what a big job it was to supply ammunition, gasoline and rations to a battalion of more than 700 men and 54 medium tanks and 17 light tanks. One of the sad parts of our training experience was the treatment received by our black tankers when they left the post area. These men were in the uniform of their country and were later to fight and some die for their country. Even so, they were constantly mistreated and verbally abused by some elements of the civilian population. It is remarkable that they could continue to train diligently. The thing that kept them going was their determination to show the world that they could fight in tanks and win.[4]

The battalion's distinctive insignia has a snarling panther head with the motto, "Come Out Fighting." Captain Ivan Harrison helped to design this. He recalls:

When Joe Louis fought Max Schmeling the second time, when he knocked him out, in all of the newspapers they asked how Joe was going to fight Schmeling. He said, "I'm going to come out fighting!" Joe Louis said that. "I'm going to come out fighting," and we picked that up with a draftsman in the battalion. He was from Ypsilanti, Michigan and I tried to locate him. He helped to design the panther. That thing went to the Department of Heraldry in Washington and they would kick it back. We had to change it. There is a lot of history behind military insignia. For instance, you got to have the evil portion of it pointing away from the body and the heart. We had the two panthers snarling and we had to turn them around, the snarling portion, the evil portion. For the design of insignia you have to go through history to do it. At one time, in addition to the panther head, it had two claws. That didn't work. If you don't know anything about heraldry, forget it, but our artist just kept sending it back. We finally got it through. It took a couple of years before it was approved and adopted as our official military insignia.[5]

Shortages of enlisted personnel were filled on January 7, 1944, when 128 men came to the battalion from the Armored Force Replacement Center. The battalion had an authorized strength of 39 officers, three warrant officers, and 713 enlisted men, which included a medical detachment.

During the early months of 1944, a few more African Americans officers joined the battalion. Warrant Officer Clarence I. Godbold from the 92nd Infantry Division became the personnel officer and 2nd Lieutenant John Roosevelt Robinson from the Cavalry Replacement Center became a platoon leader and the morale officer.

2nd Lieutenant Robinson recalls training with the 761st:

> Impressed with what they considered to be an honest approach, the men really threw themselves into their work. During maneuvers, I was in constant communication with the sergeant I had placed in command. I had a two-way radio in my tank and we always talked things over. He did a wonderful job of explaining things to me and I learned as I went along. We got along splendidly and everyone worked as a team.
>
> Finally one day, I was called to the quarters of my chief, Colonel Bates. I did not know what was coming, so you could have knocked me down with a feather when he said: "Robinson, I want to commend you and your outfit on your work down here. You have the best record of all the outfits at the camp and I am singling you out for special mention."
>
> Well, I didn't know what to say. I had gotten to first base on an error and managed to steal all the way home. I decided to tell the truth. I don't know who was more surprised, I, who had never expected a word of praise for an officer transferred from a horse outfit to a mechanized group, or he, when he heard how I had placed the sergeant in charge. He finally said, "Robinson, I don't care how you accomplished what you did, but the fact of the matter is that you still have the best outfit of all down here. That's all that counts. You have found a way to make your outfit tops and that's all I ask." I left that interview as happy as I had ever been in my life.

Jackie Robinson at Fort Riley, Kansas, in April 1942. Here he unsuccessfully applied to Officer Candidate School. He asked Sergeant Joe Louis, the world heavyweight boxing champion, to intervene. The matter was brought to the War Department. Soon Jackie Robinson and the other African Americans at the fort were admitted to OCS (courtesy Jackie Robinson Post #252).

Shortly afterwards he asked me to go overseas with him as his morale officer. I told him I would think it over. Let me explain that I had a chipped bone in my ankle and was on limited duty. I did not have to go overseas if I did not want to go. The Army asked me to sign waivers relieving them of any responsibility in the event of injuries that might occur to me overseas because of the bad ankle.... I remember that I had not really made up my mind about going when something happened that almost changed the entire course of my life.[6]

On July 6, 2nd Lieutenant Robinson, on a bus from Camp Hood to the local town of Belton, refused to move to the back of the bus when ordered to do so by a civilian bus driver. Court-martial charges ensued but could not proceed because Lt. Colonel Paul L. Bates would not consent to the charges. The top brass at Camp Hood subsequently transferred 2nd Lieutenant Robinson to the 758th Tank Battalion, where its commander immediately signed the court-martial consent.

Lt. Colonel Bates describes this incident:

> The worst thing here was the bus situation. The only recreation areas they had was off post here in Killeen, a very small town, and Belton and Temple. The bus drivers took a vicious pleasure on the last bus at night, which was always full of soldiers. They were always in the back area or standing. Getting about two or three miles from the post and say the bus was overloaded, some of you have to get out. They would make six or eight of them get out and walk back to post. They clearly enjoyed it! The day came and it actually happened about six weeks before we went overseas when one of our Negro officers came out of the Negro officer's club, got on the bus along with a Negress who was so light that she looked like a white woman. She was the wife of an officer friend of his. Instead of going to the back of the bus he sat down in about the middle of the bus. Two more stops and the bus was filled with workers leaving here and somebody pointed out that a Negro officer was not sitting in the back of the bus, he was sitting in the middle of the bus with a white woman.
>
> The driver went back and told the man he would have to go to the back of the bus. The man refused to go to the back of the bus. He had a short temper, a short fuse, he refused to go back and told the bus driver he had a choice of either driving the bus himself or he would drive it. The bus driver got on the radio, called the dispatch and said he had an uppity kind of Negro here and I'm going to drive to the MP station, have them wait there for us.
>
> They started asking him questions and many of the white people on the bus began yelling that he used bad language, he was disrespectful to the bus driver. The MP was a captain and two enlisted men. The captain and the enlisted men called him nigger. This is a

black officer. They sure were talking to the wrong man. That was Jackie Robinson who later became the star baseball player. Jackie Robinson at that time was the only man from UCLA with four letters in four major sports and that is true still today.

He came here from Fort Riley. He had gone to OCS and got an appointment to Fort Riley. At Fort Riley, he didn't want to go out for football. They asked him to go out for football, which he did. And then it came time to play Fort Leonard Wood and Fort Leonard Wood sent the word back that their team would not play a team with a Negro on it. This is what it was like for us! After the game was over, the coach came around to him because he did not report to practice. He said, "I will not play anymore unless you assure me this incident will never happen on any future games." He said, "We can't do that." Jackie Robinson said, "I won't play." A Lt. Colonel, who was a special services officer got with him and said, "If you don't play we will transfer you to another post where you'll wish you did play." And I got him. They transferred him to the 761st Tank Battalion.

He was interesting, a colorful person. He livened up all of us a lot when we had pick-up softball games. I remember when the officers were playing softball against him. Everyone in the infield went out about 50 yards further because when the ball came by it looked like a saucer instead of a round ball.

Back to the bus incident, with all this shouting they took him into the station. They had a woman there who would take down his story of what happened. He would start to answer a question asked by the captain MP. He would never get an answer out, this woman would interrupt and contradict him. She would then repeat what some of the passengers said about him. He did threaten one of the enlisted men because of the way he was talking to him.

The next day I was called into Group Headquarters and they had heard of the incident in the worst light possibly imaginable and said there was probably a court-martial pending. I went back to my head-quarters and found Jackie there waiting. He told me his story. I then told him that I think the best thing for you to do is, you have accrued leave, put in a request for a ten-day leave. I will sign it. You go home to Pasadena, California, where the entire atmosphere is different. Think about it, line up and do whatever you can to help yourself because there is pretty well going to be a court-martial.

Copies of telegrams came from the War Department. They said, "We are being deluged with letters upholding the character and pop-ularity of this man. Proceed in court-martial with great care." You would think that they would have dropped it.[7]

The trial opened on August 2, 1943, and lasted for 17 days, in which time the 761st departed Camp Hood. Twenty-five-year-old Jackie Robinson was charged with the violation of the 63rd and 64th Articles of War. The first charge specified: "Lieutenant Robinson behaved with disrespect toward Captain Gerald M. Bear, Corps Military Police, by contemptuously bowing to him and giving several sloppy salutes while repeating, O'kay Sir, O'kay Sir in an insolent, impertinent and rude manner." The second charge specified: "Lieutenant Robinson having received a lawful command by Captain Bear to remain in a receiving room at the MP station disobeyed such order." Lieutenant Robinson was not charged for his actions on the bus.

Lt. Colonel Paul Bates remembers the trial:

> I spent quite a bit of time there and it was the first time in my life I was ever called prejudiced. Because after my testimony, the prosecuting attorney recommended that all of my testimony should be thrown out because I was too prejudiced in favor of the defendant. Isn't that a beautiful way to use that word?
>
> The beautiful part of it was that Jackie was a very intelligent individual and when the first defense appointee from the Judge Advocate General came to him, Jackie asked him: "What chances do I have of getting out of this?" He said, "I think you have very little." Jackie said, "I don't want you. I want somebody who believes in me." The next man who came was a man named Cline. Jackie asked him the same question. He said, "No doubt about it ... this is exaggerated beyond belief. I will defend you and you will get off."
>
> At the beginning of the trial there were many, many witnesses who were on the bus who made many derogatory statements about him, about the bad language he used.... It did look pretty bad until this very smart lawyer asked this enlisted man who claimed that Jackie Robinson had threatened to injure him. He asked if he had ever called Jackie Robinson a nigger. He said, "Under no circumstances." "Did you ever use the word?" He said, "No, I never used it." "Did any of you ever use that word?" (Well, they all did actually.) He said, "No, none of us ever did." "I want you to tell me and this is very, very important so that we can punish this man properly. I want you to tell me the exact words he used when he threatened you." "If you ever call me a nigger again, I'll break you in two."
>
> At that the president of the court stood up and the others did and they had the charges and specifications read. And to everyone of them he just said: "Not guilty, not guilty." We lost Jackie then.
>
> I didn't expect to stay in the Army and if they were going to throw me out that would be as good a cause as any. Well, we left here with a bitter taste in our mouths. Yes, he got off but it never should have happened![8]

Jackie Robinson recalled how his military career ended up after the acquittal: "My CO sent me to the hospital for a physical checkup and they changed my status to permanent limited service. After that I kicked around the tank destroyers doing a little bit of everything. Then I wound up as a lieutenant in an infantry battalion at Camp Breckinridge. In October 1944 I was given a 30-day leave and put on inactive duty.... What I'd like to know is, do I have to go back into active duty to get separated or will they just notify me that I'm out?"[9]

4

Destination E.T.O.

Since June 9, 1944, the 761st Tank Battalion remained on full alert for overseas movement. This was three days after the D-Day invasion where more than 1,000 air transports dropped paratroopers in the early morning hours to secure the flanks of the assault area. Amphibious crafts landed some 130,000 troops on five beaches along 50 miles of French Normandy coast. The British and Canadians landed on Gold, Juno, and Sword beaches, while the Americans landed on Utah and Omaha beaches. After bombing enemy targets, the U.S. Army Air Forces and the British Royal Air Force controlled the skies. Rangers climbed cliffs, engineers destroyed beach obstacles, and quartermasters stockpiled supplies in the largest beach invasion in military history.

While making preparations to join the great battle, the Panthers received news that Lt. General Leslie J. McNair had been killed in Normandy during a bombing raid. Although heavy-hearted, the 761st Tank Battalion became more determined to reward the late general's faith in them.

Brig. General Ernest A. Dawley, the commanding general of the Tank Destroyer Center, gave the Panthers a farewell speech. He expounded the various things that would and could happen during combat for which there would be no obvious explanation and just couldn't be figured out. He went on to say, "Just lay it to the Fog of War!" He concluded by saying that he believed the 761st Tank Battalion would do fine things in battle and, "when you get in there, put in an extra round of ammunition, and fire it for General Dawley!"[1]

On August 1, an advance party departed Camp Hood bound for Camp Kilmer, New Jersey. Major Charles M. Wingo, Warrant Officer Mark Henderson, and Tech. Sergeant William H. Newkirk made up the advance party. Eight days later the main body departed Camp Hood bound for Camp Shanks, New York, the Port of Embarkation (POE).

"I was about to get on a train from Temple to go home to Chicago on leave before we were shipped to Europe," Johnny Holmes recalls. "I went into a restaurant to buy some sandwiches to take with me. I was in uniform. There were 20 or 30 people in there. I saw a few black people in the back of the restaurant near some garbage cans and a stack of Coca-Cola crates, but I didn't know why they were there. I had just walked in the front door the way I had back home." Then the following conversation took place: Owner: "What you want, boy?" Soldier: "I'm not a boy! I'm a United States soldier." Owner: "So what do you want?" Soldier: "I want a couple of sandwiches to go." Owner: "All right but you've got to go around to the back door to get them." Soldier: "Back there where the garbage cans are? I don't want them then." Owner: "Well then, get the hell out of here, nigger!" As he said that, Holmes remembers: "Every white person in the place grabbed their knives and their forks and raised up like they were coming after me. I backed up to the door and said I'm going. I hadn't had anything to eat in 14 hours, and I never got a bite from Temple to St. Louis. It was damn near two days."[2]

The battalion arrived at Camp Shanks, New York, on August 13, and departed for England on August 27. Few if any of the Panthers had ever crossed a body of water larger than one of the Great Lakes, but they all got on board when the blue-green Atlantic Ocean loomed over the horizon. They were anxious and worried, knowing that they might never return. These African American men were about to cross the same ocean that their African ancestors crossed in chains.

The battalion sailed on the HMS *Esperance Bay* and arrived at the port of Avonmouth, England, on September 8. Upon arrival, the battalion had a strength of 36 officers, two warrant officers, and 676 enlisted men — well trained, disciplined, and ready for combat.

At completion of the voyage the transport commander gave Lt. Colonel Paul L. Bates a letter of commendation: "I wish to express my appreciation to you and your officers for your hearty cooperation in making this voyage most successful and pleasant. I commend your unit for its discipline, military courtesy, high morale, and soldierly conduct throughout the voyage. It has been by far one of the best disciplined units of its kind on this ship since the undersigned has been transport commander. My staff and I wish you Godspeed in your future missions, and the best of luck and success to final victory." It was signed by Captain Peter W. Jacoby.[3]

Upon arrival, the battalion proceeded to Wimbourne, England, and began last-minute preparations. There the Panthers received assignment orders to the Ninth Army and placed on alert to stand by in readiness for movement within notice of six hours.

Private First Class Joseph E. Wilson describes his journey from Camp Hood to the ETO before he joined the 761st Tank Battalion later in the war:

> Being a member of the 679th Tank Destroyer Battalion, located at
> North Camp Hood near Gatesville, Texas, I became aware of what a
> tank was and the lethal pain this British invention could inflict on its

enemy. This was the summer of 1943. I arrived with those who had completed basic training at Camp Wheeler near Macon Georgia, in the anti-tank specialty.

Traveling on a troop train from Georgia and through the westward south, the vastness of my country awed and re-educated me. This is my country, I felt, but other Americans felt that my slice of the American Pie should not equal theirs. This enigma took up residence in my mind and refused to abate, even to now.

My sojourn at Camp Hood proved too much for me and I volunteered for immediate combat duty. With the rank of Private First Class (praying for corporal), I became a member of Battery C, 686th Field Artillery Battalion. This medium artillery unit fired the 155 millimeter shell (98 lbs.) in the vicinity of nine miles, with devastating effect.

I joined the unit at Table Rock Camp. We lived in tents and had to be trucked into the main post at Camp Hood for showers, PX, movies, church activities, etc. The long awaited journey to the hot war began. We loaded for bear and struck out for the POE. Troop trains in those days were a common sight. It was not unusual to see troop trains of ten or 20 rail cars loaded with soldiers passing through your town.

Our troop train left Texas and found itself negotiating the heights of the Rocky Mountains. These were sights we learned about in school, but to experience your train parked on a vertically inclined side track waiting for a speeding passenger bullet to whiz by dealt a fatal blow to the pleasure of the trip. Old Smoky clickety clacked through countless hamlets, towns, and notable cities. Memories gathered, the excitement soared when Old Smoky passed through Milwaukee, Wisconsin, where I first saw the light of day and later Gary, Indiana, my hometown. Leaning out of the window, I saw no one I recognized. What a letdown!

Old Smoky sped on spewing soot and ashes through open windows until cities lying behind were Cleveland, Buffalo, and New York City. We soon learned that this place where Old Smoky came to rest on a side track was our destination, Camp Shanks, New York, the POE.

During our ten-day stay, we Cosmolined our guns and equipment and prepared for the ocean voyage which lay ahead. Setting out across the Atlantic, we were not alone, for as far as one could see, troop ships laden with troops and their equipment were in a common unit, a convoy.

Wind, rain, and fog were our reliable companions, and thanks to them I was able to appreciate a natural phenomena, a natural work of God, the Gulf Stream. The ocean water, no longer green, had turned to a dark blue, representing deep water, an ocean desert, but not a watery wasteland. Entering these northbound rivers of warm water we noticed that the gloomy weather vanished, enabling us to enjoy weather you would expect in the tropics.

Our ocean voyage ended when we docked and disembarked at Southampton, England. Hours later, we found ourselves being whisked west to the southern port of Wales, a small hamlet called Ponty Pool. We moved into Quonset huts at the Polo Grounds.[4]

5

Last-Minute Preparations for Battle

While the Panthers made last-minute adjustments to equipment, a gut-wrenching sense of responsibility fell on their shoulders. The time was approaching when the late Lt. General Leslie J. McNair would be vindicated or discredited for his faith in the black tankers.

The 761st Tank Battalion was relieved from the Ninth Army and assigned to Patton's Third Army on October 5, 1944. A "bastard" battalion, it was self sustained and up for grabs by any division in the Third Army. Individual companies, platoons, and tanks would be constantly shifted to and from various units within the division.

Lt. Colonel Paul L. Bates received a letter of instruction to separate unit commanders in the Third Army from Lt. General George S. Patton, Jr., regarding leadership: "Each, in his appropriate sphere, will lead in person. Any commander who fails to obtain his objective, and who is not dead or seriously wounded, has not done his full duty!"

The battalion was composed of Service Company, Headquarters Company, Companies Able, Baker, Charlie and Dog, along with a medical detachment. Service Company took charge of maintenance, administration, and transportation. Headquarters Company had the 105 millimeter assault gun platoon, the 81 millimeter mortar platoon, and the reconnaissance platoon. Companies Able, Baker, and Charlie operated with the Sherman medium tanks. Dog Company, the "Mosquito Fleet," operated with the M-5 light tanks.

The configuration of the Army at this time was the "Tri-System." With few exceptions, each unit had three elements along with supporting units. For example, each army had three corps; each corps had three divisions; each division had three regiments; each regiment had three battalions; each battalion had three companies; each company had three platoons; etc. The 761st Tank Battalion, a medium

Company Commanders of the 761st Tank Battalion enjoy a meal before crossing the English Channel and going into combat. *Clockwise from left:* David J. Williams II (Able); J. R. Lawson (Baker); Irvin McHenry (Charlie); Richard English (Dog); Ivan Harrison (H.Q.), and August Bremer (Service). Wimbourne, England, September 27, 1944 (National Archives photograph 111-SC-194875).

tank battalion, operated with three medium tank companies—Able, Baker, and Charlie. They also had three supporting companies—Dog, Service, and Headquarters. When the 761st attached to a division, each of the medium tank companies would be assigned to one of the division's three regiments.

Private E. G. McConnell recalls:

> When we met the British they seemed to be very cheerful people with no hate in them. This was quite different from back home. At that time we were young chow hounds, we never could get enough to eat. There was a farm next to where we were so a bunch of us got on our bellies and started crawling in that direction. We cut down greens

and then we started going for the corn. When we got there someone said, "Someone's coming!" Then we ducked back to where the greens were and laid on our bellies. The next thing I heard, in an English accent, "Hi, Yanks." Here stood a farmer. I looked up and he had his two sons with him. He asked what we were doing on the ground. I knew nothing else to say but the truth. I told him we were stealing the greens and the corn. The old farmer started laughing. He said, "What for?" We said we were hungry. He and his two sons started laughing again. He told us that those crops are for feeding hogs. I found out then that the British did not eat corn, they raised it for their livestock. His kids made out like crazy because we gave them candy and chewing gum and went back to the barracks to get more. The farmer let us know that we were welcome anytime we wanted to get something but next time we could stand up. We were so embarrassed.[1]

Franklin Garrido describes the social conditions in England: "I felt hostility from white American enlisted men and officers because they didn't want the English girls to go after the Negro soldiers. They told them stories, just as Johnny Holmes said, "We had tails, we were ignorant, and the only reason we had tanks was because we were bringing them up to the front for the white boys. They were the ones who put out the bad rumors, but I will say this, they failed. Many of the black soldiers had English girlfriends, some of them got married."[2]

The African American soldiers were fighting a war before they went to the real war. The British citizens were absolutely amazed when they witnessed white American soldiers, in mob fashion, closing down dance halls where black soldiers danced with British girls. When a young black soldier got together with a young white girl, that girl would be encouraged by white soldiers to say she was raped. If she did, the American MPs would viciously beat a confession out of the black soldier. A number of black soldiers were subsequently court-martialed, convicted, and sentenced by unanimous vote to hang by the neck until dead.

Political editor Cecil King of the British *Daily Mirror* newspaper stated in his private diary: "The feeling is fairly common that Negroes are nicer and better behaved than the ordinary Yank. So there is some indignation when Negro soldiers are condemned to death for raping English girls. In the most recent case the evidence would surely have resulted in acquittal in an English court. In the far more numerous cases of rape or murder by white American soldiers, the punishment, if any, is of a wholly different order of severity."[3]

On October 7, the 761st Tank Battalion received new tanks and equipment and departed Wimbourne, England, for Weymouth along the English Channel. Two days later they departed England for France. They landed at Omaha Beach on the Normandy Peninsula. When their tanks rolled ashore, it was a momentous day in military history. There had been black soldiers in France in World War I, but

Dog Company 761st Tank Battalion making last-minute adjustments to equipment before leaving England to go into combat. *Left to right* (front row): Maxie Henry, Judge Favors, Jack Gilbert, Albert Fullwood, John Winbush; (rear) Elmo Johnson, Mathew L. Johnson, and Arthor E. Richie. September 27, 1944, Wimbourne, England (National Archives photograph).

this was the first time that African Americans had ever been on foreign soil in their tanks. They were going to fight over the same ground that their fathers had fought on just 26 years before. The time was near!

Upon arrival, the battalion attached to the 26th "Yankee" Infantry Division in the XII Corps in France. The 26th Division was commanded by Maj. General Willard S. Paul. XII Corps was commanded Maj. General Manton S. Eddy.

The Panthers began a mounted field march to the front on October 22. They traveled approximately 400 miles in six days consuming nearly 70,000 gallons of gasoline and 700 gallons of oil. There were no vehicular losses, and only one tank arrived a day late, due to mechanical failure. On October 28, the battalion arrived at Saint Nicholas-de-Port, just east of Nancy, France.

On October 31, Maj. General Willard S. Paul welcomed the 761st Tank Battalion from on top of a half-track: "I am damned glad to have you with us. We have been expecting you for a long time, and I am sure that you are going to give a good account of yourselves. I've got a 'Big Hill Up There' that I want you to take, and I believe that you are going to do a great job of it."

On November 2, the Panthers received another welcome, this time from "Ole Blood & Guts" himself. Lieutenant William Blake remembers: "We were in battalion formation when the order came down to man all guns. Suddenly a bunch of jeeps loaded with MPs and .50 caliber machine guns rolled in and took up strategic positions. Then a single jeep came dashing up and stopped beside an armor scout car. A three-star general jumped from the jeep and vaulted up on the hood of the armored car and when I saw his two ivory-handled pistols I knew I was looking at Lt. General George S. Patton, Jr."[4]

Patton addressed the 761st Tank Battalion: "Men, you're the first Negro tankers to ever fight in the American Army. I would never have asked for you if you weren't good. I have nothing but the best in my Army. I don't care what color you are, so long as you go up there and kill those kraut sonsabitches. Everyone has their eyes on you and is expecting great things from you. Most of all, your race is looking forward to your success. Don't let them down, and, damn you, don't let me down!... They say it is patriotic to die for your country, well, let's see how many patriots we can make out of those German sonsabitches."[5]

Silence fell over the formation until Corporal Howard "Big Tit" Richardson turned to his CO and said: "Sir, that old man is crazy as hell. Did you see the way his eyes roll around when he talks? No bullshit about the Hornet. That's for damn sure. I'm more afraid of him than I am of those krauts. That boy in Sicily [a malingerer] was lucky he just got slapped. The old man could have had him shot!"[6]

Patton climbed down from the half-track and walked over to E.G. McConnell. "He climbed up on top of my tank," McConnell recalls, "to inspect this new high velocity gun we had on there. Then he climbed down on the commander's side and looked me straight in the eye, with gray eyes, he said, 'Listen, boy, I want you to shoot every gawd damn thing you see — church steeples, water towers, houses, old ladies, children, haystacks — every gawd damn thing you see. This is war! You hear me boy?' I said, 'Yes General!'"[7]

The Panthers were shocked to discover that Patton had a very high-pitched voice and almost sounded like a woman. They now understood why he used so much profanity — so he would be taken seriously and not perceived as a sissy.

At Third Army Headquarters, Patton commented on his inspection of the 761st Tank Battalion: "They gave a very good first impression, but I have no faith in the inherent fighting ability of the race."[8]

Since September, Patton's Third Army was at a standstill in front of Metz. Patton built up supplies and personnel for a major offensive while the Germans dug in deeper and built more concrete fortifications in anticipation of the coming offensive. The area assigned to the 26th Infantry Division embraced several key towns along the supply routes southeast of Metz. Untaken in 1,000 years, Metz had some 22 forts around it. The German defenders were standing off the 5th, 90th, and 95th Infantry Divisions, which were poised to attack Metz from three sides.

The Panthers took up positions at the Line of Departure (LD) near Athanville, France. The temperature was cold, the skies cloudy, and rain fell lightly. Because the U.S. Army Air Forces had damaged the Dieuze Dam with aerial bombings, the area around the LD and the enemy defenses was flooded by waters of the Seille River. Heavy mud made the terrain difficult for tank operations.

In the predawn hours of November 8, the Panthers encountered a roadblock at the LD. A herd of cattle blocked the intersection, causing a traffic pileup. The French cattle herder, possibly a collaborator, was personally arrested by Lt. Colonel Paul L. Bates. Just as the crossroads cleared, an enemy artillery barrage fell, disabling one tank. Then an enemy patrol opened fire on the column, seriously wounding Bates.

Maj. General Willard Paul's words rang in the ears of the Panthers. They knew the "Big Hill Up There" loomed on the horizon. The morning was only a few hours away.

6

The Big Hill Up There

At 0600 hours on the morning of November 8, 1944, the 761st Tank Battalion, while attached to the 26th Infantry Division, jumped off in a two-pronged attack. The enemy expected an attack on Dieuze, but the Panthers attacked in the direction of Moyenvic and Vic-sur-Seille.

With Lt. Colonel Bates seriously wounded and out of action, the responsibility of command fell on the slender shoulders of his executive officer, Major Charles Wingo. Paul Bates describes the situation:

> None of our men went psycho that I know of. The only one that went psycho was a white officer, my executive officer. There was this terrible day when the whole Third Army was making a big attack and it was delayed, and delayed and delayed for a week. At the last few hours before the attack, a patrol came back and said there is ground out there unpassable for tanks. The direction of the tank attack was changed 30 degrees and we got the word out by radio as they were moving toward the line of departure. I hurried up in a jeep and got up to the line of departure. It was barely breaking daylight and I stood there. I knew they knew me and I was making sure they were going in the right direction. They all went by, waved, buttoned up and kept going. When we got on by, a German patrol nailed me with a burp gun. Unfortunately, that day I went down and my XO cracked up.[1]

1st Lieutenant John D. Long, who in a few days became Baker Company's commanding officer after his white commanding officer was removed, shows his disgust with the XO's actions: "The next man in command, Major Wingo, the morning of the attack, turned his tank around and went hell-bent in the opposite direction. He just plain chickened and that SOB was evacuated for combat fatigue. Hell, we hadn't even been in battle yet." Long went on to describe his own philosophy: "Not for God and country, but for me and my people. This was my motivation, pure

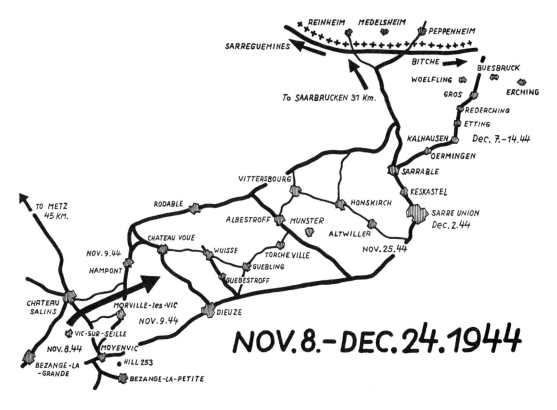

This map was drawn by William Kaiser, Jr., the bow gunner in Charlie Company's "Cool Stud" tank. Kaiser's maps were officially used by battalion headquarters for reporting purposes (National Archives).

and simple, when I entered the Army. I swore to myself there would never be a headline saying my men and I chickened. A soldier, in time of war, is supposed to accept the idea of dying. That's what he's there for; live with it and forget it. I expected to get killed, but whatever happened I was determined to die an officer and a gentleman."[2]

Private E. G. McConnell recalls his baptism of fire:

I had my two dog tags and a lucky half-dollar piece that was hanging along with my dog tags. I had my little prayer book that Moms had given me. We heard that Lt. Colonel Bates had gotten himself shot up. We were so hurt by this because this man gave us the pride to keep going forward and not to hurt ourselves by getting involved with those crackers and all of that hate back in the States. Our assignment, the three tanks of Headquarters Company, was to guard the supply train and we stayed just beyond the front and we were up on high ground. As we looked off into the distance a couple of miles, we saw some tanks of the 761st involved in a bitter tank battle. We saw several tanks burning. We saw infantry pinned down and wounded. The supply train had stopped and we were looking down on all of this. We didn't know what to make of it, yet I wondered why they didn't give us an order to fire smoke down there to distract them so that some of our guys could get out of there. It was a hellhole down there. Nothing happened. Then I got out of my tank. Major Wingo was in Smitty's tank. Headquarters company had three tanks to carry the battalion's high-ranking officers. We didn't know where the acting battalion commander, Major Wingo, had gone. We knew tank tactics and we could have given them cover but we dared not shoot. I asked Smitty where was the major. He said he went to the rear. As we found out, this major, who was a staunch bigot, deserted the 761st Tank Battalion. This was one time when we really needed leadership. Anyway, Smitty gave me Wingo's trench coat and he kept Wingo's binoculars. I remember earlier as we were coming towards the front, Wingo kept shouting over the radio, 'I want absolute radio silence. You boys keep quiet on those radios.' So someone opened up their radio and said, 'Yo Mama!' That brought a chuckle out of everyone because he was very much disliked but we dared not used the radios after that.[3]

Leading black soldiers into battle became a psychological paradox for many white officers, especially if they were prejudiced. They would exchange tales of black cowardice at their officer's clubs. As it turned out, the "redneck" officer spooked himself with his own stories.

Elements of the 101st and 104th Infantry Regiments of the 26th Infantry Division with a detachment of combat engineers followed Able Company's spearhead through the line of resistance. Captain David J. Williams II led two tank platoons in the direction of Vic-sur-Seille, followed by elements of the 104th Regiment. 1st Lieutenant Charles H. Barbour, Jr., led a tank platoon in the direction of Moyenvic, followed by elements of the 101st Regiment. Traversing through minefields, three tanks were lost to mines before reaching their first objective.

The dashing young Captain Williams, a Yaleman and scion of the Pittsburgh Williamses, eased tensions by radioing to his men in Cool Cat Harlemese: "Now, looka here, ya cats, we gotta hit it down the main drag and hip some of those unhepped cats on the other side. So let's roll down ole Seventh Ave, and knock 'em, Jack!" 1st Lieutenant Joseph Kahoe's tank platoon moved out first with Platoon Sergeant Ruben Rivers in the lead tank.

Rivers encountered a roadblock that held up the advance. With utter disregard for his personal safety, he courageously dismounted from his tank in the face of direct enemy small arms and mortar fire, attached a cable to the roadblock and had it moved off the road. As the tank backed up, pulling the large tree clear of the road, several puffs of smoke were seen as the mines exploded. His prompt action prevented a serious delay in the offensive operation, and was instrumental to the success of the assault.

This task force came up against the crack 11th Panzer Division, which was reinforced by 12,000 reserve troops, 30 big guns, and a large number of tanks. This unit was one of the finest formations in the *Wehrmacht,* with a long tradition of victory on the Russian Front and in North Africa. Supporting this panzer division were the 361st and 559th *Volksgrenadier* divisions, which by comparison were not as formidable, but still deadly.

After traveling a few hundred yards, the ear-piercing whine of the German 88s whistled into range. The first shell exploded off to the right, leaving a cloud of black smoke. Then came the staccato of machine gun fire and the steel bullets clanking ineffectually off the sides of the tanks. This was reassuring, one thing that could not harm the Panthers. If the enemy had no armor-piercing shells or if the HE (high explosive) shells did not explode too close over the turret tops, they were safe. But danger was everywhere. Private First Class Floyd Dade recalls: "We were fighting to take this town when our tank got hit with a round of armor-piercing ammunition from an 88. It cut off our .50 caliber gun mount from the turret top."[4]

The inside of a tank, potentially an iron coffin, was a hell of a place to be. When an armor-piercing shell penetrated a tank, slivers of white-hot metal fragments flew throughout the tank's interior, striking everyone. These flying fragments would rip a man apart and splatter blood and human flesh all over the tank's white interior. The hellish part about it is that once it got in there, there wasn't a damned thing that could be done about it.

Staff Sergeant Chester Jones from the 961st Tank Ordnance Company recalls: "When you opened the hatches of the wrecked tanks that could be repaired, some of the most ghastly sights you could imagine were exposed; what were once human beings were scrambled all over the interior of these tanks. You didn't stop to figure out which leg or arm went with which remains, if there were a whole torso. You just put it in a plastic container and cleaned the spattered brains and blood from the inside of the vehicle. I was a tank mechanic, but cleaning out those wrecks went with the job...."[5]

The tank drivers did an excellent job of keeping their tanks out of harm's way. They learned that Ripsaw's first shot is long, the next shot is short, and the following shots are right in your lap. It paid not to be there when those on-target shells came in. Although the drivers did not get the praise that the tank commanders and gunners got, they made their tanks elusive targets and thus saved many tanks and their crews.

Private Clifford C. Adams, an aidman in the 761st Tank Battalion's medical detachment, was hit by fragments from an exploding shell. He died a few hours

Staff Sergeant Harvey Woodard's M4A3-E8 Sherman Medium Tank negotiates the muddy terrain. It is armed with a .30 caliber machine gun mounted to fire along the same axis as the main armament, a 76 millimeter cannon. It is also armed with a .30 caliber machine gun in the bow and a .50 caliber antiaircraft machine gun on the turret. This tank has a five man crew and is powered by a 500-horsepower Ford gas engine. It has a top speed of 35 mph and a range of 100 miles. Nancy France, November 8, 1944 (National Archive photograph).

later, the first Panther to be killed in action. Corporal Floyd Humphrey was beside Adams when the shell hit. He said, "I was lucky."[6]

The second prong of the attack jumped off with elements of the 602nd and 691st Tank Destroyer Battalions, Company K of the 101st Infantry Regiment, a platoon of combat engineers, and the remainder of the 761st Tank Battalion. The 761st's assault gun, mortar, and reconnaissance platoons remained in strategic reserve. The 4th Armored Division stood by on alert to exploit any breakthroughs made by this task force, designated provisional Task Force A. Lt. Colonel Peter J. Kopcsak, commanding officer of the 602nd Tank Destroyer Battalion, commanded this task force.

Members of the 761st Tank Battalion, Nancy, France, November 8, 1944. *Top left:* Tank Commander Harvey Woodard asessing the terrain and situation (National Archives photograph 111-SC-196110). *Top right:* Tank Gunner Carlton Chapman manning the .50 caliber antiaircraft machine gun (National Archives photograph 111-SC-196107). *Bottom left:* Assistant driver and bow gunner Nathaniel Simmons at the ready with his .45 caliber (grease gun) submachine gun (National Archives photograph 111-SC-196109). *Bottom right:* Cannoneer L. C. Byrd, likewise at the ready (National Archives photograph 111-SC-196108).

Tank Driver Claude Mann, a "Panther Wrapped in Cold Steel" (National Archives photograph 111-SC-19106).

Charlie Company with 12 tanks, commanded by Captain Irvin McHenry, took Hill 253 and Bezange-la-Petite after a furious battle. Spearheading for the 328th Infantry Regiment, Charlie Company lost three tanks, a complete tank crew dead, and two tankers wounded.

Staff Sergeant Harvey Woodard and his tank crew were killed under mysterious circumstances. Not a single man inside the tank had been hit by a shell fragment or by a machine gun bullet. When the tank was opened, every man in the crew was sitting in his assigned position, with eyes staring, pupils dilated, and no fear showing on their faces. But every man in the crew was dead. The tank was buttoned up and had no damage to the exterior or interior. All was in order. What snuffed out Woodard and his crew? That was the question that nobody could answer with certainty. The cause could have been the concussion from a burst of HE (high explosive) just over the turret top, which sucked out all of the air and sent shock waves through the tank. More than likely it was carbon monoxide exposure, which was common in those tanks.

It was during this difficult operation near Bezange-la-Petite, against fresh troops from the enemy's 361st Volksgrenadier Division, that Corporal Alfred L. Wilson, a medical aidman from the 328th Infantry Regiment, earned the Medal of Honor. He was the only member of the 26th Infantry Division to receive the nation's highest award during World War II. The citation reads:

> He volunteered to assist as an aid man for a company other than his own, which was suffering casualties from constant artillery fire. He administered to the wounded and returned to his own company when a shell injured a number of his men. While treating his comrades he was seriously wounded, but refused to be evacuated by litter bearers sent to relieve him. In spite of great pain and loss of blood, he continued to administer first aid until he was too weak to stand. Crawling from one patient to another, he continued his work until excessive loss of blood prevented him from moving. He then verbally directed unskilled enlisted men in continuing the first aid for the wounded. Still refusing assistance for himself, he remained to instruct others in dressing the wounds of his comrades until he was unable to speak above a whisper and finally lapsed into unconsciousness. The effects of his injury later caused his death. By steadfastly remaining at the scene without regard for his own safety, Corporal Wilson through distinguished devotion to duty and personal sacrifice helped to save the lives of at least 10 wounded men.[7]

Private Harry K. Tyree describes his baptism of fire: "I will never forget that first day of combat in [Sergeant] Crecy's tank. I was driving. We pulled out and crossed this little bridge and made a left-hand turn. Shells and mortars were jumping all over the place.... That was one heck of a day. I peeped out through the

761st field officers await action near Nancy, France, on November 8, 1944. *From left:* Cpt. Ivan Harrison, H.Q. Co. C.O.; Cpt. Irvin McHenry, C. Co. C.O.; and 2nd Lt. James C. Lightfoot, the 81 MM Mortar Platoon Leader (National Archives photograph).

periscope with shells jumping and the infantry guys would just disappear. Zroom! Gone! Oh God!"[8]

Private E. G. McConnell went on to describe in detail the remainder of his first day in combat:

> It was now getting late in the afternoon and the sun was shining. While we were waiting there I was talking to Trezzvant Anderson, the man who wrote *Come Out Fighting*. He was a war correspondent. I saw this injured German across the road. Having been a Boy Scout, I knew first aid. I went over to see him. He would raise up on his arms, he was on his belly. How pitiful he looked. His whole damned jaw was hanging. I got the first aid kit out of the tank and Trezzvant Anderson went along with me over to him. We crawled over to where

2nd Lt. Jay E. Johnson, the 761st Tank Battalion's Motor Officer, led Charlie Company's first platoon into their baptism of fire. He was seriously wounded and temporarily blinded by a shell burst (National Archives photograph 111-SC-196104).

he was, near a ditch. We got up close and really looked at him. I saw how messed up his face was with no mouth, just top teeth and blood pouring everywhere. I didn't know what to do. The only thing I saw that I could do anything with in the first-aid kit was the gauze. Trez-zvant Anderson had his whiskey flask with him and he had brandy in it. I dipped the gauze pad in the brandy and dabbed up around [the German's] wounds and I could see the appreciation in his eyes. Oh my God, I wondered out loud. There were no ambulances around, they were down below in the field where all of the fighting was going on. All of a sudden they started shelling us. We retreated back to our tank and got in and we left that poor soul out there. There was nothing we could do for him. We couldn't even give him an aspirin because he had no way of swallowing. Then I happened to see a scout car, a half-track from some other unit. This half-track diverted from its driving on the road and deliberately went off the road and ran over this guy we were trying to help. I couldn't believe this. This was war. After that, I saw many dead up close, American soldiers scattered all over just lying in the mud. [Other Americans] usually took the infantryman's rifle with the bayonet on it and stuck it in the ground and put the helmet on top of it to mark where a body was. Then we saw the stream of ambulances coming out of there — jeeps, trucks, everything with wounded lying all over — on top where the windshields were and on the backs — all over. Then we saw Americans walking back and we saw a few German POWs walking back. Now I realized this is war — total war. My prayer book that I still have today, it seemed that every chance I had I opened up this book and I prayed to God and asked Him to save me. I had never had a girlfriend in my entire life. I went into the military at 16. I didn't know what it was to kiss a girl except at a party where you played spin the bottle. I prayed and I said, "My dear God. I'm too young to die like this. Please dear God, don't let me die." My prayers were answered.[9]

The 761st Tank Battalion had just undergone its "Baptism of Fire"; the "Big Hill Up There" was finally taken. Everybody was scared and only a liar would deny it. After the fearsome 88s had oriented them, the battle got underway in earnest. When the day was over, Bezange-la-Petite, Bezange-la-Grande, and Hill 253 all had fallen to the Americans. One hell of a time was had by the Panthers and everyone else involved before the sun set on France that bloody 8th day of November, 1944.

7

The Living Nightmare
of Bloody Hell

At the crack of dawn on November 9, 1944, the 761st assaulted Vic-sur-Seille, Moyenvic, and Morville-les-Vic. The light tanks of Dog Company conducted screening operations in an area around Salival. Here Sergeant Crecy came out of a wooded area where antitank fire caught him in the open and took his tank out from under him. He immediately recovered and took over a vehicle armed only with a .30 caliber machine gun. Still under heavy fire, he liquidated the enemy antitank crew that had knocked out his tank, and aided in the annihilation of enemy forward observers, whose direction of artillery fire had the American infantry pinned down. This swift action permitted the foot soldiers to advance.[1]

Private Harry K. Tyree describes the hit on his tank: "We were with the 26th Division. We pulled out of the woods and picked up a 26th Division lieutenant. This lieutenant got into the assistant driver's seat. The lieutenant wanted to go into the woods and look over this hill. As soon as I got up to the front of the patch of woods something went BOOM! A damn shell hit the assistant driver's side. It was a 75 millimeter armor-piercing shell. It hit the ground first and then hit the tank. It tore the whole suspension system on the right side out. I had one track working. I put the sucker in reverse and floored it! It wiggled its way back into the woods. [Sergeant] Crecy jumped up and said, 'I'm going to get 'em!' That lieutenant, I don't know what the hell happened to him. I never did see him again."[2]

Lt. Colonel Paul L. Bates describes this fixed resolve never to quit: "These men were such terrific fighters. They would do unusual things. They hated the Germans so much, I think they had a lot of hatred in their hearts when they left here [Camp Hood]. They hated them so much that a man would get shot out of a tank; he would be a sergeant; he would go over to another sergeant he outranked or a corporal and using their language to get out of that tank. 'I know where that guy is, I'm going to get him. You don't know where that guy is.' He would take that tank over, get a covered position and knock it out. They fought like that. They were great gunners."[3]

As the 761st converged on Morville-les-Vic, heavy artillery and mortar fire greeted them. The enemy had an artillery officer's candidate school in Marsal only four kilometers to the east. From this location, 88 millimeter shells could be lobbed with ease and accuracy. Eager OCS students worked overtime trying to make good records for themselves and gain glory in the eyes of their superiors. The piercing whine of the 88 "Ripsaw" filled the air.

The situation became worse with the fall of snow. The muddy ground was soon covered with a white mantle against which the dark outlines of the Sherman tanks were clear. This same snow covered the already concealed enemy positions, making them nearly impossible to detect.

Later that day Lt. Colonel Hollis E. Hunt from the 17th Armored Group replaced the wounded Lt. Colonel Bates as battalion commander. Major John F. George, also from the 17th Armored Group, became the battalion S-3 (staff operations officer).

The Panthers took up positions around Morville-les-Vic with Able Company on the east, Charlie Company on the northwest, and Baker Company in the middle poised to go in. Dog Company conducted screening operations from the direction of Salival. After the tanks battered the town thoroughly, the doughboys—American infantry—attempted to break in behind the tanks of Baker Company. Barricades and antitank fire held up the advance.

When Baker Company finally overcame the barricades, a few tanks got into town only to be stopped dead in their tracks by a fury of antitank fire. Enemy antitank and machine gun fire came from all directions. The enemy was cleverly positioned in upper story rooms, basements, and around street corners. The doughboys suffered heavy casualties.

The situation became desperate. Several times the enemy forced the Panthers to relinquish their hold on Morville-les-Vic. Approximately two-thirds of the way through the town, the second tank took a direct hit from a *Panzerfaust* (bazooka) and caught fire. The tank commander, Sergeant Roy King, was hit by machine gun fire and killed as he exited the right turret hatch. Private First Class Nathaniel Ross, Jr., came out through the left turret hatch. He was severely wounded. Technician James T. Whitby and Private John McNeil exited from the bottom escape hatch, hauling their .45 caliber submachine guns. Corporal Herbert Porter, wounded by the hit on the tank, exited last. Minutes later, Whitby reentered the burning tank through the bottom escape hatch. He manned the .30 caliber machine gun and snuffed out several German machine guns and a *Panzerfaust* team in upstairs windows. This action permitted the awaiting doughboys to reenter and begin clearing the town.

In the high grounds, Dog Company assisted the infantry in gaining a foothold northwest of Morville-les-Vic. In a furious battle during this operation they broke up an enemy counterattack. Staff Sergeant Jack Gilbert and his tank crew had to abandon their tank after being hit by antitank fire. The enemy captured and held this tank until Gilbert and his crew recaptured it. In another tank, Private First Class Obie Smith personally accounted for 20 enemy dead with his machine gun.

Meanwhile, Sergeant Crecy's new tank bogged down in the mud. Crecy dismounted and fearlessly faced machine gun fire to extricate his tank. In the course of his work he saw the advancing American infantry crossing open terrain and getting picked off. He climbed up on the rear of his immobilized tank and held the enemy at bay with his .30 caliber machine gun while the foot soldiers escaped. Crecy's driver, Harry K. Tyree, describes how Crecy got tank and crew out of that tight spot:

> When we took out of this wooded area up on the front line, my foot was shaking and carrying on. I'll tell you one thing, Crecy and I worked really well together because I had my headset on, we had throat mics and stuff like that. We started up this hill and Crecy said, "Take it easy, Ty, take it easy." I'm creeping, the light tank had two Cadillac motors in it, and I can't see anything because I'm down and he's up. I'm going up and he says, "Easy, easy, easy." We made it up, not quite to the top, when I heard, "Whing! Whing! Whing!" "Back up! Back up!" I kicked it in reverse and backed it up. Turley and them were over to our right and got stuck going down into a tank trap. We backed up down that hill and went into a little ditch. I couldn't see anything. He said "Right, left" and I'm following his directions. On our tanks we had such small tracks. It was so easy to get stuck, unlike the German tanks that had wide tracks. They could go through the mud and almost anywhere. Crecy said, "Can you get out?" I said, "I'll try," and rocked it a little bit and then Crecy said, "I'll get one of the other tanks to pull us out." I told Crecy, "I'm not going out there." I peeped out there. I had some new boots that I bought in England on the side of the turret, and saw the German machine guns eating them up. He got out there, fired at the enemy, and then attached a cable and had somebody pull us out. I stayed in my position as the driver.[4]

Meanwhile, Charlie Company attacked with such swiftness that a bridge over the Seille River was crossed before the enemy could destroy it. Charlie rumbled right into Morville-les-Vic and then caught hell. 2nd Lieutenant Kenneth W. Coleman was leading his tank platoon in the attack when his tank fell to antitank fire, blocking the road and halting the advance. Coleman, the type who never got excited, immediately dismounted and courageously led his crew on foot under heavy artillery and small arms fire. They battled against a much larger enemy force

Tank Commander Warren G. H. Crecy on the mic (courtesy E. G. McConnell).

and actually drove them from their positions. This outstanding feat enabled his tank platoon to proceed. Lt. Colonel Paul L. Bates describes Coleman's skill in battle: "Lieutenant Coleman, they were pinned down by fire, his men were getting hit. He went forward with a submachine gun and found the machine gun nest, wiped it out. He later got killed."[5]

Charlie Company then ran into a hellish antitank ditch that extended from the woods at the edge of the high grounds to the road in the open country. They came over a steep hill and down into the trap. Unable to pull back over the steep hill they became sitting targets. It was later reported by 26th Infantry Division Headquarters that a hasty briefing about such hazards had taken place, and that details of the antitank defenses had not been given full attention.

Less than 50 yards behind the tank trap stood cleverly concealed concrete pill boxes covered with snow. Antitank guns and rocket launcher teams unleashed hell on the immobilized tanks. The Panthers were knocked out one by one down the line. Seven tanks were put out of commission. Nine enlisted men and one officer lost their lives.

1st Sergeant Samuel Turley, fighting as tank platoon leader, organized tank crews into dismounted combat teams. The field manual was thrown to the winds

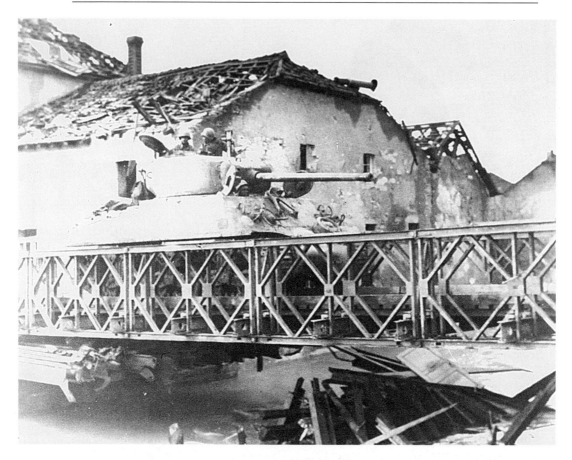

An Able Company 761st tank crosses the Seille River via a recently erected Bailey Bridge on November 9, 1944 (U.S. Army Signal Corps photograph, courtesy Patton Museum, Fort Knox).

for this was not a textbook situation. Upon dismounting his burning tank Turley removed the tank's machine gun, then returned fire by shooting the heavy weapon from his hip. Some of his men crawled under their disabled tanks with their machine guns and placed withering fire upon enemy positions. The dismounted teams held off the enemy counterattack while crews from other trapped and burning tanks escaped along the tank ditch.

Corporal Raleigh Hill, a Charlie Company bow-gunner, recalls: "A German shell hit our tank and set it on fire. We were loaded with ammunition, so much that we couldn't escape through the bottom hatch, we had to come out through the top. The Germans had us well covered with a machine gun that pinned us down inside the tank. We almost couldn't get out when the ammunition started exploding. Then Love King's tank came up and he saw my tank burst. He trained his guns on that German machine gun and 88 and knocked them out. We were hit coming out and they had to carry us to a field hospital."[6]

The escaping Panthers crawled tooth and nail in the freezing, muddy waters of the ditch, beneath rain and snow. Red-hot shell fragments fell all around, steaming up the water as the earth shook from the explosions. The situation became hopeless as artillery began walking a line towards the ditch. The entire atmosphere filled with screams of death, followed by prolonged moans. Then the stench of death and burning bodies caused some survivors to discharge the contents of their stomachs.

Corporal Dwight Simpson, scrambling for his life, saw Technician Horatio Scott, who was seriously wounded and unable to move. With total disregard for his personal safety, Simpson weaved through artillery fire and moved Scott away from his burning tank. He immediately administered life-saving first aid and remained with Scott until dark. Under the cover of darkness he evacuated his wounded comrade 300 yards to the rear for further treatment.

Pinned down and unable to return fire, Turley ordered the retreat of this men. Under heavy artillery and small arms fire he emerged and covered their retreat with such accurate fire that the enemy gunners had to take cover. This selfless action allowed his men to escape with their lives.

Trezzvant Anderson, the war correspondent from the Negro press attached to the 761st, describes the climax of Turley's supreme devotion to duty and skill in battle on that fated day: "We couldn't even put our guns up over the top of the ditch to fire for Ripsaw [the German 88s] had us covered…. Turley was doing one of the most wonderful things ever, when he was killed. Standing behind the ditch, straight up, with a machine gun, and with an ammo belt around his neck, Turley was spraying the enemy with machine gun shots as fast as they could come out of the muzzle of the red hot barrel. He stood there covering for his men, and then fell, cut through the middle by German machine gun bullets that ripped through his body, as he stood there, firing the MG to the last! Not with a tripod, not mounted, but in his hands! That's how Turley went down, and as his body crumpled to the earth, his finger still gripped that trigger. We made it! And then an 88 HE shell hit the spot where Turley was, and the last we saw was pieces of the machine gun and Turley flying in every direction, as the explosion tore the earth, and all around it, to shreds. But we made it!"[7]

Lt. Colonel Paul L. Bates describes Turley's heroics: "C Company in the dim light went into a tank trap and seven tanks were destroyed there. The men were heroes by the moment. The first sergeant of the company, instead of staying behind, routed a bow gunner and went with them. His tank was disabled; he dismounted with a machine gun and a belt of ammunition. He provided covering fire, his men got away, he got killed."[8]

Captain Ivan Harrison was on the other side of the Seille River with a relief force:

World War II German artillery on display today at the U.S. Army Ordnance Museum, Aberdeen Proving Grounds, Maryland. *Top left:* "Ripsaw," the fearsome PAK-43 long-range 88 millimeter antitank gun. *Top right:* 105 millimeter howitzer. *Bottom left:* "Screaming Meemie" *Nebelwerfer* multi-rocket launcher (M-41 150 millimeter). *Bottom right:* Front view of the "Ripsaw" 88 millimeter (courtesy U.S. Army Ordnance Museum Aberdeen Proving Grounds, Maryland).

Right where they crossed that river, I backed my tank up and got close to the buildings. They were shooting heavy artillery at us and the slates on the roofs came down and splattered all over the streets and on top of my tank. I'm watching this through my periscope. Coleman's tank had already been hit and he came back to jump on another tank and go back in. He was crossing that bridge and he got disgusted and sat down. I was looking right at him and Boom! They put more artillery on it and shot him off the bridge. I never guessed why but he just stopped and sat on the edge of the bridge. That is when they killed those men working on the bridge. A white lieutenant who had a platoon up there trying to rebuild the bridge ran down the road. He was shell-shocked! I had my head out of the tank looking. He was so shook up he fell to his knees right by my tank and started praying! I think that shook me up more than anything. I said, "This is hell!" This man, he's running; he fell to his knees and he had a lot of men killed on that bridge where Coleman got killed. I wanted to get the hell out of there myself. That was the most frightening day of my life because we hadn't been there very long and all of those people were getting killed. It was rough and dangerous in places like the Bulge [Ardennes Forest] but I was never shook up like that.[9]

Charlie Company was nearly annihilated by the time help finally arrived. The 105 millimeter assault gun platoon and the 81 millimeter mortar platoon opened fire on enemy positions with devastating effect. Spotter planes picked up an enemy column of approximately 30 vehicles and 200 soldiers enroute to Morville-les-Vic. 1st Lieutenant Charles "Pop" Gates conducted an indirect fire mission that trapped and destroyed the enemy relief column.

(Charles Gates received the nickname "Pop" when his assault gun platoon acquired the call handle, "Father." They would say, "Call 'Pops' and his little sons and they will get the job done." There was also a player on the Renaissance Basketball Team with the name Pop Gates.)

Meanwhile, far out on the left flank, Able Company had completed its mission of capturing Chateau Salines with the 104th Infantry Regiment. This was the first major town to be encompassed by the 26th Infantry Division. As the infantry occupied the town and established a headquarters for the XII Corps, Able Company headed east toward Morville.

As night began to fall, the Panthers received orders to head back. During the return trip tracers ricocheted from the tanks, lighting up the night.

During that evening Lieutenant William Blake was sent out for immediate liaison duty: "When we entered the city I had just got oriented to a building that was between me and the direction from which Jerry's artillery shells were coming when I received orders to report to the regimental command post for instructions. It was pitch dark and the only way I could find my way up the streets was to hug to the buildings as I went along. Just as I got outside my building a German shell landed on the outskirts of the village. This made me feel pretty good for I figured Jerry didn't have the range yet, and I'd be able to make it to the command post before he got it. But I guess I was wrong for about that time I heard one scream over my head and I flattened out on the ground close up beside the building. The shell landed on top of the building and a big pile of debris fell in the middle of my back as I lay there. The concussion stunned me and I laid there for quite a while. Finally I got myself together and began crawling on to the command post."[10]

After Lieutenant Blake arrived at the command post he did not inform anyone of his injuries. For eight days he performed liaison duties for tank and infantry

Charlie Company survivors of the "Living Nightmare of Bloody Hell," Dwight Simpson and Daniel "Club Foot" Cardell (courtesy E. G. McConnell).

coordination before he finally sought medical attention. At the aid station it was discovered that he had suffered serious injuries to his spinal column, and would have to be evacuated to the United States for treatment.

Trezzvant Anderson sums up the Battle of Morville-les-Vic: "'Such bravery I had never before seen!' That's the way a captured German officer put it, after the memorable 9th of November, 1944, when the soil of France was dyed a deeper red with the blood of those daring colored Americans, and Jerry kicked hell out of Company C! It was a living nightmare of bloody hell at Morville-les-Vic. The town was taken, but it was only after a bitter battle, replete with the heroism from America's first Negro tankers, bidding for the place in the sun."[11]

8

Hill 309

As the Panthers pushed on, Platoon Sergeant Johnnie Stevens ran across an infantry platoon pinned down by heavy machine gun fire:

> This lieutenant came up to me and asked if I could put a few rounds of HE on top of a hill. I said, "Are you kidding? I'll blow that son of a bitch apart!" My gunner was good. He was the best! The best gunner in the United States Army. I never had to bracket range with him. He knew what I was thinking. He would lay that shell into the target. He gave me what I asked for every time. After Joe Kiah, my gunner, blew the top of that hill off, the infantry lieutenant thanked us and we went on our way.
>
> One day Joe Kiah knocked out an enemy tank at a distance of over 500 yards. He was the proudest man in the world then. He looked up at me and said, "Sarge, how did I do?" I said, "You stink!" He said, "Why?" "Because, you should have got him on the first shot!" We laughed, that was a joke between us.
>
> I had a good crew and a good platoon. Paul Murphy, my cover man, is my daughter's godfather. We made a pact. If we get out of this alive, whoever gets married first, the other will become the godfather of the first child.[1]

On November 10, 1944, Able Company rumbled through Morville-les-Vic with the infantry. They continued to press forward together as the enemy withdrew slowly in a well-planned and executed retreat still giving stiff resistance. The 4th Armored Division stood by ready to attack should the enemy show signs of making a full retreat.

General F. W. von Mellenthin, the German Chief of Staff for Army Group G in France, describes their orderly withdrawal: "Our plans were based on the principle of elastic defense, whose value had been fully proved in the great [post–1942] battles in Russia. Troops packed into forward positions were doomed to destruction

James Mason and Johnnie Stevens, Jr., in 1944. Captain D. J. Williams recalls: "I had some tough guys — Johnnie Stevens — who would cut your throat in a minute. A tough, nasty staff sergeant. He was a maverick. I said, 'Johnnie, I should have court-martialed you, but you were too good a fighter'" (courtesy Johnnie Stevens, Jr.).

by artillery and air bombardment, so we issued instructions that when an attack appeared imminent the forward troops were to withdraw to a line some miles in the rear. Only patrols were to remain in the forward area. In this way the enemy might be induced to off load his destructive fire on empty trenches, and our troops could be conserved for the main battle."[2]

On November 11, Johnnie Stevens led Able Company's 3rd platoon in an assault on Hill 309 near the town of Wuisse:

> This was the worst! I remember Hill 309 because I lost so much on Hill 309. My tank was knocked out, I had a crew member killed. Shivers's tank was knocked out and I lost a lot of men on that hill. I was worried about Joe Kiah, my gunner; James Peoples, my driver; and Emerson Hadnot, my bow gunner, because they were my crew. I came out with three of my crew members. I watched George Shivers's tank go up, I watched him when he got hit. I didn't know how many guys got killed, but I found out later that Shivers got killed. He was

George Shivers, a tank commander who was killed in action on Hill 309 on November 11, 1944 (courtesy Margaret Crecy).

in my platoon, one of my tank commanders. He got hit. I saw that before I got hit. Ivery Fox was out there, but I don't remember what happened to Fox because I got hit after Shivers. Nelson, I don't know what happened to him and his crew because I was hit, I was wounded, but I knew my platoon took a beating on that hill that day. We took one helluva beating up there because we were told there was nothing up there. I led my platoon up there and what the hell, all of a sudden hell broke loose and we got shot up all over the damn place. The 26th Division's recon had told us there was nothing there, which often happens in combat. Maybe they moved them up after the recon people checked it out, but there was no reason for me to leave all those dead men on the field.

The 26th Infantry Division lost a lot of infantrymen that day. A lot of people died on that day because somebody made a mistake. I came out with three of my crew members, the other had been killed. We were laying in the field, and the Germans started dropping mortar fire. Because, you see, they want to kill tankers. Tankers kill too many people, and when you come out of those tanks, they're going to make sure they kill you. I had been hit pretty hard. My combat suit was all covered with blood, and I was laying in a ditch. A tall sergeant from the 26th Division calls out to me, "Hey, Sarge, you hit?" I said, "I'm hit hard as hell." He jumped over the other side of the embankment and he took his arms and put them under me and he just shoved me over the embankment where I was safe from the mortar fire. And before he could duck back down himself, a German raised up about 15 yards away and with his burp gun, he cut that sergeant half in two. After I got out of the hospital, I tried to find out the sergeant's name. He should have been posthumously cited. This has always bugged me. I could never find out who this guy was. I received some letters from Minnesota, places like that where people think they know who it was, but the timing wasn't right. It was November 11 at 11 o'clock. I didn't want to say who it was unless I could prove it and I never had a witness.[3]

It was during this vicious battle that Captain Garland "Doc" Adamson, M.D., the 761st Tank Battalion's medical officer, proceeded on foot through an artillery barrage from the aid station to the wounded tankers. There he efficiently gave life-saving medical treatment in total disregard for his own personal safety. For his strong devotion to duty, courage, and solicitude for his wounded comrades, he was awarded the Bronze Star. "Doc" was approximately 50 years old then, the unit's oldest member. Before joining the Army he taught obstetrics and gynecology at Meharry Medical School in Tennessee.

During this battle the enemy's artillery found the battalion command post and bivouac area. The barrage disrupted the lines of communications between the joint tank and infantry elements, causing confusion.

Captain Garland "Doc" Adamson, M.D., November 1944 (National Archives photograph 111-SC-196102).

On November 12, 1st Lieutenant Joseph O. Kahoe, Jr.'s tank platoon, along with elements of the 104th Infantry Regiment, counterattacked. They spotted the anti-tank guns and wiped them out. They took Wuisse around 1400 hours on November 13 and defended the town during the night.

Kahoe, the son of a dry-cleaner, had developed into an intrepid platoon leader and a brilliant field commander. He had joined the Army in 1935 at the age of 18 and groomed horses as a $21-a-month cavalry private. He re-enlisted in 1942 with the hopes of going to OCS. As the only black officer candidate in his class, he graduated and became a 2nd lieutenant.

On November 14, the battle-weary Panthers limped over to Ham Pont, regrouped and performed maintenance. Johnnie Stevens was in the hospital having 11 pieces of shrapnel removed from his legs.

9

The Baddest Man in the 761st

On the second day of battle, Sergeant Crecy's sworn friend, Technician Horatio Scott, was wounded and evacuated to a hospital. He sent word back to Harding (that's what Crecy's close friends called him). He said, "Harding, I'm okay and I'll be back soon."[1] He could not live up to his word. He died and went into a grave in a foreign land.

Margaret Crecy affectionately recalls her husband's best friends: "We were friends, we were the greatest of friends. Scotty [Horatio Scott] and I were the same age. We were the buddies. All of their spare time, the four of us would spend together. That was Jordan, Scotty, Harding, and I. They went home with us. We weren't that far away from Temple. On the weekends we would go and they would come with us. If Harding had duty and couldn't come home, Scotty and Jordan would come into town and take care of me. We were a foursome. Scotty wasn't his only best buddy."[2]

When word of Scott's death reached Crecy, he became infuriated and took out after the enemy with vengeance. Trezzvant Anderson describes Crecy's motivation:

> To look at Warren G. H. Crecy (the "G. H." stands for Gamaliel Harding), you'd never think that here was a "killer" who had slain more men than any man in the 761st. He extracted a toll of lives from the enemy that would have formed the composition of three or four companies, with his machine guns alone. And yet he is such a quiet, easygoing, meek-looking fellow that you'd think that the fuzz which a youngster tries to cultivate for a mustache would never grow on his baby-skinned chin. And that he'd never use a word stronger than "damn!" But here was a youth, who went so primatively savage on the battlefield that his only thought was to "kill, kill and kill," and he poured his rain of death pellets into German bodies with so much reckless abandon and joy that he was the nemesis of all the foes of the 761st. And other men craved to ride with Crecy, and share the reckless

thrill of killing the hated enemy that had killed their comrades. And he is now living on borrowed time. By all human equations Warren G. H. Crecy should have been dead long ago, and should have had the Congressional Medal of Honor, at least...! It's either for revenge, or to kill to keep from being killed, that makes men do great things on the field of battle. That was what made Warren G. H. Crecy the killingest killer in the 761st Tank Battalion, Revenge! For others it was the same, or "If I don't kill them, they will kill me." And so, it was Jerry who had to get it, for it was coming to him, from these men of the 761st Tank Battalion![3]

Warren G. H. Crecy (courtesy Margaret Crecy).

Platoon Sergeant Johnnie Stevens from Able Company remembers Crecy: "Crecy was always in on everything. Whenever there was a fight or something going on, Warren Crecy was there. I don't know what it was about the guy, but he had a way of doing things. You see, I trained Crecy in Texas. I used to tell him: 'Crecy! Man, you're gung ho!' He wanted to do everything better than anybody else. The guy just seemed to have no fear. Not having fear means this, you're afraid but you don't want to die. You want to kill the other guy before you die. I was afraid all the time. Afraid of dying like everybody else. Any man who goes into combat and says he's not afraid is a liar!"[4]

Harry K. Tyree affectionately remembers his friend and former tank commander: "He was such a nice guy, you would never think that he would turn out to be such a hellcat. One of his buddies got killed and he went berserk! But he was such a beautiful guy. I was really proud when the day came when Crecy got his bars and we could salute him."[5]

Captain Philip W. Latimer, the battalion S-4 (supply officer), remembers Crecy: "Many of the men referred to him as the 'Baddest Man in the 761st.' I never saw him in action, but everyone who did gave enthusiastic support to the idea that he was a great fighter."[6]

Sergeant Crecy would often pull his tank far ahead of the infantry, leaving himself open to the dreaded *Panzerfaust*. He would eliminate enemy machine gun emplacements whose fire had the infantry pinned down. Several times he had his

Best friends — Warren G. H. Crecy *(left)* and Horatio Scott (courtesy Margaret Crecy).

tank shot out from under him. Although wounded, he returned fire from an exposed position outside of the tank, using the tank's anti-aircraft machine gun. This enabled the foot soldiers to advance or escape. Then he would take over another vehicle, not always a tank, and get right back into the battle. He fought like that throughout the war. Captain Edwin W. Reynolds, a 761st staff operations officer, recalls: "Sergeant Crecy in D Company really showed them something. When his tank got knocked out, he stood on the turret and fired a machine gun. He killed a lot of them."[7]

Crecy's concentration on destroying the enemy was so intense that on many occasions he personally liquidated so many enemy soldiers that they could not be counted. It seems that the more enemy fire he drew, the harder he fought. After the battle he had to be pried away from his machine gun. He received the Silver Star for his actions around Morville-les-Vic.

There are clear indications that racial discrimination and inadvertent neglect on the part of those in authority may have been a factor in denials of the Distinguished Service Cross or the Medal of Honor. The climate created by the Army commanders could only have made it difficult to provide proper recognition for a "colored" soldier. The accomplishments of Sergeant Crecy were quite impressive. The high enemy casualties and destruction of their equipment were achieved despite personal wounds, documented adverse weather conditions, and problems in logistics peculiar only to a dispersed "colored" outfit attached to several other units in a segregated Army. With no controlling headquarters element, it would have been extremely difficult for the outfit to compile timely statistical information necessary to prepare well documented and timely recommendations.

The battalion commander, Lt. Colonel Paul L. Bates, later commented on this situation: "I sincerely hope no one believes that no one received a CMH [Congressional Medal of Honor] simply because no one took the time to investigate, do the paperwork, follow up, and keep following up. That is sheer idiocy and complete lack of understanding all the things that need to be done to fight, maintain vehicles, tend the sick and wounded, provide food, medicine, ammunition, gasoline, service weapons, replace parts, and sometimes to find time to eat and sleep. I come from a sizable, loving family. The only mail I ever received was while in the hospital. It might give you some idea of the dependability of paperwork once it leaves your hands. Decorations, medals up through a Silver Star, only have to travel up one level of command, from battalion to division for approval. Others have a very long way to go in distance, time, and number of people."

Bates further pointed out: "During World War II we entered combat with over 700 men and received 200 while in Holland. In 183 days of combat, this multiplicity of men coming and going (killed or wounded) moving through attachments to seven divisions, changing armies four times with all that reporting in and out, moving through six different countries, putting in recommendations for medals

Daniel Cardell and Warren G. H. Crecy showing off their recently captured German-officer PPK pistols (courtesy E. G. McConnell).

that were discarded simply because we were black and moving out of the unit's jurisdiction loosely describes our situation."[8]

Charles "Pop" Gates, who later became Crecy's company commander, recalls: "We started out with 750 men. All through the 183 days, we had 34 men killed in action. We had 293 who received Purple Hearts. We had 60 who received Bronze Stars. We had 11 who received Silver Stars. Remember, these awards were granted through the divisions with whom we'd been attached. A division naturally is gonna take care of its own first. So for us to have received that many awards meant to me that any man who received a Bronze Star should have received a Silver Star and any man who received a Silver Star should have received a Congressional Medal of Honor. Because we got only the crumbs. So we must have done a very creditable job. They were very well trained and disciplined. We had a job to do and they did their best."[9]

Despite this lack of recognition, Crecy devoted himself to his duty with a zealous pride that went back to his childhood. A graduate of Solomon M. Coles High School in Corpus Christi, Texas, he was a "blood and guts" football player. At 150 pounds, his coach said that pound for pound he was the greatest player he had ever

Crecy's Charlie Company tank (courtesy E. G. McConnell).

coached. On April 12, 1942, Crecy was 17 years old when he enlisted in the Army at Fort Sam Houston, Texas. Margaret Crecy remembers: "We grew up together. He proposed to me, I was nine and he was 12. Our families were friends and he came over one Sunday after Mass. He was dressed up and had flowers and ice cream for my mother and she said, 'Oh, Harding.' We never called him Warren, it was always Harding. He said, 'I come to ask for your youngest daughter in marriage. When she is 18 I'm going to marry her.' He was always a very positive person. As a boy he took pride in everything he owned and anything he did because he was always a man."[10]

10

Ruben Rivers Leads the Way

It was rough during that fall of 1944, with the rain, the mud, the cold driving sleet, and the ferocity with which the crack Nazi troops bitterly contested every inch of ground. With terrain thickly sown with mines and cleverly concealed anti-tank positions, the Panthers smashed through the French towns of Obreck, Dedeline, and Chateau Voue with Platoon Sergeant Ruben Rivers leading the way for Able Company.

2nd Lieutenant Robert Hammond, Jr., recalled communicating by radio with Rivers: "Don't go into that town, Sergeant, it's too hot in there." The lieutenant's radio crackled and Rivers's response came back in a respectful tone of voice: "I'm sorry, sir, I'm already through that town!"[1] In this stretch Rivers became adept at liquidating the enemy with his .50 caliber machine gun. The dashing young Oklahoman from the small town of Hotulka, near Tecumseh, became a legend in his battalion. He was Able Company's finest sergeant, a proper and quiet gentleman respected by all for his guts and calmness under fire. Everyone swore that he would receive the battalion's first battlefield commission.

The 26th Infantry Division's objective was to take the town of Benestroff, with the 761st Tank Battalion spearheading the advance. Benestroff, a vital railroad and communications center, served enemy operations east of Metz. Patton's Third Army had other divisions simultaneously closing in on Metz. As the pincer movement closed up, the 26th Infantry Division eliminated any possibility of relief to the hard-pressed enemy.

On November 16, 1944, Able Company led an early morning attack on Guebling by spearheading for the 2nd Battalion, 101st Infantry Regiment. The railroad town of Guebling was situated in the center of a four-mile-wide valley surrounded by wooded ridges. At the bottom of the ridge stood approximately three miles of open terrain that had been churned up by an earlier failed attempt by CCB (Combat Command B), a tank brigade of the 4th Armored Division. The freezing temperatures caused the churned-up mud to harden, providing excellent traction for the tanks. Still, the Panthers felt uneasy as they passed by CCB's burned out Sherman tanks.

Lieutenant William Blake, who at this time was Stateside recovering from spinal cord injuries, remembers the crack 4th Armored Division: "We would be on our way up to attack and we'd meet the 4th Armored Division going back the other way. After this happened a couple of times, we began to get curious because we figured they must be retreating since they were always going the other way. Finally we found out how they were operating. A day before we were to attack the Germans, Lt. General Patton would select a strongly fortified town about 15 miles behind the German lines and tell his 4th Armored boys to go out and 'blast the hell out of it.' Those guys would take off in their tanks and fight their way through the Jerry lines to the town and do just what he told them to. The next day when we hit the Germans the 4th would fight their way back from behind the German lines and join us on the frontal attack. Boy, that's a real outfit."[2]

Ruben Rivers, 1944 (courtesy Anese Rivers Woodfork).

Able Company approached Guebling with 11 tanks and split into two tank platoons that would lead the way for the infantry. Hammond took the first platoon of five tanks, with Rivers in the lead tank. 1st Lieutenant Joseph Kahoe led the second platoon with six tanks, including Able Company's headquarters tank. As the second platoon reached the summit of a gentle slope, a concentrated barrage of enemy artillery fire met them. Kahoe lost his tank and had to be evacuated along with a member of his crew. Kahoe's remaining tank crew members escaped injury and returned to the command post, picked up another tank, and rejoined the platoon. Kahoe's tank platoon pulled back, changed direction, and joined Hammond's platoon as the infantry followed.

On the way into Guebling, Rivers's tank ran over a double teller anti-tank mine. The explosion was so great that it blew off the right track, the volute springs and the undercarriage. The tank was tossed sideways. Staff Sergeant Ray Roberson and Corporal Homer Bracy of the 761st medical detachment heard the explosion, jumped in their jeep, and drove down along the tank column until they reached the lead tank. There they found Rivers behind the tank holding his leg. There was a gash in his right leg where the knee used to be, and a bone stuck out through his torn pants leg. The medics cleaned and dressed the wound and attempted to inject Rivers with morphine. They told the commanding officer that Rivers must be evacuated immediately. Rivers refused. He also refused the morphine in order to remain alert. Rivers pulled himself to his feet, pushed past the commanding officer, and jumped up on the second tank where he told Sergeant Conway to get out because he was taking over. Conway then took his sub-machine gun and took up positions with the infantry. At that moment a hail of enemy mortar fire came in, marking the tanks with smoke for the heavy artillery. Orders were given to disperse and take cover in and around Guebling's railroad station complex. Rivers's new tank was driven by Technician Jonathan B. Hall. Private First Class Frank Towers was the bow gunner, Private First Class Ivory V. Hilliard was the loader, and Private Everett Robinson was the cannoneer.

The commanding officer, Captain David J. Williams II, recalls what happened: "With the morphine needle in my right hand about a half inch from Sergeant Rivers's leg, I could have told my sergeant to hold him down. I said, 'Ruben, you're going back. You've got a million-dollar wound. You're going back to Tecumseh. You're getting out of this. You got a Silver Star and Purple Heart.' He says, 'Captain, you're going to need me.' I said, 'I'm giving you a direct order! You're going back!' I said, 'Medics, get the stretcher.' He pushed the needle away and got up. He said, 'This is one order, the only order I'll ever disobey.' I said, 'Listen to me, once across that bridge there is no coming back, they're over on our right flank.' And I said that the 4th Armored Division with 30 tanks got murdered here. So he pushed by me, goes to another tank, Henry Conway's, orders him out and gets in his turret. At that time they were marking us with smoke and I said, 'well, medics, you go back. I'll see Sergeant Rivers tonight.' So we took the little place and waited for the engineers to put the bridge in."[3]

At dusk, on November 16, Captain Williams paid a visit to each tank, as was his custom. Accompanied by his driver, Corporal Howard "Big Tit" Richardson and two medics, they found Rivers's tank behind the house nearest to where the combat engineers worked. It was obvious that Rivers suffered extreme pain even though he did not complain. After the shock wore off, the pain must have been excruciating. The medics told Williams to get Rivers out of there and Williams gave Rivers another direct order. Rivers again refused and said, "Captain, you're going to need me." Williams later remarked: "Well, he was good and he probably would have been an officer. No, he probably would have been company commander."[4]

On November 17, the combat engineers worked, sweated, and died constructing

Opposite and above: German *Panzerjaegers* (tank destroyers) on display today at the U.S. Army Ordnance Museum, Aberdeen Proving Grounds, Maryland. *Opposite top:* "Elephant" Stu 6 Tank Destroyer armed with an 88 millimeter antitank gun. *Opposite bottom: Jagdpanzer* armed with an 88 millimeter antitank gun. *Above:* Hetzer (Baiter) *Jagdpanzer* armed with a 75 millimeter antitank gun.

a prefabricated Bailey bridge while the Panthers and doughboys exchanged fire with the enemy. Despite the intense firefight, the combat engineers completed the bridge late that afternoon and Rivers led the way across.

As the Panthers entered Guebling, Rivers, despite his serious wounds, engaged two enemy tanks and battled them until they withdrew.

Rivers and a companion tank commanded by Sergeant Walter James took up firing positions on a gentle slope that offered a field of fire on Bougaltroff. 2nd Lieutenant Hammond and a companion tank took up positions in an orchard area in the low grounds. Captain Williams and the remaining tanks took up positions inside Guebling, as the snow and sleet continued to fall.

Private First Class Floyd Dade, Jr., recalls entering Guebling: "We were heading for Guebling and 2nd Lieutenant Hammond ordered us to the center of the town and he took the left flank which was on the outskirts. The picture that you see in the *Stars and Stripes* on November 27, 1944, is our tank shielded behind a knocked out tank of the 4th Armored Division. As the Germans would fire, the rounds would go over the knocked out tank and hit the buildings. So we were

Private First Class Floyd Dade, Jr. (courtesy Mr. and Mrs. Floyd Dade, Jr.).

covered pretty good. Our mission was to guard the crossroads about 500 yards away. We zeroed in on the crossroads in case the enemy counterattacked.

"That night all hell broke loose. The 26th Infantry Division had a company that got captured and the Germans took their uniforms and returned to infiltrate our lines. The Germans were sending up flares. As the flare would light up the terrain, it was a beautiful sight to see the infantry frozen in position, then they would hit the dirt. You could hear gunfire of the German burp guns and American .30 caliber machine guns and M-1s. They fought all night until daybreak."[5]

Before dawn on November 18, Captain Williams and the medical team again visited each tank. When they visited Rivers they found him poker faced, but it was obvious that he was in extreme pain. The medics reexamined what was left of Rivers's leg and discovered that infection had set in.

Captain Williams reflects on this: "CCB of the 4th Armored Division got murdered in the same place and I thought, here it comes our turn. That night after we took the town of Guebling, I went up to see him again... I said, 'Ruben! Richardson will take you back tonight. I'm giving you another order.' He says, 'Captain, you know better than that.... This is going to be tough! Another two days won't make any difference.' The medic says: 'Listen, he's got gangrene!' I said, 'Ruben,' and then they started to shell us and I went back to my tank."[6] Throughout November 18, both sides held and defended their positions.

At dawn on November 19, the assault on Bougaltroff began in earnest. Staff Sergeant Weston's tank led off as the infantry began infiltrating past the tanks. When the Panthers came from behind cover, the morning air outside Guebling was lit up by tracers from enemy anti-tank positions. Captain Williams's tank followed behind Weston's, leading two other tanks in column. Weston's tank received a direct hit that disabled his 76 millimeter gun. The Panthers began to be knocked out, one by one. Williams immediately radioed all tanks on the move to pull back. Rivers, along with his companion tank, spotted the enemy's antitank positions from their covered position behind a slope. They immediately came from behind cover and placed a concentrated barrage of fire on enemy Mark IV Panther Tanks and

94

Panzerjaegers. This allowed the trapped Panthers and doughboys to escape with their lives. Captain Williams saw tracers hit 2nd Lieutenant Hammond's tank and Hammond's companion tank. He then ordered all tanks to pull back. He ordered Rivers and James to take cover behind the crest of the hill, as division artillery intensified their "time on target" fire mission. Again and again he tried to get a response. Helpless, filled with agitation and dismay, Williams tried to radio them, knowing that neither would ever answer: "Move back, Rivers!"[7] Rivers, in a frenzied firefight shooting out tracers from his 76 millimeter cannon like a machine gun, probably didn't hear Captain Williams. The Panthers heard Rivers over the radio: "I see them. We'll fight them."[8] Rivers kept firing on the enemy until tracers were seen going into his turret. "Pull up, driver! Pull back, driver! Oh, Lord," were Rivers's last words before his tank exploded. At that moment the Panzerjaegers began to go after Rivers's companion tank. Sergeant James immediately pulled his tank to cover behind the crest of the hill.

Trezzvant Anderson describes the hit on Ruben Rivers's tank: "From the comparatively close range of 200 yards, the Germans threw two high-explosive shots that scored. The first shot hit near the front of the tank and penetrated, striking two of the men beside Rivers. Robinson, the cannoneer, was wounded and Hilliard, the gunner, was killed, by the ricocheting fragments confined inside the steel walls of the tank, and Rivers was also hit. The second shot scored into the tank. The first one had blown Rivers's brains out against the back of the tank, and the second went into his head, emerging from the rear. And the intrepid leader was no more. Hilliard's body was discovered two days later."

Anderson went on to write: "Technician Roderick Ewing, of Oklahoma City, Oklahoma, was also killed that day. And the platoon leader, 2nd Lieutenant Robert C. Hammond, Jr., of Cleveland, Ohio, also went down, dying a heroic death, as he was bringing out the .50 caliber machine gun, to cover the escape of crewmen from the other disabled tanks. He was shot down firing at the enemy."[9]

Private First Class Floyd Dade, Jr., recalls: "Early that morning, when the fog lifted in the hedge grove, in front of 2nd Lieutenant Hammond's tank about 200 yards away was a Tiger tank. The Tiger fired one round that hit the gunsight on [Hammond's] tank. The 2nd Lieutenant and his gunner were killed."[10]

Captain David J. Williams II recalls the aftermath:

> A runner came up and said, "Colonel Lyons from the infantry just lost his eye and a leg, you're in charge!" I told the runner to get the grunts back and hide in the cellars, they have too much for us. Another bundle of joy, the infantry said, "They are coming around behind us." I said, "Once you're in the houses, let them attack." I had the cannon company from the infantry there. War is strange. Suddenly there was a lull, silence. The medics started checking the tanks. My job was to identify my dead. In my company we had a rule to go

95

after the wounded because tank wounds are terrible, they're vehicular. If they get out of that tank, there is a leg off....

Then along comes Lt. Colonel Hunt, who took Bates's place. He is standing in a half-track looking immaculate and he says, "Williams, you had quite a battle here." I said, "Yes sir!" Then the TD Captain said, "Listen, this company stayed in there." I didn't have much of a company left and there was infantry all over the place. The infantry takes terrible casualties. I said, "I want to put Sergeant Rivers in for the Congressional Medal of Honor." He said, "What did he do? He got the Silver Star already." I said, "Sir, that was for November 8. He's up in that tank there." He said, "Well, put it in writing." He didn't show any interest.... It was subtly told to me not to put anything in over the Silver Star. We called it the battalion commander's good conduct medal; I got one. Once they saw 761st with "N" behind it; Silver Star. I didn't deserve any more.[11]

At 1300 hours, the Panthers and what remained of the infantry were pinched out. Ruben Rivers did not have to die on that cold, dreary November morning but he continued to take his tank into the thick of every battle. It became a popular theme that when Able Company entered battle, Rivers led the way. He was always there first. He was expected to receive the first Battlefield Commission.

Captain Williams was now about to come up close and personal with the enemy:

We had a rule in A Company not to leave wounded out there, without legs and such, to die alone. It was for morale purposes and it was nothing heroic but a company commander had to set the example. I knew what was coming. Me, Big Tit, Chico, Henry Conway, we went out. The enemy was about 150 yards away and I knew there was an observation post and machine gun nest. I went over to Vinton Hudson and he said, "Am I going to die, Captain?" I said "No, you'll be home." It wasn't bleeding that much and Ray dusted it with sulfur, splinted it, and put a patch on. I said, "Ray, you better give him the morphine." Then I looked over to some trees and I saw a German soldier I thought was dead. I saw him raise his hand about 10 yards away. I said, "Ray, follow me." I signaled the stretcher bearer to take Vinton back. So I crawled over on my belly and I said, "*Was ist los mit dir?*" He replied, "*Ich bin verwunded,*" and pointed to his shoulder. Ray cut the jacket away, dusted it and put a compress on it. I signaled another stretcher up and put him on it. We walked away and as I got to the trees, I looked around and a German officer stood up and saluted. I saluted him back. This was the 11th Panzer Division, a very noble division. We got them back and Vinton lived. I remember saying to the German soldier in German, you'll like Camp Hood, Texas. And I got a letter from him! "Dear *Hauptman*, You were right. I like Camp Hood, Texas." I remember when I sent him off, I said, "*Krieg*

The remains of four German Panzers and two 761st Sherman tanks lie in the open field between Guebling and Bougaltrof, casualties of the fierce November 19 battle. This photograph was taken on November 25, 1944. In the left foreground is a bomb crater filled with rainwater (National Archives photograph).

ist endet für dich." The war is over for you. He was a German gefreiter. The poor son of a bitch, he got the luckiest break of his life. The Germans didn't fire at us even though Ray had given our Red Cross flag to the infantry. I said, "Where the hell is your vest? They can't see that cross on your helmet!"[12]

Two weeks later, the Rivers family received the following Western Union telegram: "To Mrs. Lillian Rivers. Rte One Box 57 Tecumseh, Oklahoma = The Secretary of War desires me to express his deepest regret that your son Staff Sergeant Ruben Rivers was killed in action on Nineteen November in France. Letter follows = Dunlop Acting the Adjutant General." Then the following letter from the 761st Tank Battalion's commanding officer, Lt. Colonel Hollis A. Hunt, arrived:

The Silver Star, the first one ever presented at Will Rogers Airfield, was awarded to the parents of Staff Sergeant Ruben Rivers on May 30, 1945. *Left to right:* Colonel John F. Boodle, Mr. Willie Rivers, Willie Rivers, Jr., and Mrs. Lillian Rivers (courtesy Anese Rivers Woodfork).

IN GRATEFUL MEMORY OF

Staff Sergeant Ruben Rivers, A.S.No. 38063493,

WHO DIED IN THE SERVICE OF HIS COUNTRY AT

in the European Area, November 19, 1944.

HE STANDS IN THE UNBROKEN LINE OF PATRIOTS WHO HAVE DARED TO DIE

THAT FREEDOM MIGHT LIVE, AND GROW, AND INCREASE ITS BLESSINGS.

FREEDOM LIVES, AND THROUGH IT, HE LIVES—

IN A WAY THAT HUMBLES THE UNDERTAKINGS OF MOST MEN

Franklin D Roosevelt

PRESIDENT OF THE UNITED STATES OF AMERICA

Courtesy Mrs. Anese Rivers Woodfork.

Left: Clerk Typist Charles P. Ashby (courtesy Charles P. Ashby). *Right:* Anese Rivers, Ruben's younger sister (courtesy Anese Rivers Woodfork).

My dear Mrs. Rivers,

I know only too well that words cannot bring comfort to your aching heart in these hours of loss; however, as your son's battalion commander, I want to tell you that all of us who remain in this battalion grieve with you in the loss of our comrade.

Your son, Staff Sergeant Ruben Rivers, 38063493, was killed in action on 19 November 1944 during our attack on Guebling, France. He was buried in the Province of Lorraine, France, after an appropriate service at which a Protestant Chaplain officiated. You may secure more detailed information concerning the location of the grave and the disposal of your son's remains and effects by communicating directly with the Quartermaster General, Army Service Forces, Washington 25, DC.

He did his duty splendidly and was loved and admired by all who knew him. We will not forget.

He gave his life in the service of his country and these simple words cannot lighten our sorrow, but they bring great pride and inspiration to us all.[13]

Although no documentary evidence could be found, Captain Williams maintained that he recommended Ruben Rivers for the Medal of Honor on November 20, 1944. The company clerk, Technician Charles P. Ashby, in a sworn affidavit stated: "…while serving as the person charged with the responsibility for preparing and processing recommendations for awards and decorations for the 761st Tank Battalion, did process and forward through proper channels for further review, a recommendation for the posthumous award of the Congressional Medal of Honor for Staff Sergeant Ruben Rivers, for acts of heroism 'above and beyond the call of duty,' while at a location near the town Guebling, France, November 20, 1944." Yet Rivers received no Medal of Honor; in fact, of the 1.2 million African Americans who served in World War II, none received any of the 433 Medals of Honor awarded.[14] This became, as the black poet Langston Hughes once said, a "dream deferred."

Anese Rivers Woodfork, a younger sister of Ruben Rivers, describes seeing him for the last time:

> I'm one of six sisters of Ruben Rivers. There are nine of us still living, three brothers and six sisters. One thing that I can say about my brother that nobody knows about, I was the last of his family to see him when he left the little Oklahoma town and the muddy road where he left from. He had to walk back to the station because the roads were so bad that he could not go by car. I stood there and looked at my brother. I was just a young teen, but I really cried because I loved my brother. When he left he kept waving. He waved and he waved and he waved…. So I feel proud that I really was the last sister to see him.
>
> I remember when World War II broke out. We were sitting in a classroom and when they announced that a world war had broken out, it was like a bomb or something hit. We were just young teens, but we realized what a tragedy that was. My mother had three sons to go to World War II: my oldest brother Robert, second Ruben, then Dewey. Dewey is no longer with us, but my oldest brother Robert is still here and he remembers everything. As a matter of fact, he said he was there two days after Ruben was killed and he tried to tell us about it, but for some reason my brother did not want to talk about it anymore. The thing that I really regret is, my mother wanted to have my brother's body sent back home, but my father said, "No, it will bring back sorrow again." I used to hear my mother crying. She was crying for her son, I know that.
>
> I feel that my brother is somewhere up in the elements floating

David J. Williams II points out the sights along the way as he goes with the 106th Cavalry Reconnaissance Squadron to reconnoiter a path for his Able Company tanks. Albestroff, France, November 22, 1944 (courtesy David J. Williams II).

around for I believe in wandering spirits. He was a religious person, so am I. My mother and father brought us up religiously. I feel that he is floating up in the elements somewhere and if he should receive the Congressional Medal of Honor, which I really feel he deserves, his soul will come home to rest. I know that he was a leader, he wanted to make someone proud of him. There is something else I just heard, race. He never mentioned race because he was a man, an honorable man. I think that his chief ambition was to be a leader, a man. He fought for a country that actually did not recognize him. He was not recognized as a man or a soldier, but he still fought for his country. I keep wondering today, was that really his country that he was fighting for? Well, maybe I can feel a little bitter, but I'm not, because I am a religious person and maybe it truly will happen. If he should receive this honor, his soul will come home to rest.[14]

With heavy losses, Able Company limped several miles southeast and regrouped at Marimont. The maintenance section worked feverishly to get the remaining tanks ready for the next mission while the men rested, cleaned themselves, and dealt with their continual cases of dysentery.

On the morning of November 21, Captain Williams was awakened by Corporal Walter Lewis, who invited him to a memorial service given by the men. They wanted to say their own personal prayers and just be together. Williams recalls:

> I walked quickly with him to the weather beaten, ancient stone church and sat next to him in the last row of benches. Every head was bowed. There were no sounds except for quiet weeping. I, too, bowed my head. I thanked God for them, for their loyalty and brotherhood. I not only prayed for our dead, but also for those who had fallen in the other companies. I thought about 1st Sergeant Turley and the heroic way he died. I remembered so clearly how kind he had been to a very young, uncertain 2nd Lieutenant in April 1942. I thought about the gentle, sensitive Lieutenant Hammond and the stoic, fearless Sergeant Rivers. I wondered about Sergeant Johnnie Stevens and where he was wearing his defiant, confident expression. Had Vinton Hudson survived his terrible leg wound? Herbert McCullock … Shivers … Campbell.…
>
> I prayed for Roderick Ewing, who like Rivers, was from Oklahoma. He was such a good baseball player. I shivered when I thought about Ivory Hilliard running in panic and pain toward the enemy lines and found a day and a half later curled up in an abandoned enemy trench. What must his last thoughts have been? If only he had stayed near the tank. I prayed for our wounded, too. I prayed that they would recover and be sent home, not back up here, even though our depleted ranks needed them. Lastly, I prayed that somehow what was left of us would get through. We were one now. No barriers between these black men and me. No more suspicions, no more hatred, no more contempt. Only love and respect.
>
> Before I left that church, I at last understood in part their great pride, the black man's pride, that had kept him from insanity through the centuries of humiliation and exploitation. I saw how this small company of soldiers was rising above their nightmare at home to pass the deadliest manhood rite ever devised. I knew deep inside my soul that these men had helped me find my manhood, also.[15]

Despite their heavy losses, Able Company pushed on. Embittered over the loss of their comrades and sworn friends from their training days back at Claiborne and Hood, they battled the enemy with an unrelenting fury. Corporal Otis Johnson, Technician Ivery Fox, Private First Class Louis Gains, and Private Homer Nealy — Staff Sergeant Ruben Rivers's original tank crew — knocked out two enemy tanks at a range of approximately 1,600 yards. They fired only one round for each of those tanks of the 113th Panzer Brigade.

11

The Hot Spot at Honskirch

On November 20, 1944, Charlie Company supported the 2nd Battalion, 328th Infantry Regiment, for an assault on Kerprich. Four assault guns and four medium tanks shelled the town while the doughboys attempted to break in. Captain Irvin McHenry, Charlie Company's commanding officer, broke his hand in his cannon's recoil. 1st Lieutenant Charles "Pop" Gates from Headquarters Company took his place. The infantry entered Kerprich that evening and began to clear it.

On November 22, Charlie Company entered Torchville unopposed. From Torchville they drove through Bois-de-Hessling to the western edge of Munster. One section of assault guns moved south and shelled the town. As night fell, the doughboys occupied a portion of Munster and the enemy controlled the remainder. For the following two days Charlie Company remained in Munster firing on enemy sniper and mortar positions while the doughboys fought house to house and room to room in a bloody street fight.

The Panthers continued spearheading for the 26th Infantry Division, leading the way through mine fields, barricades, and fortified enemy positions. From the Saint Suzanne Farms they pushed the enemy back through Marimont, Guenestroff, Guebestroff, and Vergaville, then began preparations for an offensive against Benestroff and Dieuze.

The assault gun platoon unleashed a fire mission on Dieuze with such pinpoint accuracy and devastation that Maj. General Williard S. Paul said that he had never seen such a demonstration of firing by weapons of that type.

The battered enemy withdrew from that town and the infantry entered and began clearing it. Before the last house was cleared, the enemy counterattacked in force and a vicious battle ensued. When the smoke cleared the enemy occupied the town again. Another attack kicked the enemy out — this time for good.

Combat Command A of the 4th Armored Division entered Dieuze as previously planned. Trezzvant Anderson describes what happened: "The 4th Armored Division was reported to have 'taken' the town of Dieuze, according to *Yank*

Private Clark, a Charlie Company tank driver, sporting his captured German Luger pistol (courtesy E. G. McConnell).

magazine, but they failed to say that all the heavy work was done by the 761st Tank Battalion, which battered the town into submission, or at least the assault gun platoon did the most beautiful piece of firing it ever performed there at Dieuze, and that after they had gotten to the town, the 761st Tank Battalion followed its instructions to let Combat Command A, of the 4th Armored come through after the 761st had done the job! But, that's what happened at Dieuze. And Jerry kicked hell out of us again at Honskirch! Yep, it was no walkaway!"[1]

With the fall of Dieuze, the Panthers rolled through more than 20 miles of the Forest-de-Bride and launched an assault against Benestroff, the objective. Division Headquarters chose the 26th Reconnaissance Troop and a platoon of M-5 light tanks from the "Mosquito Fleet" to enter the town first. A French woman with a white flag appeared at the town's edge and shortly thereafter the Germans capitulated.

The onslaught advanced to the German border, smashing through Bidestroff, Bassing, Inswiller, Nebing, Neufvillage, and Albestroff. Patton wanted to break into Hitler's Third Reich at as many points as possible.

The 81 millimeter mortar platoon got into action at 0200 hours on November 25. They fired continuously throughout the early morning and set a small village on fire with WP (white phosphorous) mortar shells. Soon, enemy forward observers spotted their position and a 10-minute artillery barrage followed. When the smoke cleared, five Panthers and a large number of doughboys had to be evacuated to an aid station.

Elsewhere on November 25, five Charlie Company tanks, four assault guns, and elements of the 328th Infantry Regiment based in the town of Torchville, launched an early-morning attack toward Honskirch. With the terrain still muddy from the cracking of the Dieuze Dam, they took Vittersbourg without losses. The attack shifted toward Honskirch at 1535 hours.

Private E. G. McConnell recalls the events leading up to the assault on Honskirch:

> What I recall of that attack that day, we had two crossroads and a town to take. The town was the last, which was Honskirch. We were able to take both crossroads. One crossroad I recall very vividly, having stopped in there, and this place was a pub or something. There were a number of dead Germans, some sitting at a table, some on the floor dead. The funny thing about this, everything seemed so familiar to me at the time, like I had been there before. I incidentally had a dream the night before that I was getting hit and was going to be killed the next day. I made an entry into my diary before the assault, a message to my mom.
>
> We went along with guns firing. We were trying to cover everything, haystacks, buildings, as we moved along with the infantry by our side. After the second crossroad we had a little lull and then we started to move out in the direction of Honskirch. I was praying like a devil the whole damn time. We waited for a short time and at that time I found that our gun had jammed in recoil. So I'm damned glad for that lull. I said to myself maybe this is what was going to kill me. We could have fired this gun and it would have exploded and blown up the whole damned tank. We worked and freed up one of the hydraulic recoil things. I forgot exactly what I did.
>
> Well, we started out again and we got to within 600 yards to that place and then we got a call to withdraw, which we did. We withdrew and while back there we waited and waited and didn't know what the delay was about. We heard they were going to shell it.[2]

Several hours later, as the tanks led the way down a road to Honskirch, they were greeted by enemy artillery and antitank fire. The last tank in the column was knocked out, trapping the others. Then, one by one, all five of the leading tanks were taken out. Hearts pounded as the Panthers opened fire and continued firing until it was their turn to get hit.

THE MECHANISM OF PENETRATION

WHEN THE SHOT STRIKES THE TARGET IT FIRST DEFLECTS TOWARDS THE PLATE AWAY FROM ITS LINE OF FLIGHT (LEFT) IT THEN PIERCES THE PLATE (CENTER) AND THEN ROTATES TO PENETRATE ALMOST AT RIGHT ANGLES (RIGHT)

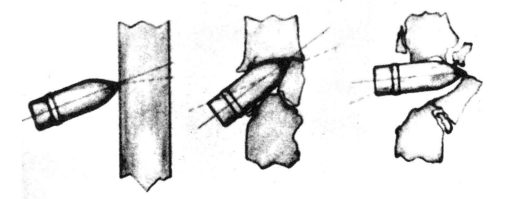

IT IS THIS CONVOLUTED PATH WHICH DEMANDS CAREFUL HEAT TREATMENT OF THE SHOT BODY TO PREVENT IT SHEARING OFF.

Top: E. G. McConnell (courtesy E. G. McConnell). *Bottom:* German armor-piercing shells were the greatest threat to the Panthers in their tanks. This diagram shows how the shells were able to penetrate the tanks' armored sides (courtesy U.S. Army Ordnance Museum, Aberdeen Proving Grounds, Maryland).

E. G. McConnell recalls the slaughter at Honskirch:

Finally, after quite a long delay, I forgot exactly how long, we were told to continue the advance. It seems as we approached, the day had clouded up some and it was sort of late afternoon. We didn't even get near that town before the first shell came streaking across the tank. We were the number-one tank. In the advancement prior, we were the second tank. We only had a crew of four. I was commanding, loading, operating the radio, and busy as all damn get out. We were shooting at every haystack, every building, every damned thing you can think of.

After that first shell came across and burst, I say about 50 feet in front of the tank, the road raised into the embankment and dirt sprayed all over us. Now we were wound up and, man, we were firing that damn gun like it was a machine gun. I was loading those shells in there so fast I didn't have time to look and see just what was happening. I got up on the .50 caliber machine gun and was firing that as I was loading and doing every damn thing else. Then after they missed that first shot, they went for the last tank to block us on the road. The ground was marshland or something like that on the sides. I saw the last tank and I saw each tank come down. I saw them get hit and I knew we were next. When it came about, it was such a terrific force, the vibration, and I knew we were hit. I felt that my head sort of twisted and went up in the air. I saw a flash fire.

Leon Hopton describes his close call at Honskirch:

We had tanks in a column, I was in the fifth or sixth tank. As we went down, the Germans started firing. At that time of year the grounds were muddy. You couldn't drive a tank across it because it would bog down. We had to stay on the road. All of a sudden the Germans started hitting every other tank, working their way down. You can hear the guys in the tanks that had been hit on the intercom. In the meantime, the Germans worked their way up the column, the tank in front of me got hit, and Pop Gates's tank got hit. He was coming up the column trying to tell us to back out of there. Well, I wasn't hit. I had a little trailer on the back, pulling a little extra ammo. I broke that up by going back and forth, keeping a moving target. They missed me and finally I was the last tank that wasn't hit so I maneuvered back. Ford was my tank commander. We got back into the next town. There was a tank destroyer outfit picking up the wounded. In the meantime, old Motel Johnson, who was a commander of one of the assault guns, he took off, him and Hometown Hall, the gunner. They fired everything they had so they started shooting the smoke. That's all they had left. That's what saved the guys in the ditches coming back up.[4]

Sergeant Emery G. Thomas saw three wounded comrades from another tank exposed in the open terrain. After Thomas and his crew dismounted their burning tank, he courageously led a few men to the wounded while under mortar and machine gun fire. They dragged the casualties to safety and administered first aid. Then Thomas personally carried a seriously wounded man to the aid station and returned to help evacuate the others.

E. G. McConnell recalls the end of that horrible day:

Leon Hopton (courtesy E. G. McConnell).

> It was dark when I finally came around. I just thought that perhaps I was in the hereafter. There was still the chatter of machine gun fire and the occasional mortar shell dropping in. I was down on the ground. I think they threw me out of the tank. My head wasn't in the water, it was up out of the ditch. I couldn't open my eyes, that's when I thought I was in the hereafter, until I found it was the blood from my injury in my head that sealed my eyelids closed. The moans and cries of the wounded about was something else. When the medics finally got up to where we were, I remember telling them, "I'm okay, I'm okay." They wanted to put me on the litter and I said, "No, I'm okay." They had another guy who they were carrying and this one guy came up and grabbed me and went on up to this jeep. They wanted to put me on a litter and I said, "No, I'm okay, I'll ride on the back." No sooner than they started, I fell right off. I lost every damn thing and they grabbed me and put me in the jeep.[5]

Trezzvant Anderson describes the hot spot at Honskirch:

> It was Lieutenant Bruce's platoon which went forward in Company C, leading the attack. After Private James Welborn, the driver for Staff Sergeant Frank Cochrane's tank, had been killed following a hit on the vehicle, Welborn's body fell forward over the levers, and in some manner caused the tank to back up until it stopped near the

The M-7 Assault Gun motor carriage of the 105 millimeter howitzer was called the "Priest" because the machine gun position looked like a pulpit. Abraham Dildy of the Assault Gun Platoon (H.Q. Co.) mans the weapon (courtesy E. G. McConnell).

edge of the woods off the road. Private Frank Greenwood, the gunner, had both legs blown off and he was evacuated from the tank by Cochrane, who pulled his inert body to a ditch half filled with water, where they sought shelter. Greenwood's head was kept from being submerged by being rested on the heel of Cochrane's left foot and the enemy observers spotted them and began "walking" mortar shells up the ditch until they had come within 25 yards of where the men lay. Cochrane had already said his "good-byes" to the folks back home, said "The Lord's Prayer," and "The 23rd Psalm," and made that one-second kaleidoscope review of his whole life, and waited for the end, when out of the sky there came the trailing tails of white phosphorous shells being fired from the 105 Howitzer of Sergeant Robert A. Johnson's assault gun tank, aiming at the enemy mortar positions. This fire lifted the enemy's attention from

Charles "Pop" Gates (courtesy CW3 Christopher P. Navarre, Sr., USA–Ret.).

the men in the ditch, and they were able to crawl to safety, with Cochrane carrying the wounded Greenwood. But it was like a storybook affair, for Sergeant Johnson did not know that the injured men were in the ditch. He was firing white phosphorous shells simply because he didn't have any other kind! But the smoke from those shells covered the scene with a white cloud, which permitted the endangered tankers to crawl up the ditch to safety. It was a lucky accident! And hundreds of infantrymen also got out of the "hot spot" under Johnson's smoke![6]

1st Lieutenant Charles "Pop" Gates was wounded and his driver, Technician Lane Dunn, was killed. Gates pointed out: "I became very bitter in the battle of Honskirch. We had been ordered to make an attack. We were able to spot all the major defenses of the Germans. I told this colonel that our approach was very poorly organized and would be pretty tough. I delayed the attack about four hours. Finally he gave me a direct order to move my tanks straight down a road. It was in defiance to good tactics. Within five minutes, we lost five tanks. Now this colonel had been given command of an infantry regiment. All the combat experience he had was as a finance officer in the United States. He didn't know a thing about combat."[7]

Later, when asked, "Did Patton recognize you?" Gates replied, "Yes, he did. He was a person who came to the front frequently. When he'd come around us, he'd talk just as you and I are talking now. He'd start relieving people of the units to which we were attached, starting at the top. At Honskirch, he wanted to know why we lost five tanks in such a short period. Within two weeks, this colonel of whom I had spoken had been shipped back to the United States. I have respect for [Patton]. He might not have liked the Negro any more than anybody else. I know his headquarters didn't, because they never accepted our record."[8]

E. G. McConnell recalls a special greeting he received from a general while in the hospital:

Getting to the aid station, I remember the crying and the moaning of the wounded. I recall seeing stacks of GIs piled up in front of the aid station. For the next couple of days I didn't know if I was coming or going. I do recall one time I did attempt to get my helmet off and I must have passed out again. I felt the pain. I really didn't know where I was wounded. What had happened was my helmet sort of stuck on my head. The shrapnel had lodged in between my helmet and my skull. I think I was fortunate in stashing all of my V-Mail up there because it did help me.

We were evacuated to the 100th General Hospital. I don't know how long it took to get back there. It seems it was an eternity to me. I remember riding in this damned ambulance. There were four of us. I don't really remember my buddy then too much. He was conscious all the way and he saw to it that we were together. When we hit this 100th General Hospital, I remember a German POW carrying the litter out and taking us into the hospital. My buddy was in the bed to my left. This two-star general came through the ward and greeted the guys as he passed on the opposite side. "How are you, Sergeant? How are you, Private? What unit are you in? How are you feeling?" I was the only black on the ward. Then he came down on my side from my right to my left. This kid out of the 26th, my buddy, he was a young guy, too. He put up his age to get in the Army. Anyway, he got before my bed and looked over at me and said: "What's wrong with you, boy? Got the claps?" I had my head wrapped up from this head injury. I haven't had anything to hurt me that much in my life as this man's remarks. I was so dumbfounded and speechless, I couldn't say anything. But this white kid, I forgot his name now, he hollered out: "Hey, General, if he got it, he got if from your mother!"

You see, he hung with us and a lot of white soldiers couldn't imagine what kept our morale up to where we would joke and laugh on the front. We just waited for the column to stop, get out and go talk to the tank in front or tank behind. The first thing someone would say: "Hey, McConnell, you know one thing, I dreamt about your Momma last night." Oh my God. You know, it was a game, who could say the most to a person and get them to a point where you could disturb them. Maybe a fight would start or something and when somebody cracked up like that everybody would rib him to death. We would be laughing like hell. We didn't mean anything. You don't talk about white folks' mothers, see, they don't understand this. This is what kept us laughing, and this kid used to hang with us. That's why he could say it with the feeling that we could say it. And that's what he said to the general: "If he got it, he got it from your mother! Send me back to the front!" His war days were over because he was in a cast from both legs all the way up his entire body. He was in an awful lot of pain and just didn't give a damn.[9]

The Panthers suffered heavy casualties throughout the month of November 1944, with 26 men killed in action, 81 wounded in action, and 44 non-combat casualties. They also suffered heavy equipment losses, with 14 tanks destroyed and 20 damaged.

Trench foot became a crippling hindrance. The men had no opportunity for personal hygiene and foul conditions existed everywhere. The pace was so intense that when a foot began to lose sensation there was no time to stop for treatment. When time permitted, it was dark and blackout conditions did not permit using light; a stricken soldier could not see trench foot setting in. Finally, when a foot went dead and became useless, the soldier would have to be evacuated to the aid station. In some cases the limb would have to be removed. This scourge crippled many American soldiers in this campaign, especially the infantry.

At the end of the month, Lt. Colonel Hollis Hunt returned to the 17th Armored Group and Major John George assumed command of the battalion.

12

The Maginot Line

Early December 1944 found the Panthers on attack in and around the French towns of Attswiller, Pisdorf, and Sarre Union. The resistance became stiff and the enemy controlled the supply routes. The light tanks had to be called in to supply the battalion.

On December 2, Sarre Union fell after a hard-fought battle. The doughboys cleared the town and set up a perimeter defense. Shortly thereafter, German Panzers launched several counterattacks. At 1100 hours on December 3, the Panzers counterattacked in force and gained a stronghold in Sarre Union. The Panthers and doughboys suffered heavy casualties.

At 1310 hours the tanks of the 761st engaged the Panzers on the eastern edge of town. After two hours of vicious fighting the Panzers withdrew to fortified positions in and around the Maginot Line. The doughboys reentered Sarre Union, this time for keeps. The advance continued toward the Maginot Line.

The Maginot Line was built by France after World War I to prevent Germany from reinvading the French homeland. A well-planned, sophisticated, fortified bunker and tunnel system, it stretched from France's borders with Switzerland to Belgium. It was proclaimed impregnable.

When Panzer and *Wehrmacht* forces under the command of General Gerd von Rundstedt attacked France in May of 1940, they passed through the Ardennes Forest and circumvented the Maginot Line. France fell and the Maginot Line became useless. Now, four and a half years later, the Germans used the Maginot Line to defend their Reichland from invasion.

The Maginot Line came under attack by Able Company in the vicinity of Achen, Baker Company in the vicinity of Etting, and Charlie Company in the vicinity of Oermingen. This area of the Maginot Line housed a manufacturing site for the enemy's experimental jet fuel, a newly invented form of propulsion little known to the average person at the time. Factory buildings nestled along the line. The bombardment from the big guns of the 761st bounced off the thick pillbox walls.

Top: "Yankee" Division doughboys held up by enemy resistance in Sarre Union. To the right is a U.S. M-10 Tank Destroyer armed with a 90 millimeter gun. December 2, 1944 (courtesy National Archives). *Bottom:* A pillbox along the Maginot Line, 1944 (courtesy Alex R. Chamberlain Collection at the U.S. Army Military History Institute).

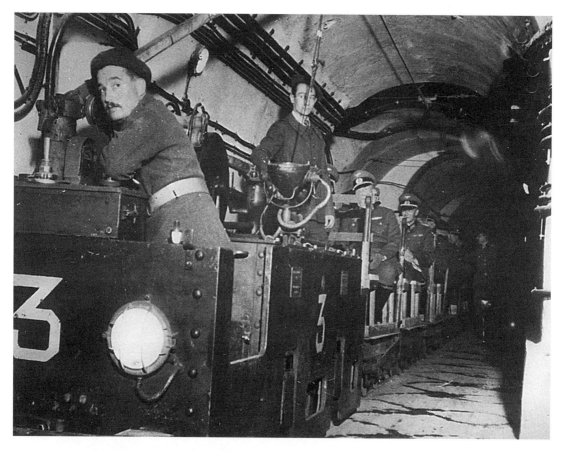

German officers are driven by French POWs inside Tunnel Hakenburg of the Maginot Line (National Archives photo 131-NO-28-4).

U.S. Army Air Forces dive bombers and explosives planted by the combat engineers were needed to demolish them. The concussion from the Panther's 76 millimeter high-explosive shells dazed the pillbox occupants long enough for the combat engineers to plant their blockbuster explosives. The results were so severe that the occupants were blown to bits.

Sergeant Walter Lewis describes the surgical aerial strikes: "We fired white phosphorus in places we wanted the planes to hit. Minutes later the P-47s came in low, so low we thought they mistook us for Jerry, as Jerry was also operating in captured Sherman Tanks.... We had radio contact with them, and when they were sure of the places we wanted them to drop their load, they gained altitude and swooped in low on the German tanks and pillboxes. We could see their 500-pound blockbusters being released from the planes. Their bombs were set at a delayed action, giving the planes time to take safe altitude. Suddenly, the earth trembled just as if there was an earthquake. The roar of the explosions was ear-splitting.

A cozy nest of warriors. Crecy and McBurney are on the far right (courtesy E. G. McConnell).

Everything became black before us. Our 32-ton tanks shook like tissue paper. We were beyond the stage of being frightened. War had made us callous and numb to feeling. It seemed like the whole world fell apart that day, and I prayed."[1]

On December 9, the Panthers crashed through the Maginot Line and assembled at Woelfling for the push into Germany. In Woelfling a bridge disintegrated beneath German mortar fire. The tanks and infantry dispersed and set up a defense. The Germans shelled direct fire every ten minutes, adding mortar fire every 20 minutes.

Air support continued, but there was little the doughboys could do because the area was heavily sown with mines and infested with booby traps. The combat engineers constructed a bridge under heavy fire and the Panthers rolled across the Blies River.

Relief came for the battle-weary doughboys of 26th Infantry Division on December 11. The newly arrived 87th "Golden Acorn" Infantry Division took over. For the 761st Tank Battalion, there was no relief.

Platoon Sergeant Johnnie Stevens recalls giving instructions to members of the 87th Infantry Division regarding tank and infantry tactics:

This infantry lieutenant introduced me. He said, "Look, this is a member of the 761st Tank Battalion. These men have done a lot of fighting. They lost a lot of men and they know what they're doing. They're experienced combat soldiers and I want you to listen." I told them, "Smoking lamp is lit, smoke 'em if you got 'em, but if you want to live, you better listen."

They had to learn what to expect from a German tank and they had to learn how to fight with a tank. I said, "The only way I can teach you is to tell you what we fear and the German tanker fears the same thing. If you go into combat tomorrow and you meet eight or ten German tanks, you're going to die! If you learn from what I tell you, then you might come out of there alive.

"What do I fear as a tanker? I fear the guy who has guts enough to run out there and take his rifle and shove it in my sprocket. You can stop a tank with a rifle. That sprocket is not going to bust that damn rifle. No way. I worry about the guy who has guts enough to run up from the rear of my tank, climb aboard, and take a hand grenade and drop it down my hatch. I worry about the guy who has guts enough to run up there and take his grenade, pull the pin and drop it in my gas tank. I worry about these things."

I showed them how we dropped the deck plate. I said, "If you're in a foxhole and you're being machine gunned and can't get out, all you have to do is, don't raise your head up. We will see you. I got a tank. We will drop our deck plate. We will run right over the foxhole and we're going to bring you up and take you inside the tank. We are going to get you out of that damned field!" I spent over three hours with them. I hope they learned enough so that some of them got back.[2]

On December 14, 1944, the 761st Tank Battalion rolled into Germany. A communiqué from SHAEF (Supreme Headquarters Allied Expeditionary Forces) reported: "Lt. General George S. Patton's Third Army infantry and armor slammed into German territory at a new point after crossing the Blies River above Sarreguemines." This was the 761st Tank Battalion and the 87th Infantry Division.

On December 9, 1944, the commanding general of XII Corps wrote the following letter of commendation for the 761st Tank Battalion:

> 1. I consider the 761st Tank Battalion to have entered combat with such conspicuous courage and success as to warrant special commendation.
> 2. The speed with which they adapted themselves to the front line under most adverse weather conditions, the gallantry which with they faced some of Germany's finest troops, and the confident spirit with which they emerged from their recent engagements in the vicinity of Dieuze, Morville-les-Vic, and Guebling entitle them surely to consider themselves the Veteran 761st. — Maj. General Manton S. Eddy.[3]

On December 14, the commanding general of the 26th Infantry Division forwarded the above letter of commendation to the 761st Tank Battalion: "It is with extreme gratification that the corps commander's commendation is forwarded to you. Your battalion has supported this division with great bravery under the most adverse weather and terrain conditions. You have my sincere wish that success may continue to follow your endeavors." Maj. General Willard S. Paul.[4]

13

The 90 Degree Turn and Race into the Bulge

Before daylight on December 16, 1944, German forces commanded by General Gerd von Rundstedt launched a Blitzkrieg counteroffensive in the West. Their objective, the strategic Belgian port of Antwerp, had to be taken at all costs. They viciously attacked in great force along their borders with Belgium and Luxembourg. They smashed through the Ardennes Forest and cut the Allied forces in half with an effect frequently compared to that of the Japanese sneak attack on Pearl Harbor.

The initial blows wiped out unsuspecting Allied outposts, leaving dazed and wounded soldiers to drift aimlessly in the snow. Rundstedt's offensive moved swiftly and bypassed stubborn pockets of resistance that could be dealt with later. German troops wearing U.S. uniforms and speaking near-perfect English infiltrated U.S. lines and created pandemonium within the ranks. The Americans soon caught on to this ruse and caught many of the German spies at crucial checkpoints, where they were unable to give the correct password or answer questions on U.S. geography and baseball. The military police executed the captured spies by firing squad.

In the middle of this offensive, the enemy's crack 1st SS Ranger Regiment spearheaded for the Sixth SS Panzer Army's thrust. This SS regiment, comprised of tanks, infantry, artillery, and combat engineers, came under the command of the infamous SS colonel Jochen Peiper, the master tank strategist. He swiftly forced his SS regiment between the U.S. 90th and 106th Infantry Divisions and shoved the U.S. 14th Cavalry Group aside. He captured approximately two-thirds of the 106th Infantry Division and massacred more than 350 American prisoners of war at Malmedy. His rapid advance came to an end only when his fuel and supply services could no longer keep up.

At Bastogne, the battle's focal point, surrounded American soldiers made a heroic stand by refusing to surrender in the face of what appeared to be impossible odds. Nearby, more American soldiers surrendered at one time and in one place than in any other episode of the European Theater of Operations.

The Battle of the Bulge became the largest, most shocking, and perplexing battle on the Western Front. It received its name from the bulging convex shape of the battle lines. There were days when nobody knew, including local townspeople, which side held a given town. Overcast days and nights obscured vision and grounded American planes. "Prisoners on both sides were captured, liberated and recaptured; on both sides, captives were killed by infuriated captors after they had surrendered."[1]

Hitler conceived this all-out counteroffensive himself against the advice of his top military experts. The Allied forces, taken by complete surprise, suffered heavy casualties.

Allied intelligence did not take Hitler's mentality into consideration. In *A Time for Trumpets,* Charles B. McDonald wrote: "Allied Intelligence had committed the most grievous sin of which an intelligence operation is capable. They looked in a mirror for the enemy and saw there only the reflections of their own intentions."

Rundstedt overwhelmed the First Army at a point where the 101st Airborne Division, assisted by elements of the 9th and 10th Armored Divisions and several smaller units, held Bastogne. During this prolonged period of disarray and distress, the 969th Field Artillery Battalion, a Negro unit, stuck to its guns and fired around the compass during the siege. The battalion's fire was enhanced by the three serviceable howitzers of the 333rd Field Artillery Battalion, as the men of the 969th manned the abandoned guns of a white artillery battalion. Casualties rose quickly as enemy tanks and infantry fired down on the 969th. All except the actual cannoneers fought back as infantry. It was here that Brig. General Anthony C. McAuliffe, Deputy Commander of the 101st Airborne Division, gave his legendary one-word reply to the German surrender demand: "Nuts!"

The 82nd Airborne Division operated in the Vielsalm — Saint Vith region on December 24. Their association recalls: "An entire U.S. armored division was retreating from the Germans in the Ardennes Forest when a sergeant in a tank destroyer spotted an American digging a foxhole. The GI, PFC Martin, 325th Glider Infantry Regiment, looked up and asked, 'Are you looking for a safe place?' 'Yeah,' answered the tanker. 'Well, buddy,' he drawled, 'just pull your vehicle behind me.... I'm the 82nd Airborne and this is as far as the bastards are going.'" The paratroopers took heavy losses and the next day they were forced to advance in the opposite direction. Two days later the 82nd was back on the offensive.

The 761st Tank Battalion, poised to strike the Siegfried Line in the vicinity of Saarbrücken and Zweibrücken, received orders to turn 90 degrees and dash into the Bulge with the Third Army. One contingent traveled by train and arrived several days ahead of the bulk of the battalion, which negotiated the steep and icy roads

This captured German photograph shows the enemy overwhelming the Allies in the Battle of the Bulge (courtesy U.S. Army Military History Institute).

World War II German armor on display at the U.S. Army Ordnance Museum, Aberdeen Proving Grounds, Maryland. *Top:* "Tiger II" (Heavy) Panzer armed with the fearsome 88 millimeter gun and two MG-34 (7.92 millimeter) machine guns. *Bottom:* "Panther" Mark IV (Medium) Panzer armed with a 75 millimeter gun and two MG-34 (7.92 millimeter) machine guns. *Next page:* "Panther" Mark II (Light) Panzer armed with two MG-34 (7.92 millimeter) machine guns.

to the battlefields in Belgium. Sergeant Robert A. Johnson, who saved the day at Honskirch, was killed in an accident when his assault gun tank slid off a slippery road.

Christmas Day 1944 was celebrated with the traditional turkey dinner at a mobile field kitchen. Unfortunately, orders came down to move out before the meals had finished cooking. Hunks of half-cooked turkeys were pulled apart and the Panthers ate their Christmas meal on the road. By this time, the German drive had penetrated the Allied lines approximately 70 miles deep and 50 miles wide. The adverse weather continued.

On the morning of December 27, 1944, elements of the 4th Armored Division entered Bastogne, ending the seven-day siege. The 590th Ambulance Company, a Negro unit, followed closely behind. They were among the first to reach the badly wounded Americans there.

The 969th Field Artillery Battalion and 33 other units would later receive the Presidential Unit Citation for their heroic performance in and around Bastogne. Maj. General Maxwell D. Taylor, the commanding general of the 101st Airborne Division, wrote the following letter to the commander of the 969th Field Artillery Battalion: "The Officers and Men of the 101st Airborne Division wish to express to your command their appreciation of the gallant support rendered by the 969th Field Artillery Battalion in the recent defense of Bastogne, Belgium. The success of this defense is attributable to the shoulder to shoulder cooperation of all units involved. This Division is proud to have shared the Battlefield with your command.

A recommendation for a unit citation of the 969th Field Artillery Battalion is being forwarded by this Headquarters."[2]

On New Year's Eve, the Panthers went into battle as the spearhead for elements of the 87th Infantry Division. The New Year celebration ended with the capture of two towns in a single day, Rondu and Nimbermont, approximately 15 miles west of Bastogne. The 87th Infantry Division reported: "The 1st Battalion, 347th Infantry, was at Remagne, the 3rd Battalion was at Moircy. Instructions were to close the highway between St. Hubert and Bastonge. Two tanks from the 761st were in front of each infantry company for the attack. On the next day, the 3rd Battalion reported that three of the tanks were burning and one was damaged beyond use."[3]

The entire area was thickly sown with mines and booby traps. The mountainous terrain was dotted with dense evergreen forest with snow waist deep in some areas. With temperatures nearing zero, the desperate Nazis retaliated with a vicious counterassault to safeguard their elaborate defensive positions at Jenneville, Bonnerue, and Pironpre. Their goal was to defend at all costs and keep open their main supply artery through Houffalize to the Bulge.

On January 3, Private Thomas S. Bragg told his commanding officer about a premonition. Captain David J. Williams II recalls: "Tom Bragg came up to me before a battle up in the Bulge. He said, 'Captain, I got to talk to you privately. My wife is having a baby now and I know I'm going to get killed.' He was always volunteering. I said, 'You go back. I'll put someone else in.' He said, 'I didn't tell you this to go back. I know it is going to be mean up here. I'm just telling you to write my wife a letter.' I said, 'Tommy, don't say that! I'm going to give you an order.' He said, 'Don't order me. I'm going to fight.' He was killed the next morning."[4]

In the vicinity of Remagne, Sergeant Walter Woodson had his tank shot out from under him by an 88 millimeter antitank gun. The delayed-action projectile ricocheted inside the steel walls of the tank and exploded behind Private Thomas Bragg, the driver, who died instantly. Lewis and his crew members, Private James Jordan and Charles Brooks, received serious wounds. Walter Lewis, in his *Diary of a Gunner,* describes the hit:

> Transmission on our two-way radio was scrambled. The Germans were on our transmission as well as Axis Sally, who was telling us about rioting in Cleveland, Ohio, and telling us to go home and doing all she could to break our morale.... She played Louis Armstrong's recording of "I Can't Give You Anything But Love, Baby".... We did not move 50 yards before we were hit! It sounded like heavy plate glass bursting into a million ear-splitting pieces.
>
> Concussion blew me out of the tank. Had my hatch not been open, all of us would have been killed by the concussion alone. I got up and ran, for I was in a state of hysteria.... My clothing was cut to

shreds. [I was] bleeding profusely.... The area was now drawing enemy fire. I ran until I was exhausted. I remember stopping at a monastery. The Germans began shelling this also, so I took off again. In my delirium, I made my way to an aid station about three kilometers from the scene of the battle, running through wooded areas infested with German snipers.... I collapsed.... When I came to my senses, I was on a litter. I was evacuated at night in a convoy of ambulances, which slowly moved through minefields and booby-trapped roads. I was operated on the next day in a hospital in Sedan, France.[5]

With the Third Army's breakthrough, the Allied Expeditionary Forces started out to prevent the enemy from reinforcing their positions. The 761st Tank Battalion closed in on Tillet intending to close the Brussels-Bastogne Highway. Bonnerue, Recongne, Remagne and Jenneville fell to the onslaught of the Panthers and doughboys. After bitter fighting the enemy pulled back to fortified positions in and around Tillet.

With extreme weather and poor road conditions, the battalion's supply train (Service Company trucks) could no longer negotiate the icy hills and trails. Dog Company again took over the supply service, using its M-5 light tanks. The mosquito fleet trundled up the icy hills loaded with ammunition and supplies and returned with the dead and wounded.

Trezzvant Anderson notes,

Sergeant James W. Nelson, of Detroit, Michigan, commander of the first Able Company tank to roll onto German soil back in December 1944 (and probably the first tank manned by Negroes to ever roll into the Reich), had been killed on January 4. Private Thomas S. Bragg, of Elizabeth, New Jersey, also of Able Company, and a popular member of the 761st orchestra (before combat), had also died that day. On the day before, January 3, Bob Johnson had died enroute to the battle he so well carried out, and on January 5, Technician Jessie J. Bond, from North Carolina, and Headquarters Company, also cashed in his chips. The 761st was winning, but it was paying for its victories with lives that could never be replaced. That was the price of war, and it made the men fight more viciously ... [the Panthers were] fighting for revenge, and it was also "COME OUT FIGHTING" or be killed! It was stark, it was grim, it was real![6]

14

The Battle of the Bulge at Tillet

The Battle of Tillet raged in early January, 1945, when the 761st Tank Battalion and elements of the 87th Infantry Division engaged units of the 113th Panzer Brigade. The Panzers had earlier annihilated nearly a complete battalion of Sherman tanks at Tillet from the newly arrived 11th Armored Division. The 761st Tank Battalion's objective was to lead the infantry into Tillet, cut off the Brussels-Bastogne Highway, and link up with the First Army.

The Germans staged one of the most brilliant defenses of the war. They set up complex defensive positions and took everything the 761st and division artillery had to offer. Fire was returned immediately with devastating accuracy. The inexperienced foot soldiers took heavy casualties in their attempt to break into Tillet.

Staff Sergeant Theodore A. Weston's tank platoon laid down a concentrated barrage of fire on a group of Panzers, forcing them to pull back. The doughboys immediately took advantage and entered the town. The Panzers braced and counterattacked. The "Ripsaw" 88s tore the doughboys apart. Equipment and body parts flew in every direction. Many of the foot soldiers seemed to just vanish from the face of earth and were reported as MIA (Missing In Action).

Trezzvant Anderson describes the leadership at the Battle of Tillet: "With Able and Charlie Companies in the fight, Captain Gates was the directing figure, but the actual combat operations fell to the hands and minds of several enlisted men, who were all staff sergeants, and platoon leaders. These men proved their ability to perform the duties of officers right there at Tillet, and before the end of the war in Europe, three of them had received battlefield commissions. The men who took over the direction of the fight were Staff Sergeants Henry H. Conway and Johnnie Stevens, both from Able Company; and Frank C. Cochrane and Moses E. Dade of Charlie Company, along with William Kitt from Baker Company."[1]

Able Company knocked out an 88 millimeter antitank gun and a self-propelled

75 millimeter gun. Dog Company took a break from supply duties and diverted enemy attention from around Tillet in an altercation at Gerimont. There they destroyed an enemy mortar position, an ammunition dump, liquidated 50 enemy soldiers and captured ten.

Charlie Company assaulted Tillet with all three tank platoons, led by their platoon sergeants, Cochrane, Dade, and Windsor. They took out eight machine gun nests, a Mark IV tank, an ammunition dump, and three antitank guns while eliminating 106 enemy soldiers. Staff Sergeant Cochrane's tank took three hits that day. With his shattered tank, he and his crew fired back and continued to advance. His entire tank platoon followed his lead.

Staff Sergeant Moses Dade's turret top flew approximately 50 feet into the air after taking a direct hit. Dade continued to lead his platoon while he and his tank crew gave the enemy hell with their remaining weapons.

Sergeant Windsor had his tank shot out from under him. Trezzvant Anderson describes this ordeal: "When their tank had been hit by an armor-piercing shell from the [113th Panzer Brigade], in the Ardennes, in January 1945, at Tillet, Belgium, these 761st Tankers crawled 5,000 yards on their bellies, through the snow, back to safety, in sub-zero temperatures. They made it, after hours of torturous crawling and alternate running! Sergeant Windsor was accompanied by PFC Leonard Smith and Sergeant William McBurney."[2] Their driver, Technician Willie J. Devore, never made it.

In another action, Staff Sergeant Conway's tank was caught on a hill by several Panzers just outside of Tillet, and had to fight there alone for more than an hour, despite having been hit. His rear hatch was blown off but the Panzers did not pass.

Meanwhile, Captain Charles "Pop" Gates, in command of a force of ten tanks with supporting infantry, launched an assault against an organized enemy defensive position following a personal forward reconnaissance. Gates gallantly led and directed the attack on foot, keeping his force going forward against heavy opposition, inflicting heavy losses on the enemy while disregarding his own personal safety. His group reached its objective after a five-hour battle up a long, gradually rising slope. At the end, only two tanks and a remnant of infantry remained of the original force.

Captain Gates had to spend a lot of time in front of his tanks. Lt. Colonel Paul L. Bates explains why by describing the training he (Bates) received under Patton as a lieutenant in the 2nd Armored Division back in 1941: "[Patton] insisted that we drive every vehicle in an armored division, fire every weapon through the smaller crew-served weapons and operate every radio. And then for his amusement on the last day there, he chose a stream with a very sandy bottom and there was a bluff about 20 feet high overlooking it. One of the vehicles we had to master that time was a motorcycle. A lot of us had never ridden one. We came down and he was there with his officers. We went into that stream with a sandy bottom and believe me, none of us got across. He harped on us about this one motto of his that

A captured photograph of a German "grunt" loaded for bear in the Bulge (courtesy U.S. Army Military History Institute).

was so important (talking to lieutenants): 'As platoon leaders, you got to treat a platoon of tanks like a piece of spaghetti. If you want to get somewhere you can't get there by pushing it. You got to get in front of it and pull it.' I can tell you that is one of the most unhealthy places you can be in your life."[3]

When the infantry finally entered Tillet, a grueling house-to-house battle ensued. The 87th Infantry Division Association describes some of the action:

> The battle of Tillet was launched early January 7 by 3rd Battalion 346th when Lieutenant Glen J. Doman, serving his first day as a platoon leader, led a 21-man assault platoon from Company K into the south portion of the town and attacked a house concealing more than 40 Germans. The attack was coordinated with Company I's approach on Tillet from the east.
>
> In a free for all fight, Lieutenant Doman's men fired rifles, machine guns, bazookas, and tossed grenades into the house. A German officer, running from the building, attempted to choke Sergeant Don Corbin. Running to Corbin's assistance, Sergeant Emil Piger emptied a full "grease" gun clip into the German.
>
> Private Warren Horton walked up to Staff Sergeant George Blankenbacker with a grenade in either hand. "Here, Sarge pull the pins for me," he said. Pins pulled, Horton heaved the grenades inside the house. A Nazi, stepping up to a window to fire his burp gun, walked directly into a bazooka shell. Nearly every German in the house was killed.
>
> When Company I struck Tillet from the east, the enemy pinned down the company with devastating fire from well protected machine gun positions. Firing his automatic rifle from his hip, Staff Sergeant Curtis F. Shoup charged forward and rushed one nest. Although hit and suffering severe wounds in his body and legs, the sergeant crawled within throwing range of the house sheltering the gun crew and killed all of the occupants with a grenade. A sniper killed Shoup as he crept toward another house.

On the evening of January 9, the enemy could no longer continue its fierce resistance and withdrew in the direction of Fosset and Roumont with the Panthers and doughboys in hot pursuit. The 87th Infantry Division set up barricades on the March — Bastogne Road and choked off this vital supply artery to the German operations in the Bulge.

"The prime supply line to the Germans surrounding the 101st Division was through Tillet," recalls platoon sergeant Johnnie Stevens, "I don't know what day it is, we're taking a beating but the guys are still pitching and whoever said the 'colored soldier' can't fight is a damn liar. We cut that supply line and we won that battle."

Trezzvant Anderson summarizes the Battle of Tillet: "But those five days

Top: The Ardennes Forest, January 1945 (courtesy E. G. McConnell). *Bottom:* The recovery vehicle, a ten-ton wrecker, rights an overturned 761st tank in the 87th Infantry Division's sector of Belgium, January 10, 1945 (courtesy U.S. Army Military History Institute).

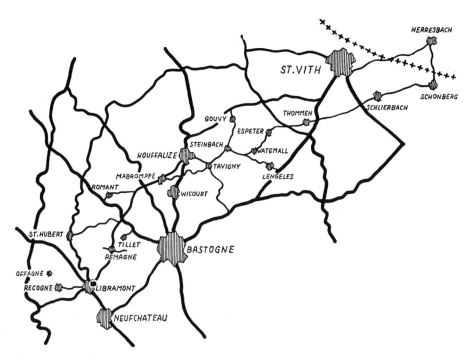

Area of operations in the Bulge. Official 761st Tank Battalion map by William Kaiser, Jr. (National Archives).

around Tillet had written their stamp on every frozen tanker, who huddled inside the steel battle wagons, half frozen, chilled and numb, yet firing and firing and firing. When Frank Cochrane's tank got hit the third time that day, he radioed back: "They've hit me 3 times, but I'm still givin 'em hell!' It had boiled down to the story of 'Kill or be Killed!' And so, for five bitter, cold, strenuous days, the 761st slugged it out there at Tillet, against the crack [113th Panzer Brigade], and in the end, it was the [113th Panzer Brigade] which withdrew before the relentless persistency of these 'veterans' of the 761st, who would not be denied the inevitable conquest which they sought, as they did their share in breaking the back of Von Rundstedt's breakthrough."[5]

On January 12, Private E. G. McConnell returned to duty from the hospital: "I was talking to my buddies. They were all sitting around gas cans and water cans. They were talking to me about who got hit and what not. A GI truck, manned by two black soldiers, pulled up. They said, 'I think we got one of your guys here.' They commenced to throw the frozen body on the ground."[6]

McConnell heard the snow crunch as the frozen corpse hit the ground. Lying in the snow were the remains of his good friend, Little Willie Devore, who, as the 761st steamed out of New York Harbor and past the Statue of Liberty, had told McConnell he wasn't coming back.

15

The Battle of the Bulge
with the Paratroopers of
the 17th Airborne

A few days before the 761st Tank Battalion attached to the 17th Airborne Division, Trooper Isadore S. Jachman single-handedly fought off a platoon of German tanks. The 17th Airborne Division Association describes his actions: "Twenty-one-year-old Sergeant Isadore Jachman, a squad leader in Company B, 513th Parachute Infantry Regiment, had been born in Berlin of Jewish parents. During the Bulge, Jachman's company ran into strong resistance while attacking near the town of Flamierge in Belgium. When German tanks arrived, the company was in grave danger of being overrun. Jachman left his position and under fire ran forward to pick up a bazooka dropped by a dead gunner, loaded it and knocked out the lead tank. Reloading, he dashed forward and hit a second tank, causing the remainder to break off the attack and withdraw. Jachman was killed by a burst from an enemy machine gun. A resident of Baltimore, Maryland, he was awarded the CMH posthumously."[1]

On January 14, 1945, the 761st Tank Battalion attached to the 17th Airborne Division just north of Bastogne at a key point on the road between Liege and Bastogne. The Panthers and the hard-hitting paratroopers fought their way to the town of Wicourt and cut the road from Liege to Bastogne, rendering another German supply artery nonexistent.

The 761st Tank Battalion prepared to support the 17th Airborne Division's plan to defend its zone and maintain contact with the enemy. One tank was lost to a mine while on routine reconnaissance between Houffalize and Vaux. These two points were considered probable places for counterattacks. The battalion commander, the staff operations officer, and the individual company commanders discussed where to employ the tanks for best results in defensive and offensive missions.

Baker Company took up positions with the 193rd Glider Infantry Regiment in the vicinity of Wicourt with ten medium tanks, three assault guns, and three light tanks. They elected not to take up defensive positions in order to have the element of surprise. The remainder of the battalion pulled back and performed emergency maintenance.

Private First Class Floyd Dade, Jr., recalls the maintenance period: "We washed our ODs and field jackets and so forth in gasoline. We also lit gasoline in 50-gallon drums to keep warm. This incident, I remember well. Steven T. Reed and I were passing a football around. I told him I was tired and quit running and catching passes. I was standing by the fire warming my hands and he threw the ball and it hit the gasoline can. Some spilled on me and I ran into the fire. I caught on fire! I knew not to run. All I could say was, put me out fellas. They wrapped me in a blanket. Each time they would remove the blanket, it would flare up again, but finally we extinguished the blaze."[2]

When the Germans retreated, they installed mines and booby traps, covered their flanks, and withdrew in an orderly fashion. The dreaded sky troopers, in baggy pants and big pockets, pursued the enemy relentlessly. With only two weeks of actual combat experience, the young paratroopers, mostly 20–21 years of age, fought like seasoned veterans. They always remembered their training: "A good soldier always moves forward, attacks, carries on."[3] Their courage, flexibility, and training won out.

On January 20, Brig. General Whitelaw, assistant division commander of the 17th Airborne Division, visited the 761st Tank Battalion to award Captain John D. Long the Bronze Star. Staff sergeants Cochrane and Kitt were awarded battlefield commissions to 2nd lieutenants. Captain Long, whose men thought that he was out of his mind, describes his leadership philosophy: "I didn't believe in asking my men to do anything that I wouldn't do myself, I always took the point. I put my finest sergeant on the point for a while for a specific reason, but I was in the next tank. I am sure my men thought I was a bastard and hated my guts, but they followed me. They were a well greased fighting machine."[4]

During this lull in the action, Master Sergeant Ernest D. Hill, Sr., was cited for meritorious service. He received the Bronze Star for keeping a maximum number of tanks and service vehicles in running condition. He accomplished this despite hazardous conditions and adverse weather, and without sufficient replacement parts or repair facilities.

Baker Company, reinforced by four assault guns, advanced toward Tavigney and still could not make contact with the enemy. They continued forward and took up defensive firing positions to repel probable counterattacks from Gouvy and Haut-billian. The balance of the battalion then moved up to the vicinity of Tavigney.

On the evening of January 23, 1945, Able Company replaced Baker Company on the line to support the 513th Parachute Infantry Regiment. With forward elements

Left to right: Jimmie Ballard, Horace Evans, and Ed Donald. "I was the lead tank under Johnny Long and remember how daring he was. At times, Johnny Long was so daring that I thought he was out of his mind" — Ed Donald (courtesy Ed Donald).

of the airborne infantry, they took to the high ground southeast of Watemall, where they engaged the enemy. The 105 millimeter assault guns opened up on a large wooded area that concealed Panzer and Wehrmacht forces. The guns aimed high and the projectiles exploded at treetop level, sending splinters and shrapnel throughout the woods. A large number of enemy soldiers surrendered.

Elements of Dog Company performed a screening action before linking up with elements of the 513th Parachute Infantry Regiment. Together they closed up pockets of resistance and took the town of Watemall. The balance of Dog Company performed supply duties because the roads were out and Service Company trucks could not maneuver through the open fields.

As rain began, the ground in the open fields became swampy beneath the snow. Eight desperately needed combat tanks became mired at one time and the recovery vehicles were hard pressed to extricate them.

Trooper Lauren Hungerford recalls the 761st and the muddy terrain: "I have one remembrance … of great importance to me. I was a sergeant with the 513th

Trooper Lauren J. Hungerford (courtesy Lauren J. Hungerford).

Parachute Infantry Regiment, 17th Airborne Division. As we moved to attack the Germans down a dirt road through the woods we came across your father's tank unit placed in the woods on the edge of a meadow. As we crossed the meadow, our column came to a halt, which was of great concern to me as we were exposed. In spite of my squad mumbling sorts of nasty words about me, I made them lay down in the deep muddy tank tracks. Immediately a heavy artillery barrage landed on us and we were one of the few squads without wounded or killed. The Germans counterattacked the next day and drove my regiment back, only to be stopped by [the 761st]. Although I was wounded later, I still am thankful for those tank tracks, as my squad survived the whole war."[5]

Trooper Bart Hagerman of the 193rd Glider Infantry Regiment compares the German Panzers to the U.S. Sherman tanks in the Bulge: "In some of the small towns, the Americans and Germans fought at point blank range, literally looking down each other's gun barrels. German tanks used diesel fuel, which was very difficult to set afire. The German Panzers were very sturdy, and it took direct hits on the gun turrets or chain drives to put them out of commission. The U.S. Sherman tanks, on the other hand, used gasoline and were very explosive. The Germans nicknamed the Sherman tank the 'Ronson' tank."[6]

Trooper Carl Arend of the 681st Glider Field Artillery Battalion remembers the tanks in the Bulge: "There was an awful lot of fighting, a lot of dead. What upset all of us, I believe, was the Tiger and Panther tanks against our gasoline Sherman tanks, that they called Sears and Roebuck coffins. Their 88 artillery was tremendous. They had *Nebelwerfers,* which we called 'screaming meemies' which were rockets. I think they shot 60 at once from tubes. There was an awful lot of artillery and tank fire."[7]

On January 24, Charlie Company, in support of the 194th Glider Infantry Regiment, crossed into Luxembourg and engaged a rear-guard unit set up for delaying action. Machine guns raked the enemy positions with a murderous blanket of fire that knocked out an anti-tank gun, a machine gun nest, and liquidated 35 enemy soldiers. This made country number four in which the Panthers fought.

As the fighting continued, the Panthers watched in awe as the paratroopers closed with the enemy. Trooper Kurt Gabel of the 513th Parachute Infantry Regiment remembers: "The platoon raced across an open field and dove into an irrigation ditch 200 yards from the highway. The unit's leader, a lieutenant, yelled for attention. White-faced paratroopers turned to him. The officer snapped: 'Fix bayonets!' A German Schmeisser kicked up snow around the ditch. A volley of rifle fire followed it. The GIs worked their bayonets onto their rifles and waited for the next order. It came soon enough. The lieutenant said: 'Let's go!' All 30 paratroopers rose up and climbed out of the ditch. They charged a row of German foxholes, their bayonets glistening in the sun, their rifles cracking as they closed the gap. The enemy returned fire, but the awesome sight of 30 Americans coming towards them with bayonets caused the Germans to fire wildly. Most of the 25 defenders leapt out of their holes. Then both forces met in a head-long clash. GIs plunged their bayonets deep. The screams of dying Germans induced their comrades to throw up their hands in surrender. One paratrooper was unable to pull his bayonet out of the German's chest. Finally, he released the latch and left the blade in."[8] This was the 2nd platoon of Company F, 513th Parachute Infantry Regiment, led by the intrepid Lieutenant Sam Calhoun.

Maj. General William M. Miley, commanding general of the 17th Airborne Division, has not forgotten the 761st Tank Battalion: "What I clearly remember is the very fine support we received from the 761st. The reason I remember it so well is because it was so much better than what we received from units previously providing support." General Miley went on to say: "My most vivid recollection of the 761st Tank Battalion was an action in support of the 194th Glider Infantry Regiment. The regiment had been stopped in its attack on a well-fortified hill. When they regrouped to renew the attack, the attack was led by one of the companies of the 761st. They led the way up the hill with so much accurate fire that the hill was seized without the loss of a single airborne soldier.... During the Ardennes operation we had very little armored unit support, but of that we had, the 761st was by far the most effective and helpful."[9]

The commander of the 17th Airborne Division, Major General William M. Miley (1897–1997) (courtesy Joe Quade and the 17th Abn. Div. Assoc.).

The towns of Gouvy and Hautbillan fell and the Panthers advanced toward Saint Vith, near the German border and the Siegfried Line. Koppingerberg and Thommen fell along the way, thus shutting down the road between Saint Vith and Bastogne. This choked off the third major enemy supply artery. Von Rundstedt's offensive began to grind to a halt.

During this period in the Bulge, Staff Sergeant Jack Gilbert needed help in repairing his M-5 light tank one evening. He saw the silhouette of an American soldier standing nearby. Gilbert called out: "Here, give me a hand with this thing, will you?" The American soldier, without hesitation, gave a hand and called two other soldiers in the shadows nearby. Gilbert received the shock of his life when he saw two silver stars on the shoulders of his helper. He was a general and the two other soldiers were colonels. When the job was done, Gilbert thanked his helpers, who smiled and took off into the night.

Trezzvant Anderson sums up this cooperative effort between the 17th "Thunder From Heaven" Airborne Division and the 761st "Black Panther" Tank Battalion: "It was pretty rough in those days, for it was the month of January, and Belgium is bad enough in October. The fog hung low over the roads, and you could hardly see your hand before your face. The Jerries were withdrawing, but they were not running like they did back in France when the Third Army broke through into the clear after Saint Lo. The enemy was determined that somebody was going to pay for that ground being bought so dearly there in The Bulge. And somebody paid, but it was the enemy. For the relentless driving of the 761st kept rocking him back and back and back, and Charlie Company got into Germany again, and closed the last route of the enemy in the Saint Vith area, fighting with the vicious, hard-hitting paratroopers of the 17th Airborne Division, who thought a helluva lot of those colored tankers, after they had worked with them for a while…. The spirit of comradeship between the men of the 761st and the men of the 17th Airborne was a beautiful thing, and they willingly risked death for each other on many occasions. And the commanding officer of 17th Airborne is reported to have remarked later that he would prefer to have five tanks from the 761st than to have any larger comparable number from any other armored unit."[10]

At 2100 hours on January 26, the 87th Infantry Division relieved the 17th Airborne Division. Able Company attached to the 346th Infantry Regiment, Charlie Company to the 347th Infantry Regiment, and the balance of the 761st Tank Battalion went into strategic reserve. There was no relief for the Panthers.

On the morning of January 27, Able company smashed into Kreigberg and Gruflange with the infantry. Together they snuffed out small pockets of resistance until they ran into mortar and artillery fire. At this point, two assault-gun tanks received hits but very little damage was done. Charlie Company moved with little opposition from Lengeler through Durier and into Oudler, where they came to a halt due to a blown bridge.

BLACK TANKERS AND WHITE PARATROOPS

Black tankers and white paratroops.
They made a lovely sight.
Unless you were a German
And then you best take flight.

Black tankers and white paratroops.
They all were color blind.
They went into the battle
With winning on their mind.

Black tankers and white paratroops
Made Patton shout with glee,
"They fight the way I want them to
They're good enough for me."

Black tankers and white paratroops
Lie buried side by side.
They gave their life for country.
They gave it all with pride.

Black tankers and white paratroops.
Our memories take us back.
Since we have been in battle
There is no white nor black.

I dedicate this poem to the brave men of the 761st Tank Battalion and the 17th Airborne Division and especially to those who made the supreme sacrifice there in the Battle of the Bulge in WWII. I am proud to have been a member of the 761st and to have been associated with the 17th.

Phil Latimer

Poem by Philip Latimer. Reprinted with permission from Lt. Col. Philip W. Latimer, USAR-Ret.

On January 28, 1945, the Battle of the Bulge was over. Two weeks earlier, the Soviet Union had launched its winter offensive on a massive scale forcing Hitler to begin the transfer of all available remnants of his forces to his Eastern Front. Hitler also ordered his Sixth SS Panzer Army out of the Ardennes and into Hungary to protect vital oil fields. Patton's Third U.S. Army linked up with Hodge's First U.S. Army and closed up the Bulge. Both sides suffered heavy casualties. The Germans lost approximately 100,000 soldiers and the Allies lost approximately 76,000 either killed, wounded, captured, or missing. With the Battle of the Bulge over, the end was in sight. It was now a matter of cracking the Siegfried Line and running the Nazis into the ground.

16

Desperately Needed Replacements

Private First Class Joseph E. Wilson, Sr., describes his baptism of fire before becoming a replacement in the 761st Tank Battalion:

On a cold January morning in 1945, our convoy formed at Le Harve. We had just crossed the English Channel from Weymouth. Traveling south, the convoy stretched so far into the distance that the lead vehicle had gone out of visual range. The bright moonlight and the snow-covered terrain almost chased away the dark night, which fell on us like a light blue blanket. Stars seemed close enough to touch and the air was cold and still. Then suddenly, out of this beautiful setting came a German twin-engine bomber spitting machine gun fire on the convoy. We thought we had driven the Heinkel bomber off only to realize our mistake in assuming such because, "Here he comes again!" was shouted as the higher flying aircraft dropped bombs on us before escaping over the horizon. I had just undergone my baptism of fire from none other than "Bed Check Charlie."

Bed Check Charlie was an enemy aircraft that loitered over the battlefield at night looking for targets of opportunity. Any sign of activity would bring Charlie down on you like a falling wall until ground-to-air fire drove him off. Light [illumination] discipline was stressed so strongly that one would not light a cigarette at night, but there were occasions when we had to ignore Charlie and carry out our mission. One dark night, while firing our 155 millimeter Howitzers, Charlie strafed my gun position. Lying in my slit trench I trembled as bullets from Charlie's guns straddled my hole in the ground. Had it not been for the fact that my slit trench was perpendicular to the line of fire, you wouldn't be reading this book.

During daylight hours we were not concerned with Charlie ... due to the presence of P-47s, P-38s, and the fighter plane that won

141

the war, the U.S. Army Air Forces P-51 Mustang. Very often we on the ground would watch dogfights between planes from the *Luftwaffe* and U.S. While we would be watching, bullets would be hitting the ground near our feet. And when the German plane was shot down, a loud cheer would go up.

Quite often in life, nothing goes as planned. Being locked in mortal combat with the world's worst nightmare provided no exception to the rule. This was a day like most days in combat, rainy, gloomy and full of uncertainty. The gun had sunk into the rain-soaked ground and it was necessary to pull the gun out of the mud and go through the process of re-laying the cannon on its original azimuth. The cold rain added another layer of misery to thwart our attempt at a Slam Bang, which was within our grasp. A Slam Bang is firing the last round of ammunition before the first round slams into the target. This could be accomplished when the fire mission called for two or three rounds.

"FIRE MISSION!" All crew members assembled at the gun. "Three rounds, shell HE (high explosive), fuse quick, base deflection, one, three, zero!" Suddenly, something other than the firing of the cannon demanded our attention. A squad of bypassed German soldiers located 200 yards off our left flank pestered us with sporadic rifle fire. Staff Sergeant Joe Willie turned to me and said: "Wilson, you had infantry basic training, take care of those krauts!" A stunned bewilderment caused my cold body to flush as I caught the M-1 rifle thrown at my chest. "Roger, Sarge!" I replied to his non-request.

Taking the prone position, I placed the first shot into the soldier on my left. The second shot killed the one on my right. The next round plunged into the throat area as he raised up in an effort to escape. The remaining squad members were cut down by other Americans who had become aware of this threat, which no longer existed. Minutes later cheers were heard throughout the battery when it was announced that the Slam Bang was right on target. None of the enemy escaped.

There were very few dull moments for Battery C, 686th Medium Field Artillery Battalion. I can recall a lull in our firing one day. All was quiet. And then a faint sound, like a drone of bees which grew louder and louder, and we looked up and saw formations of U.S. heavy bombers, B-17s and B-24s, flying overhead, so many that they nearly blotted out the light of the sun, and the sound of the engines shook the earth.

Soon the din faded into silence and this great armada was no longer in sight. We carried on our normal activities, firing our guns and dodging counter battery fire from the enemy. Something now had captured our attention. There came a rumbling louder than thunder, and it was apparent that the massive air fleet that had flown past minutes ago was releasing its bombs on enemy targets. Minutes

Cannoneer Joseph E. Wilson of C Battery, 686th Field Artillery Battalion, in front of a spotter plane, 1945 (courtesy 1SG Joseph E. Wilson, Sr., USA-Ret.).

later, that same old sound could be heard, which increased until the formation was overhead, but this time you could see a difference. There were gaps in the formation. Smoke emanated from damaged planes and it was clear that some American fliers would not be returning.

"FIRE MISSION! FIRE MISSION!" [Everyone] sprang to his assigned position to put 98-pound high explosive shells in the air. "Fickle Charlie adjust, shell HE, fuse quick, base deflection left three zero, Quadrant 15 degrees," etc. This was a fire command. Forward observers had an enemy target for us to destroy, and that was the reason for our being there. "Cease fire! Cease fire! Cease fire!" "Did he say cease fire?" "Yes." "What's going on here?" The men began to wonder aloud. Soon all were back doing what is normal between fire missions. Minutes passed and many had forgotten what happened a few minutes earlier. "FIRE MISSION! FIRE MISSION!" Excitement took charge as every cannoneer took up his position at the gun. "Fire for effect!" This meant that each of the battalion's guns would fire 12 rounds in rapid sequence. Less than five minutes later the battalion's 12 Howitzers dumped 144 high-explosive rounds on the enemy target.

The next day we moved out of our positions and displaced forward. The forward observers were proud to point out their handiwork when they explained why there was a break yesterday in the firing mission. And what we saw was devastating. It so happened that a German Army artillery unit was pulling into position when spotted by observers, who waited until the German unit had moved off the road into this wooded area and they were all in a neat package. Human body parts and equipment were blown apart and into tree trunks and all over the area. It was total devastation with no survivors. There was glee all around and we felt no remorse because the American fighting man had been traumatized by what had happened at Malmedy, Belgium [the massacre of captured American troops]— which was still fresh in our minds.[1]

On January 28, 1945, the 761st Tank Battalion advanced northeast toward Saint Vith, Belgium, to contact and relieve elements of the 7th Armored Division and XVIII Airborne Corps. The Panthers made contact at 1500 hours.

On January 29, Baker Company moved out with the 2nd Battalion, 345th Infantry Regiment, toward Schierbach, but could not enter the town due to mines and roadblocks. Charlie Company, with five tanks operational, supported a combat team from the 346th Infantry Regiment, a tank destroyer platoon, and a company of tanks from the 7th Armored Division for an excursion through the 82nd Airborne Division's sector to outflank the enemy. They accomplished this at 2300 hours.

On January 30, Baker Company spearheaded the attack on Huem by knocking out three machine gun nests placed in cellars. The foot soldiers immediately moved in and mopped up the town. As they exited Huem an enemy 75 millimeter assault gun located on the high ground started lobbing shells. The gun crew knocked out the lead tank before the other tanks ran them off. Although this was the end of enemy resistance, the advance came to a halt due to roadblocks, mines, and craters. Meanwhile, Charlie Company engaged the enemy at long range in the vicinity of Herresbach as the rest of the battalion performed emergency maintenance.

On January 31, Baker Company remained in position waiting for the combat engineers to put in a bridge leading to Schonberg. Charlie Company advanced toward Schonberg from a different location and engaged the enemy at long range because road conditions would not permit close combat.

When the month of January ended, the 761st Tank Battalion had 29 officers, three warrant officers, and 680 enlisted men accounted for. However, the actual strength was much lower due to casualties. The Panthers suffered the loss of five men killed in action, 14 wounded in action, and 22 non-battle casualties. Seventeen tanks had been lost to enemy fire and 16 needed repair due to heavy wear and

Harry K. Tyree (*standing, center*) with newly acquired friends in Hermee, Belgium, February 1945 (courtesy Harry K. Tyree).

tear on their engines and power trains caused by the steep, ice covered hills. The battalion now had 20 tanks that were combat serviceable.

Private First Class Floyd Dade, Jr. of Able Company recalls an incident around Saint Vith: "Our tank battery went dead and the driver could not start the tank. Sergeant Weston asked me to take the .30 caliber machine gun some 50 yards from the tank. I set the machine gun up and returned to get the ammunition box. On the way back to the machine gun, a mortar round hit about 25 yards from me. I could see orange smoke and feel the heat; luckily I did not get wounded! After the medic checked me, I returned and got the machine gun and brought it back to the tank. Maintenance Sergeant Murphy brought us a battery. We started the tank and joined the battle to take Saint Vith. Near the location where we were disabled, a P-51 dive bomber was circling the city and on his second run of strafing and bombing, he checked us out by circling the tank. I removed the mud from the white star so it could be seen by him. The pilot tilted his wings from side to side a couple of times for acknowledgment. We continued to fight."[2]

On February 3, the 761st Tank Battalion traveled approximately 140 miles to Hermee, Belgium, and set up a command post across the border in nearby Jabeek,

24-year-old Christopher P. Navarre, First Sergeant of the 590th Ambulance Company. He was one of the youngest first sergeants in the regular army (courtesy CW3 Christopher P. Navarre, Sr., USA-Ret.).

Holland. Orders assigned the 761st to the 95th Infantry Division, commanded by Maj. General Harry L. Twaddle.

The heavy fighting took its toll. Replacements were desperately needed. Unlike white units, the Armored Force Replacement Training Center at Fort Knox turned out no replacements for the 761st. The experimental tank battalions were meant to pacify Eleanor Roosevelt and never were intended for combat. They were called to combat duty only because well-trained separate tank battalions were needed.

Emergency replacements came from a variety of Army units. Completely untrained in tanks, these men wanted to be with the 761st because of the battalion's reputation. Most of the volunteers took a reduction in rank for this opportunity. An intense two-week training course took place in Holland. Following this, replacements received on-the-job training while in combat. The battalion commander, Major John George, planned and supervised this training program and split his time with front-line duties.

Platoon Sergeant Johnnie Stevens recalls: "There weren't enough trained replacements! So we were in a position where we were being cut to pieces, but no replacements. So we started getting people from service units, and we made tankers out of those guys in a few days. We couldn't teach them the technical things, but they could learn to be bow gunners or cannoneers in a short time."

Christopher Navarre took a reduction in rank to private for this opportunity: "They refused to let me transfer and so the only way I could go was to resign my 1st Sergeant status. I gave it up to go there because I wanted to fight and not be in a service unit any longer. I came from the 590th Ambulance Company. That was a traumatic experience and although we were taking white soldiers back to safety, they didn't appreciate blacks handling them."[3] Navarre was assigned to Charlie Company.

On February 16, Major George received a promotion to Lt. Colonel. The following day, Lt. Colonel Paul L. Bates returned and took back the command of the 761st Tank Battalion. Bates's driver told some of the men: "Everything is going to be all right now, my boy is back."[4]

On February 20, orders reassigned the 761st Tank Battalion to the 79th Infantry Division commanded by Maj. General Ira T. Wynch. Initially, Able Company attached to the 313th Infantry Regiment, Baker Company to the 315th Infantry Regiment, Charlie Company to 314th Infantry Regiment, and Dog Company to the 79th Reconnaissance Troop.

As training of replacements continued, Baker Company sent a platoon of tanks to the 314th Infantry Regiment. On February 23, they shelled the town of End in Holland and spearheaded the ensuing attack. After the town fell they took up positions overlooking the Ruhr River and launched several diversionary attacks.

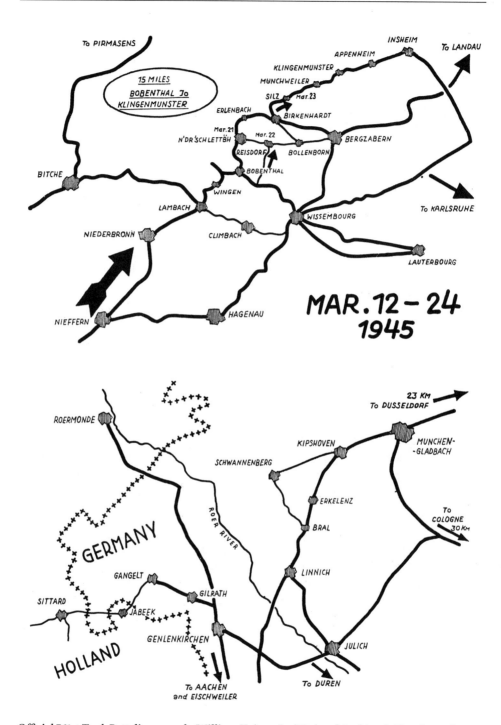

Official 761st Tank Battalion maps byWilliam Kaiser, Jr. (National Archives). *Top:* Area of operations in Task Force Rhine. *Bottom:* Area of operations around the Ruhr River.

Charlie Company, which had been designated a provisional training company, moved to the vicinity of Mheer, where they set up a firing and driving range. They trained replacement gunners and drivers.

As February 1945 came to a close, the 761st Tank Battalion had an effective strength of 33 officers, three warrant officers, and 680 enlisted men. The battalion lost ten men in non-combat mishaps but none were killed or wounded in action.

Elements of the 761st Tank Battalion smashed through Milich, near the Roermond Julich railway, and cut another enemy supply artery. The fighting continued to Erkelenz, where the Panthers positioned themselves to cross the German border for the third time.

On March 3, the Panthers crossed into the Reich at a point between Gangelt and Gilrath and assaulted the town of Schwannenberg. They mopped up small pockets of resistance and took prisoners.

On March 7, the 761st Tank Battalion along with the 79th Reconnaissance Troop, spearheaded the infantry's assault on Kipshoven in a three-pronged attack. Munchen Gladbach, home of Germany's Propaganda Minister, Josef Goebbels, fell to the combined onslaught. The Panthers found themselves 55 miles inside Hitler's Third Reich.

On March 8, the 761st Tank Battalion received orders to proceed to Saverne, France, and rejoin the Third Army. Enroute, new orders came down to join the 103rd Infantry Division in the Seventh Army. The 103rd "Cactus" Infantry Division was commanded by Maj. General Anthony C. McAuliffe, the former deputy commander of the 101st Airborne Division at Bastogne. He had given the legendary "Nuts" answer to the enemy's surrender demand when his unit was cut off and surrounded by von Rundstedt's Panzers.

The 761st Tank Battalion traveled by train through Luxembourg to Saverne, France, where they began preparations for a major offensive to pierce the Siegfried Line.

"The First U.S. Army wasn't the only American Army that got pushed back in December 1944," Trezzvant Anderson remembers, "nor was the 92nd Infantry Division the only division that lost ground it once had taken, for down there in France we had to go back and retake ground which had already been taken before — and lost — by the Americans, for the Jerries had pushed the Seventh Army around some, too, back in December. So we went to get it back — with interest. But it sure was tough, for our mission this time was: 'TO BREAK THROUGH THE SIEGFRIED LINE AND GO TO THE RHINE.'"

17

Cracking the Siegfried Line

At 1330 hours, March 12, 1945, the Panthers set up their command post in Bosselshausen, where they relieved the 48th Tank Battalion from the 103rd Infantry Division. Initially, Able Company attached to the 409th Infantry Regiment; Baker Company to the 411th Infantry Regiment; Charlie Company to the 410th Infantry Regiment; and the Assault Gun Platoon to the 928th Field Artillery Battalion. They made preparations to jump off with the 103rd "Cactus" Infantry Division in Task Force Cactus. The mission was to uncover and penetrate the Siegfried Line in the vicinity of Climbach.

This section of the Siegfried Line sat in the middle of the Hardt Mountains, where the landscape was dotted with pillboxes and dragon teeth tank obstacles. Machine gun emplacements, antitank guns, mortar positions, and artillery batteries lay waiting in the wooded hills with their guns zeroed in on the narrow passageways.

Task Force Cactus jumped off on March 14. On March 18, the task force, held up by a blown bridge northeast of Froeshwiller, was dissolved due to road conditions and difficult terrain.

During this period the 14th Armored Division prowled along the Siegfried Line probing for an opening. They made several unsuccessful attempts to break through. Once they progressed as far as Bobenthal, but enemy forces immediately repulsed their advance.

On March 20 a platoon of Charlie Company tanks spearheaded for elements of the 411th Infantry Regiment in an assault on Nieder Schlettenbach. Thirteen pillboxes and 12 machine gun nests fell along the way, and 35 enemy soldiers died. A 75 millimeter antitank gun, complete with sights and ammunition, was captured intact. This offensive came to a halt due to blown bridges. Meanwhile, about two miles south, another platoon of tanks from Charlie Company spearheaded for elements of the 409th Infantry Regiment in an assault on Reisdorf. Six pillboxes were effectively neutralized, and eight enemy soldiers were killed.

The 103rd Infantry Division's "Report After Action" describes following the

Antitank "dragon teeth" of the Siegfried Line. Photo taken by First Sergeant Takeo Susuki, Service Co. 522nd F.A. Battalion, 1945 (courtesy Takeo and Mark Susuki).

Panthers into a Siegfried town: "You crouch low, trying to keep the protection of that hot, roaring hunk of steel between you and the village. You see the turret of the Sherman swing and, suddenly, you feel the muzzle blast of the 76 as it sends a shell into the first house. Again and again the 76 fires. The other tanks fire and the noise is deafening. You are coming close to the village now, and you see the kraut mines sticking up in the sodden field. The tank, like a huge fire-spouting monster, rolls over lots of 'shu' mines and detonates them in little white puffs under the treads. God, you think, don't let 'em hit us with artillery now. Sticking out like tenpins. No cover. Mines all over the place. Caught like rats if they open up with the big stuff. The smoke screen put on the town by the artillery is thin now.... The tanks are still rolling. Suddenly, there is a blinding flash near you and you hit the ground! An antitank gun is on your tank. A guy in your squad is too close to the tank. The Sherman jerks to a stop and backs up. The GI screams in pain as the tank crushes both his legs. You yell for the medics, and you vaguely see them take over as the tank blasts back at the antitank gun to your right front. It's only 40 yards to the house now. Your squad leader looks around and then plunges away from the tank toward the building. You follow."[1]

On March 20, 1st Lieutenant Maxwell Huffman, who took over Able Company from Captain Williams, was hit by sniper fire in Nieder Schlettenbach. Huffman died of his wounds five days later.

Platoon Sergeant Johnnie Stevens recalls: "The day Huffman got killed, I told Huffman, don't go down into that gawd damned town! I don't like it. He was not my platoon leader, but he was a lieutenant and so that day he happened to be in charge. So he went down like I told him not to. He had his hatch open and you just don't do that when there are tall buildings around. A sniper can get you. He gets tied up down there. They had Mark IVs and antitank guns down there. They had everything in the town you can shake a stick at. So I went down to bail him out, then I got trapped. I got on the mic and called Murphy, Paul Murphy, my cover man. Murphy was sitting up on the hill with the rest of the platoon. I was scared as hell! The Germans were shooting up the infantry. Huffman was dead, I knew this. Barn doors opened up and antitank guns came out. They wasted us all over the place. I told Murphy, get the hell down here! All hell is breaking loose! I used to call him Corky. I said, Corky, get down here! So Murphy came down and bailed me out, with his section, with Rubley and them. If it wasn't for Murphy, I would not have made it out of that place that day because they had us trapped."[2]

On March 21, orders came down to form "Task Force Rhine," to be composed of the 761st Tank Battalion less Charlie Company; the 2nd Battalion, 409th Infantry Regiment; a reconnaissance platoon from the 614th Tank Destroyer Battalion; the 103rd Signal Company; and a detachment of combat engineers. They were ordered to the assembly area in the early-morning hours of March 22, and ordered to move rapidly through any break in the Siegfried Line and advance to the Rhine River. This task force came under the command of the 761st Tank Battalion's commander, Lt. Colonel Paul L. Bates.

Meanwhile, Charlie Company, with tank platoons dispersed and attached to elements of the 409th and 411th Infantry Regiments, continued spearheading. Together they reduced the intensity of the approaches to the Siegfried Line and would later merge with the task force for its final thrust.

At Nieder Schlettenbach, in support of the 409th, Sergeant Crecy's tank knocked out a pillbox high on a hill. The gunner who fired the 76 millimeter cannon was 1st Sergeant William R. Burroughs, who temporarily gave up his 1st Sergeant's rank to fight with Crecy. Through the open hatches of the commander's turret, Crecy immediately manned the .50 caliber machine gun and cut down a group of enemy soldiers scurrying from their burning bunker. Crecy cheated death as he ducked down and closed his hatch just as an 88 millimeter shell exploded just a few feet from his tank. This most vivid demonstration of intrepidity and skill in battle was caught on film by Sergeant George Sanders, a combat photographer with the 103rd Infantry Division.

In an action in support of the 411th, a tank platoon led by 2nd Lieutenant Frank Cochrane fought its way to Nieder Schlettenbach. Using fire and movement tactics, they rushed two tanks while the remaining tanks provided a protective cover of fire. Another pair followed in the same manner. For six hours they blasted their way past pillboxes built into the overhanging cliffs, which towered more than 100 feet above the road. The battle raged on until the following morning. When the smoke cleared on the road between Nieder Schlettenbach and Erlenbach, the platoon discovered seven pillboxes destroyed, ten machine gun nests wiped out, 12 enemy soldiers dead, and 64 ready to capitulate.

Able Company sent a tank platoon to relieve 2nd Lieutenant Cochrane's battle weary platoon on the line. Then the advance came to a halt in the vicinity of Gundershoffen due to a blown bridge. At this point all the tanks were formed together for a combined assault code-named Task Force Rhine.

The 42nd "Rainbow" Infantry Division was positioned to crack the Siegfried Line on the left flank. On the right flank was the 36th "Texas" Infantry Division. Somewhere in the area on the left flank was the 10th Armored Division, ready to exploit any opportunities through the Siegfried Line, and also to prepare the way for the "Rainbow" Division. Behind Task Force Rhine was the 14th Armored Division which would wait for these tankers to smash a hole in the Siegfried. What the 10th Armored Division was doing for the 42nd Division, the 761st Tank Battalion, a separate battalion, was to do for the 103rd Division.

Task Force Rhine remained in the assembly area south of Reisdorf until 1600 hours, at which time they jumped off. On the approach to Reisdorf a tank fell to an antitank mine. The force took up firing positions and battered the town for over an hour, in which time the infantry made its way through the high grounds and closed on the enemy in a pincer movement. Reisdorf fell, thus weakening the approaches to the Siegfried Line.

After the task force smashed through Reisdorf, it went after the pillboxes northeast of the town. Leaving them in a smoking heap, Task Force Rhine split into two columns. One headed north on a narrow dirt road that led to Birkenhardt and the other headed southeast on a well-paved road to Bollenborn. The combat teams were completely mechanized, with the footsoldiers riding on the tanks. They fired at anything that moved.

The Birkenhardt column advanced against small arms fire until they reached the northeast edge of town, where frantic antitank fire stopped their advance. They withdrew and called in a concentrated "Time On Target" artillery strike, then advanced into the smoking rubble that was once a town. Dead cows, horses, and

Top: After blasting a pillbox near Reisdorf, Sergeant Crecy traps a group of enemy soldiers between their blazing bunker and his .50 caliber machine gun bullets. Crecy wipes them all out. *Bottom:* An 88 blast from another bunker nearly takes Crecy's head off as he ducks down and closes his hatch (National Archive photographs taken by Sgt. George Sanders, Signal Corps, 103rd Infantry Division).

A knocked-out pillbox along the Siegfried Line. Photo taken by First Sergeant Takeo Susuki, Service Co 522nd, F.A. Battalion, 1945 (courtesy Takeo and Mark Susuki).

other animals littered the streets as they passed through, firing at any position that could conceal an antitank gun.

Four antitank guns were discovered in the town. The assault gun platoon snuffed out two and the other two were abandoned by their crews. At this point, the column came to a halt while the doughboys consolidated their positions.

The Bollenborn column was not as fortunate. They encountered dragon teeth that the tank-dozer simply covered with dirt; the tanks rolled right over them. They subsequently encountered an extended roadblock that the combat engineers had to clear. As the last obstacle was being pulled out of the way, a concealed 75 millimeter antitank gun set up to protect Bollenborn opened fire on the column. Direct hits completely destroyed two medium tanks. Fortunately, the crews ejected safely. With the road zeroed in, the tanks had to pull off and take cover. Heavy artillery fire rained down on the road, tearing holes large enough to hold a tank. Ten-foot-high balls of fire and smoke lifted the ground and uprooted trees. As it turned out, the artillery fire was friendly fire. A flank division had the enemy on the run and believed that the enemy used the Bollenborn road as a means of egress. The friendly flank division did not check for friendly troop positions before adjusting fire. Their 155 millimeter howitzers stopped after the error was radioed in to them. Mistakes of this sort were frequent.

The Bollenborn column withdrew and joined forces with the Birkenhardt column by now heading northwest towards Silz. Task Force Rhine was now a single cohesive fighting unit hell-bent on destroying the enemy. Every unit had an old score to settle with the Germans, such that Task Force Rhine could have been called Task Force Revenge.

With Baker Company riding point, Sergeant Ervin Latimore commanded the lead tank and 1st Lieutenant Harold B. Gary commanded the lead tank platoon. They were held in high regard by all who took part in Task Force Rhine. Refusing to be evacuated after receiving a serious wound, Sergeant Latimore continued to lead the attack. The doughboys paid tribute to him: "That tank commander in the first tank was wonderful! He overcame a hell of a lot of obstacles even before the second tank saw them."[3] Latimore received the Silver Star for his actions.

Lt. Colonel Paul L. Bates, while on foot commanding the task force and occasionally prodding the doughboys on the tanks to keep awake, was knocked unconscious by the concussion of an 88 blast. Sergeant Warren G. H. Crecy came out of his tank under artillery fire and moved his commander to a place of safety.

Private Christopher Navarre recalls Crecy's determination: "Crecy was the type of person who went from tank to tank. When his tank was knocked out he took over the next tank where the other fellows didn't do that. When our tank was knocked out we waited for another tank. Crecy alone, he had the agility and a commanding aura about him. He was a dedicated man on a mission, so in other words, you couldn't stop Crecy. As a tank commander he still did the gunner's job. If I

Task Force Rhine Commander Lt. Colonel Paul L. Bates (courtesy Col. Paul L. Bates, USA [Ret.–Dec.]).

would have been in the same tank with him, I would have lost my job as a tank gunner because Crecy would shoot the tank gun as well as the machine gun on the turret. I don't know what else that can be said to describe this outstanding soldier except that Crecy is the most inspirational and exceptional person I ever knew in battle, and I fought in Korea as well. He was destined to win. There was no such thing as losing, and if there was a case of surrender, Crecy couldn't surrender. He was that type of person. I remember saying that if anyone gets the Medal of Honor, it will be Crecy. After the war I used to call him Audie Murphy. Audie Murphy got all of this and that and I don't think he did half as much as what Crecy did. Crecy rode those tanks like a wild man!"[4]

At 1835 hours on March 22, Task Force Rhine came to a halt about 2,000 yards north of Birkenhardt due to a crater in the road. The combat engineers filled it by 1940 hours and the task force continued its advance toward Silz, where it planned to link up with the 10th Armored Division and smash through the Siegfried Line.

Darkness fell as the task force approached Silz, where it was met by enemy mortar and artillery fire. This was clear evidence that the 10th Armored Division had not made it to Silz. Alone in the middle of the Siegfried Line the task force could not turn back, no matter what the odds.

The column turned due east and blasted its way through Silz toward Munchweiler. A hit on an ammunition dump started an inferno. Sergeant William East of the 409th Infantry Regiment describes the situation:

> Soon after midnight, the tanks appeared on the outskirts of Silz. The attack was so swift, an enemy antitank gun was knocked out before its crew could man the weapon. The gun was in position and there was plenty of ammunition, but the column had knifed through the darkness so quickly the enemy was caught unprepared. The town of Silz was burning brightly from fires started by shells from the tank guns. The experienced Negro soldiers who manned the tanks employed reconnaissance by fire. Every stretch of ground along the line of march was systematically and mercilessly searched by 75mm, 76mm and 37mm cannons and .30 and .50 caliber machine guns. This was fire power with vengeance. As one of the colored gunners put it: "Man, we learned this jive from General Patton." Not to be outdone, the Cactus foot soldiers kept a steady stream of .30 caliber ammunition blazing off into the ditches and hills along the road. M-1 rifles and Browning automatics were red hot. The tanks sped unimpeded through Silz. There was an "end of the world" terror about the place. Hellish fires cast weird shadows, screams of terrified civilians mingled with the agonizing groans of the enemy wounded…. Speeding on toward Munchweiler, the armored column surprised a *Wehrmacht* column of artillery, antitank guns, and supplies that had waited too long before evacuating. This was an opportunity that had

never been encountered by the power crazed tank pilots. They sent their steel monsters bulling into the German column, strewing wreckage as they thundered forward. Tanks crushed men and horses. Cannon fire blasted trucks into twisted masses of flaming steel. Erstwhile supermen ran screaming down the road attempting to surrender.[5]

After the vengeful slaughter, dead horses, destroyed vehicles, and dead enemy soldiers blocked the road such that the tank-dozer had to be called in to clear the way.

Captain William L. O'Dea, the 761st Motor Officer, describes how his maintenance section was ambushed: "Company and battalion maintenance sections were combined and consolidated with the trains under the protection of the light tanks of Company D. These sections followed the medium tanks closely, until the town of Silz was taken. After which, the trains were ambushed by bypassed enemy infantry. The battalion maintenance platoon half-track caught the brunt of this enemy attack and fought it off with the vehicular .50 caliber machine gun until all the trucks were regrouped with the light tanks. Seven enemy riflemen surrendered to the maintenance section. There were no casualties sustained by maintenance personnel."[6]

Shortly past midnight, the task force reached Munchweiler, where it confronted more antitank fire. The Panthers laid down a heavy blanket of machine gun fire that caused the antitank gunners to flee into the night.

Task Force Rhine advanced to its final objective, the city of Klingenmunster, where it ran into considerable fire from the permanent installations guarding it. There the stench of rotting bodies, human and animal feces, and other smells of war intensified. The task force opened fire with all of its weapons and a large number of enemy soldiers capitulated. This presented another problem. With the enemy closing in on the rear of the column, it became difficult to transport the prisoners to the POW cages.

At 0150 hours on March 23, the assault into Klingenmunster began when a tank platoon from Baker Company led the doughboys into the city. They ran into heavy resistance and pulled back. The task force took up positions around the city and blasted it mercilessly until it caught fire. The force reentered the city again and began to clear it. One German soldier made the mistake of firing on a tank from an upstairs window. The undisturbed tank slowly swung its turret around, hesitated a moment in front of the window, and then blasted the room apart. Klingenmunster fell to Task Force Rhine at 0435 hours, 12 hours and 35 minutes after the main body of the task force jumped off. The path to the plains leading to the Rhine River lay clear and the 14th Armored Division began rolling through.

Operating far in advance of friendly artillery, the 761st Tank Battalion smashed through the Siegfried Line in the face of vicious enemy resistance. From March 20 to the 23rd, the 761st captured or destroyed seven enemy towns, over 400 vehicles, more than 80 heavy weapons, 200 horses, and virtually thousands of small arms.

Above and facing page: The morning after Task Force Rhine, March 23, 1945 (National Archives photograph taken by Sgt. George Sanders, Signal Corps, 103rd Infantry Division).

Further, the battalion was responsible for inflicting over 4,000 casualties against elements of 14 German divisions. No one will ever know how many casualties were inflicted from the reconnaissance by fire. Dead enemy soldiers lay in the hills and fields all the way from Birkenhardt to Klingenmunster. Over 15 miles of death and destruction lay behind the 761st when it pulled into Klingenmunster to liberate over a thousand slave laborers held by the Nazis.

The task force commander, Lt. Colonel Paul L. Bates, pointed out: "On Task Force Rhine I had about 1,800 men. This was the last of the heavy fighting and I stayed with the leading five tanks where most of the action was. There was extreme bravery, ability, and acceptance of multiple dangerous situations."[7]

Captain Philip W. Latimer, the battalion supply officer, recalls: "It was as an aftermath of this battle that my driver, Corporal Dorsey, and I claimed the capture of a village in the Rhine plain. After Klingenmunster was secured, Lt. Colonel Bates told me to go ahead to this village and choose a spot for our temporary headquarters. As we came into town, there was not a soul to be seen, however, we had not gone far before a German stepped out and waved a white flag. It turned out that he was recovering from a wound and was incapable of putting up a fight. We realized that we were the first Americans to arrive here, and we looked apprehensively at the bunker at the far end of one street. It contained a large-caliber weapon, which pointed menacingly in our direction. It took all our courage to advance even though we were fairly certain that the bunker was empty. [Dorsey and I] breathed sighs of relief when we found this to be the case."[8]

Master Sergeant Ernest D. Hill, Sr., a master tank mechanic from Service Company, described three incidents of humor and heroism during the Rhine offensive in a letter to his wife, Mrs. Hope Hill, of Chicago:

> One of our tanks got hit by a big gun in a pillbox high up on a mountain. The crew bailed out and left, except for one man. All of us thought he was hit until he showed up a couple of days later. He and an infantryman were the only GIs in the town. They had only one K-ration cracker between them. When dark came he crawled back to the tank and fired seven shots to knock out a pillbox.
>
> Another tank got knocked out in a town. So the next morning we went up to recover it. The town was quiet, except for snipers. The whole village was quiet. Not a person in sight. All of the buildings were knocked down. Dead horses, cows, and men lay around. In fact, it was too still. Then lo and behold, I heard a piano playing. I thought I was hearing ghosts or something. Finally, I recognized the song. What do you think it was? "My Momma Done Told Me!" I followed the sound. There in a shell-shattered house sat the lone inhabitant of the town. He was one of our guys from the knocked-out tank. He was decked out in a silk top hat some Jerry big shot once worn. All of the furniture and dishes were broken and lying around. Even the top of the piano was knocked off, but that didn't bother him. He just plucked right on.
>
> Another one of my boys stopped me with a broken-down tank. He said he was going to stop the first general that came by and ask him how many Germans he had to kill before he could get a new tank. He'd killed about 200 that day. (He's battle happy).
>
> The whole thing moved so fast we could hardly keep up. But we smashed through the Siegfried Line in its toughest spot, and didn't lose a man.[9]

Private Christopher Navarre recalls waiting for Master Sergeant Hill to come and repair his tank:

> After the major attack we had captured a lot of prisoners. That's when our tank threw a track and we had to pick a house in that town to wait until they came to repair the track. I took the firing pin out of the block of the main gun and the rest of the men took the machine guns out. Then we immobilized the tank and sealed it.
>
> When we went into the house the people were so frightened that they were going crazy. They were afraid of the one word that I recognized later on: "Schwarze Soldaten." I didn't know what that was until after the war: "Black Soldiers." When I sat down to eat my K-rations, I made my sign of the cross to bless the food. This frightened lady there, she grabbed my hand out of the presence of the rest of them and kissed my hand. That was a shocking experience for me

because they were all frightened. They were told that the black tankers were coming to rape them. A lot of people don't realize that the Senegalese, the French soldiers, were not blond hair, blue eyed soldiers. They were black, six or seven feet tall, and notorious warriors. When they went across the line, they returned with German heads and everything else. The Germans were aware of the black soldiers, not so much the Americans, but the French. Senegal was a province of France. I crossed paths with the Senegalese many times. I spoke French and couldn't explain that I was from Louisiana and not Senegal. I was the shortest Senegalese they ever saw.[10]

At the completion of Task Force Rhine, Maj. General Anthony C. McAuliffe sent a congratulatory message to the participants: "The first stage of our operation has been brilliantly completed. You broke through the famous Siegfried defenses and then boldly exploited your success. You have taken more than 4,700 prisoners. You have fought gallantly and intelligently, and you have led all the way. I congratulate you."[11]

On March 24, as the Panthers gathered more prisoners from the surrounding hills, Private First Class Crawford O. Pegram and his tank crew met trouble. As his light tank escorted three jeeps on a reconnaissance mission, the enemy opened fire. The vulnerable jeeps withdrew and Pegram moved his tank to a covered position behind a wall and returned fire. His tank's accurate fire destroyed two machine gun positions and pinned down one antitank gun and two bazooka teams and permitted the nearby American infantry to move in and capture the pinned-down enemy soldiers. While moving forward his tank was fired on again by a well-concealed antitank gun. Pegram's tank took cover and he immediately dismounted to locate the hidden gun. Upon his return the enemy cut him off from his tank with small-arms fire. He low-crawled to higher ground and met a group of doughboys with a mortar. He pointed to the enemy positions and the crew quickly set the mortar in position and fired five rounds that forced the enemy to abandon their antitank gun. Pegram then returned to his tank, picked up with the jeeps, and continued the reconnaissance mission.

Meanwhile, at the command post, orders came down through the 103rd Infantry Division stating that the 761st Tank Battalion was now attached to the 71st Infantry Division in Patton's Third Army.

During the month of March 1945, the 761st Tank Battalion fired 300 tons of ammunition and consumed 50,000 gallons of V-80 gasoline. Only five tanks were lost due to enemy action. The unit's effective strength at month's end was 33 officers, three warrant officers, and 662 enlisted men. Only one officer and six enlisted men were wounded in action. The officer, 1st Lieutenant Max Huffman, died of his wounds.

18

Mopping Up the 6th SS Mountain Division, Nord

"Well, at last we had Jerry on the run everywhere," Trezzvant Anderson remembers, "and it was just a matter of running him to death, and destroying him, and getting this damned war over, because there were some of us who wanted to get our clothes off, all of them, and get a good hot bath! And, too, this made the fifth time we had gone over into Germany, and the big idea was to make it be the last time, and let's get this damned thing over with! And besides, this time we crossed the Rhine! Man, we really 'jumped' after that.... We had to capture the 6th SS Mountain Division, Nord, for they were threatening Corps Headquarters, and that meant General Eddy, and you know we got our first battle orders under his Corps, so we just couldn't stand for that. So, off we went, over the Rhine."[1]

Private First Class Floyd Dade, Jr., of Able Company recalls being harassed by the "Ripsaw" 88s near the Rhine: "Approaching Oppenheim, we got stuck in a field for about six hours as the front moved on. There was a fence about 50 yards from my tank and I went to get some posts to put under the tracks so we could pull ourselves out. A German gun crew with an 88 antitank gun let me put down one post under the tank. Then I returned to get the other post. On my way back, they bracketed in on me. One shot went under, one shot went over, but before they could get the third shot off, I went to the right. Each shot would bury itself in the mud before exploding, making a puddle about four to five feet wide. They fired ten rounds in all. I crawled back to the tank. The retriever came and pulled us out and we joined the rest of the platoon and continued to fight."[2]

On March 30, 1945, the 761st Tank Battalion, with orders of assignment to the 71st Infantry Division, XII Corps, Third Army, crossed the Rhine River and traveled 132 miles to Langenselbold, Germany, where they reported in to the 71st Division Command Post. No time was lost getting into action when Staff Sergeant Alexander Bell shot down a *Luftwaffe* plane right outside of the CP.

Charlie Company's "Cool Stud" tank crew displaying their captured Nazi flag. *Left to right:* Goffe, gunner; W. Kaiser, cartographer; unknown bow gunner; Clark, driver; and L. Smith, loader. Photograph taken by D. Cardell, tank commander (courtesy E. G. McConnell).

Able Company attached to the 5th Infantry Regiment, Baker Company to the 14th Infantry Regiment, Charlie Company to the 66th Infantry Regiment, and Dog Company to the 71st Reconnaissance Troop. Together with division artillery, they completely surrounded the crack 6th SS Mountain Division, Nord, who prepared to break out. This unit was part of the *Waffen* SS, Hitler's elite troops, a ground force with its own chain of command independent of the *Wehrmacht.*

The initial breakout attempt occurred at dusk on April 2, when three SS convoys moved southeast to break through the American rear lines. They wedged behind 400 *Waffen* SS mountain troops that led the way with two captured American Sherman tanks, two self-propelled antitank guns, eight jeeps, and 12 "Deuce-and-a-half" [two-and-a-half-ton] trucks. The other groups also were equipped with captured American weapons and vehicles.

Able Company split up and led the infantry through the forest and circled Waldenburg. They aided in the capture of Buches and Budingen and spearheaded towards the middle of the enemy lines to force clear a supply route through the forest.

World War II German mobile firepower on display today at the U.S. Army Ordnance Museum, Aberdeen Proving Grounds, Maryland. *Top:* Grizzly Bear Sturmpanzer IV armed with a 155 millimeter howitzer assault gun. *Bottom:* STUH 42 armed with a 105 millimeter howitzer assault gun. *Facing page:* Wespe (PzkwII chassis) armed with a 105 millimeter howitzer assault gun.

Meanwhile, Baker Company advanced north to assist the infantry in mopping up bypassed pockets of resistance. Together they advanced across the bottom of a ravine and over a small stream under small-arms fire. Two tanks became stuck in the mud and another tank lost a track. Private First Class Irving Boone of the 14th Infantry Regiment recalls: "...I was particularly impressed by the black officer down in the ravine giving hand signals to get the tank drivers through the stumps and other obstacles ... all the while there was heavy firing from both sides."[3]

Baker Company and the infantry finally reached the other side of the ravine and emerged at the crest of an embankment overlooking the Nieder Mockstadt — Ober Mockstadt Road. There they came face to face with the reckless and desperate German forces attempting to break out. There was no stopping the SS, who had eight mobile artillery pieces placed on a hill along the road to cover their convoy as it rumbled by. They preferred death to surrender. Lieutenant

Gary's tank platoon went after the artillery and Captain Long's tanks fired on the trucks in the convoy. The foot soldiers engaged the SS in a fierce firefight.

As the first tank crested the embankment and started across an open field with its cannon ablaze, the SS artillery immediately bracketed in on it. Hatches flew open and the crew members abandoned their tank just as it was hit and let loose clouds of greasy black smoke. The next tank tried to stay below the crest line. It fired on the convoy until it took a hit on its gun barrel. Once again the hatches flew open and greasy black smoke poured out as the men scrambled to safety. Only one tanker was injured. The others pulled him to safety and then took up positions with the infantry as the driver crawled back into the smoldering tank and backed it out of the line of fire.

By this time the doughboys began to run short of ammunition. Orders came down for them to save three rounds per weapon. The traffic on the road had stopped and darkness began to fall as the cannonless tank led the way back through the ravine, past tank retrievers that worked to get the disabled Shermans out of the mud. After this initial clash, the SS broke up into small groups and attempted to escape.

Charlie Company faced north to take up positions south and east of the enemy's position, setting a trap to capture the retreating SS. Captain Charles "Pop" Gates describes what happened when they finally came out of the woods: "On one combat mission, we were having difficulty getting the Germans out of the woods. We kept firing low. Finally I told 'em, Gentlemen, raise your fire so it will explode up in the trees. That'll send more shrapnel around, also some trees down, and get those people out of those woods. They came out waving white flags and calling, 'Kameraden.' I told the men to remain in their tanks with the hatches buttoned up, and when the enemy got abreast of 'em, just direct 'em back to the infantry. Well, some guy opened up his hatch a little bit early. The Germans looked and they said, 'Schwarze Soldaten!' (Black Soldiers!) That word just went through the bunch and they started runnin' back to the damn woods. We figured, we'll be damned if you're gonna get back to those woods. Finally, they figured they'd better go along with these black soldiers."[4]

The German Army couldn't see how the Panthers could be in so many places. To be sure, each company was split into three platoons and each platoon was split into two sections; all were scattered throughout the division. The Germans had the Panthers plotted on their maps. A captured German officer asked Captain Charles "Pop" Gates, "How many Negro Panzer divisions *are* there?"

In another altercation, Dog Company performed screening and reconnaissance missions in coordination with the 71st Reconnaissance Troop. Technician Leonard "Chico" Holland led six light tanks in the capture of an enemy radio station and two fully stocked armored supply dumps near Lake Rotenbach. Dog and the 71st wiped out an estimated 200 enemy infantrymen.

The assault gun platoon split into two sections. Lieutenant James R. Burgess, Jr., took the first section and covered the forward movement of the 608th Field Artillery Battalion. The other section, commanded by Staff Sergeant Richard L. Sparks, laid 105s in on enemy positions in the heavily wooded areas around Spielberg, Streitburg, and Leisenwald.

When Sparks reported to the commander of the 66th Infantry Regiment to escort a convoy, the colonel told Sparks: "Convoy? We're going out to fight!" Without batting an eye, Sparks replied: "Okay, sir, let's go, then!"

While the infantry prepared to attack Leisenwald, Infantry Private First Class Matthews was laying communications wire when he noticed something unusual. In a field near the village he spotted four German soldiers with *panzerfausts* waiting to ambush the tanks. Realizing that the destruction of any of the four tanks supporting the infantry could result in the failure of the mission, he immediately went to warn the tankers. In order to reach the tanks he had to cross an open field and expose himself to enemy fire. Matthews worked his way to where the tanks were preparing for attack. Under his direction a few well-placed shells from an assault gun eliminated all four German soldiers. For his heroism and initiative, Matthews received the Silver Star.

On the way into Leisenwald, the infantry encountered small-arms fire and reinforced pillboxes. The two assault gun tanks neutralized the pillboxes and the infantry entered the town. The doughboys engaged the SS in a bitter house-to-house battle that lasted well into the night. The enemy forces at Leisenwald capitulated at around 2200 hours.

This village was typical of those encountered to the east of the Rhine. Americans dubbed them "cow towns." The smell of manure was everywhere. Standing on the narrow winding roads inside the villages were sturdily built stone houses whose outer walls were lined with neatly stacked firewood. The assault guns left most of Leisenwald's stone houses in a smoldering heap and the neatly stacked firewood was strewn all over the place. Instead of the familiar manure smell, the stench of decomposing bodies filled the air. Leisenwald's streets were heavily littered with dead German soldiers, a reflection of the bitter fighting of the previous night. The houses left standing were filled with wounded German soldiers being attended to by their medical personnel, who paid scant heed to their captors as they went about their work.

The doughboys captured a German payroll and dutifully forwarded it to regimental headquarters. They also recaptured ten U.S. "Deuce-and-a-half" trucks and had no intentions of surrendering these vehicles which they considered rightful "spoils of war." Thereafter, they moved about quickly.

By April 4, the entire 6th SS Mountain Division, Nord, was either destroyed, captured, or in a state of pandemonium. The Germans ran for their lives. With the threat to XII Corps Headquarters eliminated, the Panthers and doughboys, in hot pursuit of the enemy, moved east toward Fulda. Lieutenant Gary's tank platoon chased after a German general. Unable to catch him, they cleared a wooded area to Fulda by knocking out ten machine gun nests set up for delaying action. The German machine gunners gave their lives to save their general from capture.

19

The Drive Across
the Third Reich

With the Wehrmacht in disarray and soldiers capitulating by the thousands, the enemy could no longer launch a major offensive. Some units offered an extraordinary miscellany of Luftwaffe personnel, police, old men, boys, and even special battalions composed of men with stomach troubles or men with ear ailments. Even well-equipped units from Germany had received virtually no training and came straight from the parade ground to the battlefield. Small units of *Volksgrenadiers* offered sporadic resistance and larger units of the enemy's finer troops made good stands before they tore and ran. Unfortunately, some of the SS made a deadly exception.

Occasionally, fanatic SS troops were encountered who preferred death to surrender. On the drive between Fulda and Meiningen, Sergeant Jonathan B. Hall witnessed an SS officer who was wounded and incapable of putting up a fight pull a razor and slash his own throat from ear to ear rather than surrender to these black tankers. Hall and his crewmen watched in disbelief as the young SS officer slowly bled and choked to death on the ground in front of their tank.

On April 7, 1945, the Panthers reached Meiningen. Nearby, in a salt mine outside of Merkers, combat engineers from the XII Corps were about to discover the famous Nazi gold cache. Directly inside the underground vault stood canvas bags filled with precious metals, Reichsmarks, American dollars, British pounds, French francs, and Norwegian crowns neatly arranged and stacked waist high. Along the rear wall stood suitcases that had burst open and had been hastily taped shut. Inside were family heirlooms taken from Jewish families arriving at Nazi concentration camps. Priceless paintings by Rembrandt, Raphael and Renoir were packed in crates. With the fall of approximately 80 percent of Germany's gold reserve, the beleaguered German soldiers could no longer be paid.

The drive across the Third Reich led through one historic town after another.

The Panthers gave the retreating enemy no rest. Together with the 71st Infantry Division, they smashed through Hildberghausen, Herbertsdorf, Eishausen, and Oberlauter and found themselves in storybook land on the outskirts of Coburg, approximately 50 miles from the Czechoslovakian border.

The fine spring weather added to the region's natural beauty. In the midst of medieval castles and villages, fluffy clouds hung suspended in a beautiful blue sky. Trees and flowers blossomed. This land was long associated with the development of nobles who later became kings of several nations. The English had a long relationship with these monarchists. King George III, their descendent, was the one who gave the American colonies a hard time in the 1770s.

German resistance stiffened along the outskirts of Coburg as mortar fire fell on the Panthers. The Luftwaffe got into the action until U.S. Army Air Forces fighters drove them off. Machine gun nests, mortar positions and *Panzerfausts* fell along the way to Coburg, a route that had been surrounded by the 761st Tank Battalion, 71st Infantry Division, and Combat Command B of the 11th Armored Division. The commander of the 5th Infantry Regiment issued a surrender ultimatum to the civil authorities of Coburg. The *Bürgermeister* (mayor) and a female interpreter approached the 5th Infantry Regiment to surrender. This sensible decision spared the historic town and picturesque castle a great deal of damage.

On April 12, the infantry entered Coburg and began ridding the town of snipers behind the cover of Dog Company's light tanks. The tanks' 37 millimeter cannon blasted out several upper story rooms where snipers had been spotted. A lieutenant from the 5th Infantry Regiment was killed by sniper fire from a small hospital before the town was cleared. A few diehard enemy troops seemed determined to preserve this historic spot for the Third Reich.

In Coburg it was discovered that the German citizens were very fond of uniforms and dearly loved to strut around in them. There were a few embarrassing moments when the doughboys took uniformed German civilians to their regimental command post for interrogation. The railway agents, postal workers, and other civilian workers looked like German military officers. The German society was rank-and-uniform happy.

Coburg's local firemen fought to contain a number of fires that had been started by the bombings. Equipped with *Wehrmacht* helmets, they gave the appearance of German soldiers and nearly came under attack.

After clearing the town of snipers, the Panthers enjoyed fresh eggs, chicken, and wine in the town square. They sat in the shadow of a monument to a Dominican Friar of African descent who had been canonized a century earlier. They enjoyed the spirits from a liberated cognac cellar. When they went sightseeing the camera enthusiasts had a field day taking pictures.

To add to the comfort, the Panthers enjoyed refreshing hot baths and had quilted feather beds to sleep in. One tanker commented: "Yes sir, this is the life."[1]

The "Mosquito Fleet" after clearing out scattered pockets of snipers in Coburg on April 12, 1945. Note white flags hanging from windows (National Archives photograph 208-AA-32P-10).

They were roused shortly after sleep descended. "We have a fire mission!" With the enemy on the run, Maj. General Willard G. Wyman, commander of the 71st Infantry Division, wanted to run the fleeing Germans into the ground before they had the opportunity to regroup. He gave orders to attack Bayreuth, a key city along the Berlin-Munich *Autobahn*. The sleep-deprived tankers piled into their battle wagons and moved out on the double.

Later, on April 12 the Panthers received the sad news that President Roosevelt had died suddenly of a massive cerebral hemorrhage at his cottage in Warm Springs, Georgia. FDR had been posing for a portrait when at 1300 hours on April 11 he said: "I have a terrific headache." At 1315 hours he fainted and at 1535 hours he died without having regained consciousness. Vice President Harry S Truman took the oath of office at 1908 hours and became the 33rd President of the United States.

The death of FDR subdued the Panthers, but the war continued. There was no time for a formal gathering or a memorial service to honor their fallen Commander-in-Chief. They had to remain in hot pursuit of the enemy to prevent them from regrouping and fortifying their positions.

When the news of FDR's passing reached Berlin, Josef Goebbels, Hitler's Minister of Propaganda, became ecstatic. He immediately called Hitler to congratulate him. Some astrological hocus pocus assured him that the president's death foretold the turning point of the war. Meanwhile, the Ninth Army crossed the Elb River about 50 miles west of Berlin while the Soviets closed in from the east.

On April 14, Kulmbach came under attack by the Panthers and the 71st Infantry Division. Baker Company knocked out one armored car, 15 machine gun nests, liquidated over 100 enemy soldiers, and captured 200. Charlie Company accounted for 19 enemy vehicles destroyed, 125 enemy soldiers dead, and the capture of two complete battalions, along with an unattached company. Charlie Company also liberated two American officers and one enlisted man who had been held captive.

The tankers and infantrymen had become skilled at combined operations. The tanks fired on specific targets in the town as the infantry moved in. Company B of the 66th Infantry Regiment entered Kulmbach under this fire, followed by other infantry units. There they found a warehouse crammed with stolen food, drinks, and treasures from countries previously occupied by the Nazis. They found no enemy soldiers in the town, only civilians looting the place.

Kulmbach fell on April 14, which marked the beginning of stiff resistance from that point to the city of Bayreuth, where a major battle ensued. In this stretch Corporal Fred Brown, the gunner in Baker Company's Tank Number 6, was wounded by an 88mm artillery shell that exploded directly overhead as he was attempting to reenter the tank. He later died of his wounds.

In this stretch, Baker Company spearheaded for the 14th Infantry Regiment. 1st Lieutenant Harold B. Gary's tank platoon engaged enemy armor and knocked out one Panzer, forcing the enemy to destroy four of their remaining tanks to avoid capture. When the smoke cleared, 75 enemy soldiers lay dead and 200 capitulated.

As the fighting raged outside Bayreuth, 66th Infantry Regiment troops attacked Bindlach Airport to the north. In a wooded area nearby, they uncovered another large airfield and an aeronautical school defended by Luftwaffe personnel.

The doughboys had to cross a wide open field and did so courageously while under heavy machine gun fire. The Panthers and the infantry's heavy weapons placed a concentrated barrage on the enemy machine gun nests as the doughboys made their way underneath this fire. They would run, hit the dirt, and get up and run again. Many of the doughboys never got up to run again. Every yard felt like a mile. When the remaining foot soldiers made it to the buildings, the tank and heavy weapons fire ceased as the infantry went through the area taking prisoners and shooting the rest. When they thought enemy soldiers could be inside a building, they set fire to it and waited for the Germans to come out.

Charlie Company silenced nine machine gun nests in this support of the infantry. 1st Sergeant William R. Burroughs who dismounted from his tank to personally locate a machine gun nest that had the doughboys pinned down, was shot over the left eye. He had to be evacuated and later lost that eye. A record keeper from the 66th Infantry Regiment noted that 520 prisoners had been taken; no effort was made to determine the exorbitant number of enemy dead.

Bayreuth was now surrounded by the 11th Armored Division, the 65th Infantry Division, the 71st Infantry Division, and the 761st Tank Battalion. Together they hurled steel into the city with devastating effect. Unfortunately, the enemy spurned a surrender ultimatum and the barrage continued. After two days of shelling, Bayreuth could no longer withstand the bombardment. On April 16, the commander of the city's enemy defenders surrendered to the commander of the 14th Infantry Regiment.

Also on April 16, Task Force Weidenmark, with the objective of extending the Third Army's Eastern Front to Czechoslovakia, jumped off with two assault gun teams and five Dog Company light tanks supported by tank destroyers and infantry. Their drive into enemy territory went without major incident as white flags appeared from windows along the way. On rare occasions, they ran into sporadic machine gun fire.

The task force came across recently freed Russian prisoners of war. It was a pathetic sight: hundreds of frail, emaciated men with bones showing through their skin supporting each other from falling. They looked at their *Amerikanetski* allies, but could not greet them due to their near-death condition.

The task force posted security guards along the way to hold their captured territory. They advanced to within sight of the Czechoslovakian border before heading back to the command post near Bayreuth. Upon completion of Task Force Weidenmark, the 761st Tank Battalion became the sole spearhead for the 71st Infantry Division's drive south to Austria.

The Panthers rolled down the *Autobahn,* firing on enemy soldiers hidden in the woods. They destroyed enemy aircraft placed along the highway and shot out search and landing lights.

In an attempt to prevent the enemy from escaping or fortifying their positions, elements of the 66th Infantry Regiment launched an attack without tank support. As they crossed an open field they were pinned down by heavy machine gun and *panzerfaust* fire. It became necessary to call for tank support and in a coordinated assault with Charlie Company tanks, they breached the enemy's outer defenses. The infantry took heavy casualties in this fierce firefight but the wood-frame buildings were soon burning from direct hits by 76 millimeter white phosphorous shells. The German soldiers who escaped the fires became easy targets for the sharp-shooting doughboys who waited outside.

On April 18, in the vicinity of Neuhaus, Platoon Sergeant Johnnie Stevens aided the doughboys in overcoming a machine gun nest. Stevens describes what happened:

> I was ordered up to support a part of the 71st Division. This lieutenant came back and said: "We're tied down on the hill." I said where are they? He spotted them for me on the hill. We pulled up, I brought my tank into hull defilade [protective position]. I told Joe Kiah, who was my gunner, Kiah, I'm going out there to see what the hell is going on because there was shooting all over the place. Kiah said, "Sarge, you crazy son of a bitch! Don't go out there!" I said, Kiah, cover me damn it! I crawled forward maybe about 50 yards. I can see that the infantry is tied down in this field and can't get out of there. I happened to notice a machine gun nest to the left. They had not seen me and I knew they didn't see me, but the lieutenant saw me. He knew I was moving in. There in between my tank and the machine gun nest, Joe Kiah is covering for me, I can't get back to the tank, I've got no choice. If I try to get back to my tank, they are going to wipe me out. I was about 15 yards from the machine gun nest and they hadn't seen me because I was crawling. So what I did, I grabbed some grenades and started throwing them and sprayed the machine gun nest. Nine guys died there. When the infantry saw what I was doing, all of these white boys started firing and advancing. The lieutenant, I don't know who he was, he was leading them on and in about three minutes we took the objective. Nine men dead, 36 captured, and that was it. They wrote it up that I had a platoon. I had no platoon! I had one tank. I can tell you the crew members there: James Peoples, my driver; Joe Kiah, my gunner: and Emerson Hadnot, my bow gunner. We did it alone. One tank.[2]

For this action, Platoon Sergeant Stevens received the Bronze Star from the 71st Infantry Division dated June 5, 1945.

On April 19, two Charlie Company tank platoons supported elements of the 66th Infantry Regiment in their assault on Neuhaus and Velden, site of Hermann Göring's Veldenstein Castle. Here the Luftwaffe chief stored his priceless possessions (many of them stolen) in the 500-year-old castle that stood high on a bluff overlooking Neuhaus, complete with reinforced walls and tunnels. Göring saw that his property was closely guarded by the SS.

Reconnaissance reports suggested that the SS might make a last ditch stand in the Veldensteiner Forest. The 66th Infantry Regiment took Neuhaus and used the remainder of the day to make preparations for an assault on Velden.

2nd Lieutenant Frank Cochrane and 2nd Lieutenant Moses Dade took their tank platoons and spearheaded for elements of the 66th Infantry Regiment as they engaged the defenders of Göring's castle. The Panthers fired at the castle, but their shells bounced off harmlessly. The doughboys advanced up the steep hill while the

SS retreated to the nearby forest. The infantry infiltrated the castle and chased the enemy through the woods. The Panthers then swung out toward Velden and engaged enemy armor in a fierce firefight. When the smoke cleared, a Mark IV Panzer, an antitank gun, and six machine gun nests were destroyed.

After the fighting, the Panthers inspected Göring's castle. Private Christopher Navarre recalls: "The things that really impressed on my mind was the bedroom, where he had the onyx tables and the peacock at the entrance with, I think, onyx eyes. He had secret passageways behind his bed. I was also very impressed with his bathroom, which was like a big Jacuzzi, and he had all of these pornographic pictures on the walls. It was all marbled. I recall the elevator he had in the dinning room. The Germans took as much as they could before they ran off but they did not destroy anything. They didn't do like they did in France, where they had enough time to really strip the place and destroy it before leaving."[3]

Nearby, Captain Ivan Harrison remembers April 19: "When the dive bombers attacked, my mess truck, supply trucks, and all that were standing out in the street. I was over in a house and I ran out to the street to see if any of my vehicles had been hit. They hadn't been. The dive bombers missed all of them but they shot up the street. Then I just kept getting this call on the radio and it is Captain Latimer. It was my birthday and I hadn't noticed it. He shows up with a sergeant and they had a case of champagne. He said, 'Happy Birthday!'"[4]

In the evening of April 19, Major Reynolds, Captain Long, Sergeant Fields, and Technician Stanford were reported missing and presumed captured while on a reconnaissance mission in the Lindenhardt area. The battalion's entire rear echelon volunteered to go out to liberate their comrades. Only Master Sergeant Joseph Thomas remained behind; he became the acting battalion commander.

Captain John D. Long recalls his capture:

> I was captured while on reconnaissance with my jeep driver, Technical Sergeant Fred Fields. This sergeant was a big, awkward kid from Denison, Texas. He gave away my liquor, cigarettes, wore my underwear; he was real generous with my things, but he was loyal. When I sent him on an errand, only death would have kept him from following orders; I could trust him completely. Sometimes when I was going out in the jeep to look things over I'd tell him he didn't have to come along, but he always slid into the driver's seat and said, "I'm with you, sir."
>
> There was only one time that my sergeant ever hesitated about an order, but you couldn't really blame him. The unit was settling down for the night. There were wounded men with us and the medics were busy tending them. A shot rang out and one medic keeled over. Some sonofabitch had shot him right through that cross on his helmet. A second medic was killed before our guns located the sniper. When they brought the sniper in, he was bleeding to death

Christopher P. Navarre at chow time (courtesy Julia Cardell and E. G. McConnell).

from a bullet wound in his upper thigh. This was quite obvious from his color. I looked around for the other medics and they were very busy elsewhere, carefully avoiding looking in my direction. In one second, I knew I wasn't about to ask those men to tend this bastard who had chosen the conspicuous cross on the medic's helmets as a target. I told my sergeant to shoot the sniper. The kid turned ashen, then fumbled for his gun. It was an unfair order so I pulled my revolver and did it myself. Don't think it ended there. He was the first man I had killed whom I could see close up, his face, his features. For years I dreamed of him. But back to my capture. Sergeant Fields and I were cut off from the main body and taken prisoners near a town whose name I can't remember. I should, because as they led us through the town, women there got their kicks spitting on what they called the *Schwarze* captain of the elite *Schwarze* Panzer Division. I do know we ended up in a citadel called Walhalla [Memorial Hall built by King Ludwig], which I believe is near the city of Regensburg.

I expected to be killed, for our tank battalion mopped up Jerry when and wherever we encountered him and these things don't remain a secret. We took thousands of prisoners, but those who wanted a fight to the finish got just that. The fight-it-out boys were usually SS troops.

I refused to talk to non-commissioned personnel, so finally they told Fields to stand up. They were going to take him outside and shoot him. I died inside, but all I said to him was, remember you are a soldier. I'll never forget his reply: "I'm with you sir."

It turned out they were bluffing, and soon a general appeared. He asked me: "What are you doing in Germany, you rich Americans?" I answered, Sir, we found you in France! He slapped his thigh and started laughing.

To my surprise, they abandoned the citadel the next morning and left Fields and me there, unharmed. My men found us soon afterwards."[5]

On April 22, Baker Company and elements of the 14th Infantry Regiment cleared the city of Amberg. On the following day they found Captain Long, Sergeant Fields, and Technician Stanford. They did not find Major Reynolds. Several days later, the 14th Cavalry Group liberated Reynolds and he returned to duty.

Captain Long and the other black prisoners of war were fortunate not to have been captured by the SS. Black soldiers, like Jewish soldiers, had much more to fear than their comrades. There are some gruesome reports of black units that had the misfortune to capitulate to the SS.

Around April 23, in the vicinity of Auerbach, Able Company, in support of the 5th Infantry Regiment, flushed enemy soldiers from a patch of woods. As the doughboys pursued the enemy through the trees, a few tanks took up positions to prevent the enemy from crossing an open area to another patch of woods. Lieutenant Lewington "Lew" Ponder, a liaison officer from the 71st Infantry Division who stood nearby as an observer, made the following comments: "These tanks each had three weapons, a .30 caliber machine gun mounted to fire along the same axis as the main armament, a 76 millimeter cannon. There was also a .50 caliber machine gun mounted on the turret. There was a black sergeant in the turret of one of the tanks, stroking the butterfly triggers of the .50 caliber and chanting: 'Fo or mo and I uses de big gun! Fo or mo and I uses de big gun!' Naturally, I though he was referring to the .50 caliber as 'the big gun.' I was standing beside his tank when about ten Jerries broke from the woods and headed across the open space toward the other clump of trees. Bwamm!!! By 'big gun' he meant the 76 millimeter! [Because I was] standing almost opposite its muzzle he came close to blowing my head off, too! The muzzle blast shook me so that it took a second or two for my vision to clear. He had taken out three or four of the Germans, but the others were just disappearing into the woods when my eyes began to focus again. My head rang for several hours and that incident may have contributed to my eventual hearing loss. I think he could have done better with the machine guns. I know I would have been better off."[6]

Baker Company tanks engaged the enemy at Auerbach, where they captured 75 German soldiers. Charlie Company made contact with the enemy at Perkam, where they silenced three machine guns nests, took 140 prisoners, and liberated two soldiers from the American 80th Infantry Division.

The swift drive continued southeast toward Austria to meet the Soviet forces advancing from the northeast. Schwandorf, Burglengenfeld, Regenstauf, Kurn, Pirkensee, and Zeitlern fell as the Panthers closed in on the Danube River and Regensburg.

This is where the Panthers found themselves only 120 miles from the Soviets with the gap rapidly closing. As they approached the Danube River they passed through 30 miles of scenic paradise in the Sulzbach Valley. They recalled a song about the "Blue Danube" but when they got there they discovered that the river was actually a murky green. Across the Danube stood Regensburg. It was here that Browning's "Boy" of the famous poem dropped dead after his long run afoot to bring news to Napoleon. Now the Panthers were going out to get a forward command post for Patton, and Regensburg was the town where he wanted it located.

After the enemy rejected a surrender ultimatum, the assault on Regensburg began in earnest. The 761st Tank Battalion opened up with everything it had: the 105 millimeter assault guns; the 81 millimeter mortars; the 76, 75, and 37 millimeter cannons; and .50 and .30 caliber machine guns. Division artillery opened up with their 155 millimeter "Long Tom" howitzers and Baker Battery's 8-inch "Barking Bitch" cannons. As the big guns saturated the enemy's fortifications, the doughboys crossed the Danube on assault boats and stormed the city, where they

A blown bridge over the Danube River. Photograph taken by First Sergeant Takeo Susuki, Service Co. 522nd, F.A. Battalion, April 1945 (courtesy Takeo and Mark Susuki).

engaged the enemy in bitter house-to-house street fighting. Regensburg fell on April 26, and it was now a matter of mopping up scattered pockets of resistance.

Gefreiter (first rank above airman) Willi H. Jaehne recalls the events leading to his capture near Straubing after the tanks of the 761st chased his unit through Bavaria:

> I was drafted when I was 17 in April 1944. I was sent to a place near Frankfurt-an-der-Oder for Luftwaffe boot camp. After boot camp we were sent to Bloise, France. There I took a refresher course in flight engineering that they rushed us through. This is when the Allies landed at the beach on June 6, one day after my birthday.
>
> We were then sent down to Montelimar at the Rhone River. I was assigned to a Junker 88 aircraft as the flight engineer. We

completed a few missions before our plane was bombed and destroyed. We received no replacement for it was late in the war. We all knew it couldn't last very much longer.

We were then sent to Strasbourg and on the way our truck got ambushed by the French Resistance fighters. Our truck fell over and I received a concussion and fragments in my body. I was taken to a field hospital in Colmar.

Upon release, my unit was dissolved and they sent me to Fuerth, which is near Nuremberg. This is where the replenishment battalions were. In the meantime the Allies crossed the Rhine as we were sent away by truck. We didn't know where we were going but as it turned out we were always a step ahead of the advancing American troops, especially the tank battalions. We made frequent stops. We went from Nuremberg over to Lauf and then down to Sulzbach-Rosenberg, Amberg, Schwandorf, Cham, Ascha, and we landed in Parkstetten. That was on the north bank of the Danube across from Straubing, on the south bank.

Our mission was to guard the bridge. Our duty was not to guard as such against unfriendly action, we were there in order to prevent unauthorized German military personnel from passing over the Danube to enter the last piece of Germany that was still unoccupied. So we had to search papers. We all knew that it would only be a week or two before the war was over, so we never found anyone who was not entitled to cross. We made up our minds, we lived through the war up to now and we didn't want to die at the last moment.

I stayed a few weeks in Parkstetten at a farmer's house. Two days before I was taken prisoner, late one evening there was a commotion. I went out to the main street and saw a large column of slave laborers being forced marched through the town by the SS. It was horrible to see those people and you couldn't do a thing, you could just look at their faces. One of them tried to flee and they shot him there. It was horrible!

For the next two days we stayed at the bridge. Then we heard tanks coming toward the bridge and we ran away from there and waited by the side. When the tanks and jeeps came, we were already waving, and they took us prisoner. There were two or three jeeps and we were a small group of about six guys, so they put us on the hoods and drove us over the fields. They took us to a point where they had prisoners deposited. From there they took us up the road in a big double trailer holding about 120 guys. Then they took the street where the SS had taken the slave laborers and we saw people lying on the side of the road who were shot and who died from exhaustion. The Americans were not very friendly here. They thought we were the culprits, but we had nothing to do with it, it was the SS![7]

182

The 761st Tank Battalion crossed the Danube River. On April 28 Able Company captured Straubing with the 5th Infantry Regiment and liberated the surviving slave laborers at a nearby camp. Baker Company took up positions in Sarching with the 14th Infantry Regiment; Charlie Company took up positions in Perkan with the 66th Infantry Regiment.

During the thrust through Bavaria, Lt. Colonel Paul L. Bates received a disturbing call from a regimental commander at the 71st Infantry Division Headquarters. This worked-up colonel complained that some of his infantrymen, caught in a mine field, had been abandoned by a 761st tank crew. Bates immediately went to the alleged scene of desertion. There he found upwards to twenty dead doughboys and a disabled tank. Bates replied: "You tell the guys that if you hit a mine, get the hell out of the tank as fast as you can. Because [an artillery shell] is going to hit you because they want to burn that tank up or explode it so it can't be repaired and used again. We beat it into their heads that when you get out of the tank, you'll see your tread marks and you can walk away by walking in those treads, because if any mines were there, they would already have detonated. I went back to division headquarters and told them that whoever complained is a goddamned fool. He's simply got badly trained soldiers. You're going against a fortified position, so you know damn well there's going to be a mine field. If you've got any sense, you tell your infantry to go behind the tanks; it's a shield. Walk down the tread marks. Don't blame my tankers, they did what they were supposed to do, but you didn't tell your people what they were supposed to do. So the guy says, 'Well, you know, it's all right. It's all right.' Those are the kind of thanks they gave you."[8]

On April 28, 1945, Italian dictator Benito Mussolini took his final breath in front of a firing squad imposed upon him by Italian partisans. His 25-year-old mistress, Claretta Petacci, and 16 other Fascists perished by his side. Their bodies were taken to Milan and dumped into Milan Square. There, a howling mob kicked and spat on *Il Duce's* remains in the city where Italian Fascism was born.

On April 30, 1945, Adolf Hitler committed suicide with his new bride Eva Braun in his underground command bunker as Berlin burned above. The *Führer*, age 56, died 12 years and three months after he established the Third Reich that was to have endured a thousand years. The day before his death, Hitler appointed Grand Admiral Karl Dönitz, Germany's naval Commander-in-Chief, as his successor.

During the following day, German radio played gloomy music interrupted by *"Achtung!"* warnings that an important announcement would follow. A three-minute silence preceded the announcement and the phantom voice of a German resister broke in on the air waves: "This is a day of rejoicing for the German people!" The announcement finally came: "It is announced that our Führer, Adolf Hitler, this afternoon at his command post in the Reich's Chancellery, fighting till his last breath against Bolshevism, fell for Germany." Hitler's successor personally

German crossing guards before they blew the bridge and ran.

read a proclamation while the phantom voice interrupted each reference he made to the *Führer's* heroic death: "Nonsense! He was one of the world's greatest criminals." Grand Admiral Dönitz demanded discipline and obedience to him as Hitler's successor. He went on to say: "My first task is to save the German people from annihilation by the advancing Bolshevist enemy. The military struggle will continue only with this aim. Inasmuch and as long as the attainment of this aim is being hindered by the British and the Americans, we shall have to fight against them." With this news, waves of suicides, desertions, and executions swept the German ranks.

Hitler died three days after his Axis partner in crime, Benito Mussolini. He had modeled his Third Reich on Mussolini's Fascist hierarchy. Together, the two dictators forced the Western world into the grimmest war it has ever known.

At the end of April 1945, the 761st Tank Battalion had an effective strength of 38 officers, three warrant officers, and 642 enlisted men. Corporal Fred L. Brown died of his wounds on April 14. One officer and seven enlisted men were wounded in action. The battalion suffered 33 non-battle casualties and lost one assault gun tank, two medium tanks, and two light tanks. The drive continued.

20

Face to Face with the Holocaust

The 761st Tank Battalion, along with the 71st Infantry Division, began uncovering a fraction of the numerous hellholes the Nazis operated in their forced labor and concentration camp system first started at Dachau. Twelve years earlier, the following announcement appeared in the *Münchner Neuesten Nachrichten:* "On Wednesday, March 22, 1933, the first concentration camp will be opened in the vicinity of Dachau. It can accommodate 5,000 people. We have adopted this measure, undeterred by paltry scruples, in the conviction that our action will help to restore calm to our country and is in the best interests of our people." Signed by Heinrich Himmler, Commissioner of Police for the City of Munich.[1]

As Germany's borders expanded, the *Konzentrationslagers* (concentration camps) grew. The people sent to these camps included Poles, Gypsies, Jehovah's Witnesses, Communists, Social Democrats, Soviet prisoners, trade unionists, homosexuals, the mentally challenged, criminals, and anyone deemed undesirable by the Reich. However, the Nazis reserved their most fanatic hatred for the Jews, whom they regarded as "race defilers."

The main camp of Dachau stood in the Seventh Army's zone of operation, approximately 50 miles west of the 761st Tank Battalion's position when the camp was officially liberated by the 42nd "Rainbow" Infantry Division. Brig. General Hening Linden, with an interpreter and a representative of the Red Cross, accepted the white flag of surrender from an SS lieutenant. Together with other units, the "Rainbow" Division liberated over 30,000 inmates on April 29, 1945.

Dachau did not actually form a part of the town Dachau; it stood in the town of Prittlbach. The first camps that the Panthers helped to uncover came under the general jurisdiction of Dachau and those uncovered in Austria came under Mauthausen.

What is still generally misunderstood is the fact that each major concentration camp had upwards to 40 branch camps or subordinate facilities. The International Red Cross estimated that there were as many as 2,000 locations where the Nazis held people against their will. On April 26, 1945, three days prior to the liberation of Dachau's main camp, the final roll call balance sheet reported 30,442 inmates in the main camp and 37,223 inmates in the branch camps. The branch camps of Dachau were collectively called Dachau.

Samuel Pisar, who had been imprisoned first in Poland at Auschwitz and then in Germany at Buchenwald, was transported to a Dachau branch camp late in 1944: "We arrived in winter and there were a few barracks but no other facilities. So we had to dig the ground and pour the cement and cut the logs. And it was freezing cold and we were very hungry. The German SS men were our guards.... There was tremendous violence going on here, every day and night. They had vicious German shepherd dogs, and it was no fun. Many of my friends died right there. And of course, I still don't know how I made it. I was barely 15 years old."[2]

Pisar pointed out: "This was a hard-labor camp, people died here through hard work, hunger, punishment, freezing cold.... [The guards] were the greatest monsters that ever lived. Sadistic, violent. Kill a human being at the drop of a hat. [They] didn't have gas chambers; here the executions were by firing squad and through hanging."[3]

It is estimated that between 6 and 10 million people, mostly Jews, perished throughout Europe in Nazi concentration and extermination camps. The aged, the very young, and the infirm were killed shortly after arrival. The strong were usually detailed out as laborers in factories, mines, and work camps until they too became useless due to hunger, disease, and overwork. The Nazis estimated that the average life expectancy of an internee would be nine months.

Jan Domagala, a Polish inmate at Dachau recalls, "'If the miracle should happen that you live to tell the tale, write it down and tell the world what they did to us.' That was the most sacred will of the comrades who died in our arms or were removed by the 'invalids-transport' to be gassed. That was the will of brothers and true friends, of the numbered-men (*Nummermenschen*, the men who seemed to have no names, but only numbers), whose ashes escaped through the chimneys and covered the fields of a foreign country."[4]

During the final days of the war, a gut-wrenching sense of uncertainty and fear descended over the camps as the sound of artillery fire came closer. American planes flew in low and destroyed military targets. News spread through the camps that SS Chief Heinrich Himmler had ordered the liquidation of the inmates in keeping with Hitler's goal of a *Judenfrei* (Jew free) planet. This news drove many of the inmates mad. Fortunately, this plan was not carried out. Commandant Weiss, the Inspector General of Dachau's main and branch camps, did not permit the execution of Himmler's orders to shell and burn the camps together with all inmates. Weiss was later captured, tried, and executed by the Allies.

As the Allies advanced closer to the concentration camps in Bavaria, the SS employed the death-march strategy. Prisoners were forced-marched from the branch camps to the main facility of Dachau and then to the south. They lacked food and water, and struggled along in wooden clogs and flimsy striped prison garb. Their SS guards took a vicious pleasure in taking pot shots at them. The marchers learned to pay scant heed to the shootings, knowing that if they turned around, they too would be shot.

Samuel Pisar will never forget his march:

> I don't know the exact date, because not only did I have no watch and no sense of time, but I was hallucinating with hunger. We knew we were close to the end of the war because we could hear cannon shots in the distance.... And we saw American and British planes flying in for bombing missions. And while to our captors this was something that inspired fear, to us it was a message of hope. [The move] back to Dachau was a place where they would be extremely likely to do away with us. They lined us up and marched us away. The main roads were clogged by [German] military convoys, so they had to take us the long way through side roads, forests, fields.
>
> While many were falling like flies from exhaustion, from hunger, we kept at it. And one bright morning, three American planes came down very low, thinking we were a military column, and started strafing us. The guards hit the dirt, and Nico, who was the oldest of the three of us, suddenly said to Ben and me. "Get up and run after me." And we started to run. As we discovered later, 14 of us made a break for the forest as the American planes were machine-gunning the entire column. And as we ran, nine were shot. Of the five who made it into the forest, Nico, Ben, and yours truly were among them. And we ran and ran and ran until we couldn't run any longer. And deep in the forest, we stopped. It was early spring, and we simply fell asleep, and we must have slept for hours and hours, because we woke up in the middle of the night.
>
> We were tired, and there was danger all over the place. Suddenly we came upon a barn. So we broke in and discovered it was paradise, full of straw and it had a loft upstairs, so we climbed up and went to sleep. And we slept and slept and slept. We decided not to take any risks. We decided this was where we could try and sit it out. Occasionally I would go out and steal some food from the farms. I was a young kid and I had already stolen for myself some Bavarian leather pants. I looked like a peasant boy, except that my head was completely shaved. But I would come back regularly with loaves of bread, eggs, which we ate raw, tomatoes and cucumbers. For once, we were not hungry, and there was water outside in a trough. Most of all we stayed still. Even though it was peaceful and quiet, it was also dangerous. From time to time, armed German soldiers would come

ORIGIN**TORS** FILE No.

SHAEF MESSAGE FORM

	CALL	CIRCUIT No.	PRIORITY	TRANSMISSION INSTRUCTIONS
		NR 21		

SPACES WITHIN HEAVY LINES FOR SIGNALS USE ONLY

FROM (A) SHAEF FWD	ORIGINATOR Supreme Commander DDE/nmr	DATE-TIME OF ORIGIN 19 April 1945

TO FOR ACTION   AGWAR

TO (W) FOR INFORMATION (INFO)   ~~SECRET~~   EYES ONLY   MESSAGE INSTRUCTIONS   G R

(REF NO.) FWD19461,   (CLASSIFICATION) ~~SECRET~~ EYES ONLY

WE CONTINUE TO UNCOVER GERMAN CONCENTRATION CAMPS FOR POLITICAL PRISONERS IN WHICH
CONDITIONS OF INDESCRIBABLE HORROR PREVAIL. FROM EISENHOWER TO GENERAL MARSHALL
FOR EYES ONLY. I HAVE VISITED ONE OF THESE MYSELF AND I ASSURE YOU THAT WHATEVER
HAS BEEN PRINTED ON THEM TO DATE HAS BEEN UNDERSTATEMENT. IF YOU WOULD SEE ANY
ADVANTAGE IN ASKING ABOUT A DOZEN LEADERS OF CONGRESS AND A DOZEN PROMINENT EDITORS
TO MAKE A SHORT VISIT TO THIS THEATER IN A COUPLE OF C-54s, I WILL ARRANGE TO HAVE
THEM CONDUCTED TO ONE OF THESE PLACES WHERE THE EVIDENCE OF BESTIALITY AND CRUELTY
IS SO OVERPOWERING AS TO LEAVE NO DOUBT IN THEIR MINDS ABOUT THE NORMAL PRACTICES
OF THE GERMANS IN THESE CAMPS. I AM HOPEFUL THAT SOME BRITISH INDIVIDUALS IN
SIMILAR CATEGORIES WILL VISIT THE NORTHERN AREA TO WITNESS SIMILAR EVIDENCE OF
ATROCITY.

~~SECRET~~   EYES ONLY

DISTRIBUTION : c/s	COORDINATED WITH :			
	THIS MESSAGE MUST BE SENT IN CYPHER IF LIABLE TO INTERCEPTION	Precedence URGENT	THI or TOR	Opr.
		ORIGINATING DIVISION SHSC	APR 19 1945 12 27	
	INITIALS	NAME AND RANK TYPED. TEL. NO.	TIME CLEARED	
	THIS MESSAGE MAY BE SENT IN CLEAR BY ANY MEANS	Lt.Col.E.R.Lee,ADC 4170		
		AUTHENTICATING SIGNATURE		
	INITIALS	ERLee		

DOD DIR. 5200.10, June 29, 1960
DECLASSIFIED
NE by WGL date 7-5-6?

U.S. Army official communication regarding German concentration camps (Presidential Library,
National Archives and Records Administration).

Lambach, Austria, May 6, 1945: German P.O.W.s remove corpses from the Lambach concentration camp, one of the camps liberated by the 761st (courtesy National Archives).

> downstairs — take a sleep, have a smoke — while we would sit paralyzed, trying to stay still. They could hear nothing. Then they would leave. No one knew we were there.[5]

A few days later, Samuel Pisar was awakened by the rumble of approaching tanks and sporadic firing of weapons. Pisar was about to meet Sergeant Bill Ellington of the 761st Tank Battalion:

> I ran down the ladder and looked out through the slats and I saw a tank. I tried to find the hated swastika, and I couldn't find it. Instead,

all I could see was a white star. What is a white star? Why a white
star? And suddenly it blew my mind; I realized that after four years
of slavery, torture, hunger, I was actually looking at the insignia of
the U.S. Army. I started to yell, "Nico, Ben! Come here and take a
look!" And like a madman, I ran out toward the tank. It was a stupid
thing to do, because I was in the middle of a battlefield. Machine
guns were barking, bullets were flying on all sides. But by then I
thought nothing could destroy me; I had taken so many risks and
been so close to death, and freedom was coming at me and I couldn't
just stand there. I couldn't stop; I was just running and running,
closer to the tank. Suddenly its cannon let out a belch. And all the
firing ceased. And as I approached, the hatch opened and a tall, hel-
meted black man climbed out. I had never seen a black man before. I
thought, maybe he has soot on his face. I didn't know how to signal
him ... how to explain that I was a prisoner, that I needed help. He
must have seen that I was weak, maybe sick-looking, with a shaven
head. But it was a dangerous situation, so the only thing I could
think of was to kneel, to put my arms around his legs and begin to
yell, in the few words of English my mother had sighed when she
prayed for our deliverance. "God Bless America!" And that he understood. He picked me up in his arms, he led me to the tank and took
me with him through the hatch and into the womb of freedom.[6]

On April 28, Able Company and elements of the 5th Infantry Regiment uncovered a branch camp near Straubing. Private First Class Bill Kern from the 5th
Infantry Regiment recalls: "Just after Regensburg we liberated a small concentration camp. We found all the SS guards had fled and the prisoners were alone. The
gate was closed with a large chain and lock holding it closed. We were unable to
break the chain, but got a Sherman tank to ram it after motioning the prisoners
to stay back. The tank knocked down the gate and half of the fence. The prisoners came running to us pleading for food. They appeared to be in a half starved
condition, but we were told not to feed them because of their condition as our food
might kill them. It was pathetic and we explained that they should 'hold on' because
the medics were bringing special food for them. I hoped the medics got food to
them in time, but we had to go on."[7]

Captain John D. Long, commanding officer of Baker Company, recalls uncovering his first concentration camp:

> War is a strange thing. You are trained to do a job, even to the killing
> of men, but you do your job. It is an impersonal thing, at least it had
> better be or you are in for a lot of trouble. This was the way I looked
> at the Germans until the day we liberated our first concentration
> camp. Have you ever seen a stack of bones with the skin stretched
> over it? At the camp, you could not tell the young from the old.

When we busted the gate, the inmates just staggered out with no purpose or direction until they saw a dead horse recently struck by a shell. Have you ever seen ants on a few grains of sugar? They tottered over to the dead carcass and threw themselves upon it, eating raw flesh. We cut ourselves back to one third rations and left all of the food we could at the camp. There was just one thing wrong, we later learned our food killed many of them. Why didn't someone tell us not to give them food? But then, what do you say to a person hardly able to stand or talk, but is begging you for food. From this incident on, Jerry was no longer an impersonal foe. The Germans were monsters! I have never found any way to find an excuse for them or any man who would do to people what I saw when we opened the gate to that camp and two others. We had just mopped them up before, but we stomped the shit out of them after the camps.[8]

During this period, 17-year-old Wolf Finkelman was relocated from the Mauthausen camp in Austria in a forced march he never forgot: "We were made to march about 30 miles with continuous beatings, starvation, and walking through various towns. The population just looked at us as if we were animals. Heavy rain was coming down, we were all drenched and cold.

We ended up in Gunskirchen. This camp was not yet finished. It was in a forest surrounded by trees with no sleeping facilities. I remember sleeping on top of some rafters, and even on top of dead bodies. There was no food, no rations for us to eat. Daily I could see literally hundreds of people dying from starvation and other causes. I decided to sleep on the outside with a few guys who cuddled up to each other. We had no blankets, the ground was very moist and it was freezing cold. I developed sores over my body."[9]

In one of the war's ironies, elements of the 442nd "Go For Broke" Regimental Combat Team, most of whom had Japanese-American family members at home in concentration/relocation camps, ran across Dachau and several branch camps. Members of its 522nd Field Artillery Battalion took part in this liberation while its 100th Infantry Battalion and supporting units traveled back to Italy.

Due to the fact that these Americans were of Japanese ancestry, their loyalty to the United States was questioned by some Americans who were influenced by hatred, prejudice, and post–Pearl Harbor hysteria. In response, the 442nd Regimental Combat Team earned the distinction as the most decorated unit of its size in United States military history. Their achievement did not come without an exorbitant cost. The combat team suffered 9,486 casualties with over 600 killed in action. Proof of their loyalty to America was given in life and limb.

Janina Cywinska, a former Dachau inmate, recalls her liberation: "I was standing with a blindfold waiting to be shot, but the shot didn't come. So I asked the woman next to me, Do you think they're trying to make us crazy so we'll run and

German P.O.W.s prepare to remove a gravely ill Jewish girl found in the barracks of the Lambach concentration camp, May 6, 1945 (National Archives photograph 208-AA-206A-2).

they won't have to feel guilty about shooting us? She said, 'Well, we're not going to run. We'll just stand here.' So we stood and stood and suddenly someone was tugging at my blindfold. He tugged this way and that way, and then he jumped up because he was short and he pulled it off. I saw him and I thought, oh, now the Japanese are going to kill us. And I didn't care anymore. I said, just kill us, get it over with. He tried to convince me that he was an American and wouldn't kill me. I said, oh, no, you're a Japanese and you're going to kill us. We went back and forth, and finally he landed on his knees, crying, with his hands over his face, and he said: 'You are free now. We are American Japanese. You are free.'"[10]

In another one of the war's ironies, Jewish-American soldiers helped to liberate black inmates from Nazi concentration camps. Germany had African colonies until World War I, and after Germany lost the war, French Algerian troops were among the occupation forces. Through interracial marriages came black German citizens. It was not only the Jews who suffered under the Nazi racial laws of 1933. "Rhineland Mulattoes" were among the first to be singled out under the sterilization program. The sterilization was not carried out by the reluctant German doctors, however, in 1937 the Gestapo took over and several hundred German children of color vanished.

Helene Brill, one of these German children of color, recalls: "I got a notice in the mail when I was 11, right after the war started. I was called in to get a physical at the headquarters of the Gestapo. I remember my foster mother was terrified that they might keep me. I think my mother was even more afraid because of the location of the physical, which was in Hitler territory. I really have to thank the doctor who did the exam. I can still see it. He patted my mother on her back and said, 'Don't worry, it's going to be OK.' I don't know if he intentionally lost my paperwork, but we never heard about it again.... I was extremely lucky that I did not get caught up in the extermination efforts."[11]

Farther south, the Panthers approached Lambach, Austria, and uncovered more evidence of Nazi atrocities. In Wels, they discovered a warehouse containing hundreds of badly decomposing bodies. The stench was sickening and in one location human heads were stacked in a macabre formation. Local Nazi officials were detailed to lay out the bodies so the burial process could begin.

Private Christopher Navarre from Charlie Company recalls: "We came into the town against no resistance. We didn't see any people of that town and we came up to the camp and the gate was open. I don't know how it got open and the survivors were pouring out as we got there. We didn't stay there very long and before we knew it, we had oncoming replacements and some infantry come up. We had a couple tanks to go around to the back. I was at the front gate with two other tanks. I got out of the tank and sat on the turret with the others. Isiah Parks, our tank commander, told us not to get down. The survivors just mulled around begging for food. We threw a few things at them, chocolates, K-rations, crackers and stuff. When we spit on the ground, they jumped at that too. I recall that! It was terrible!"[12]

Civilians from Kremsmunster reported that concentration camp guards, SS troops, and Gestapo agents had been receiving new identification papers and changing into civilian clothes for the past two or three days. The new civilians planned to hide in the woods and countryside until the advancing Allied troops passed by.

In a wooded area nearby, another hellhole was about to be uncovered. Gunskirchen Lager, one of the carefully concealed Nazi concentration camps was located just six kilometers north of Lambach, Austria. The camp was situated in the middle of a dense patch of pine forest and was well-concealed from the road as well as from the air. It was a dark *Verboten* area well suited for the atrocities committed by the SS guards and the hellish living conditions endured by the victims.

The 15,000 men, women, and children of this camp lived on a slice of bread and a bowl of thin soup per day. When the Allies approached the area, the Nazis were so busy fleeing that the inmates were not fed for four days. This was an instant death sentence for many after being in a state of near-starvation. Over 200 inmates died of starvation in two days; many would just lie on the ground and resign themselves to death.

The sudden release from these terrible camps brought on inmate hysteria, and

Photo taken near a concentration camp in Austria, May 1945. *Standing:* two unidentified dough-boys from the 5th Infantry Regiment, 71st Division, and Able company's Staff Sergeant John-nie Stevens, Jr. *Kneeling:* unidentified tanker and Corporal Floyd Dade, Jr. (*right*) (courtesy Mr. and Mrs. Floyd Dade, Jr.).

a burning desire to separate and find something to eat. Many gathered their few belongings and shuffled off with tattered clothes and feet wrapped in rags. These groups waved frantically at the passing American soldiers and made motions to their mouths. They wanted food and the opportunity to kiss the hands and feet of their American liberators. They did not know where to go or how to get there, but they knew anywhere was better than where they were. They did not get far — some a few kilometers, others only a few hundred meters. Many died along the side of the road.

Wolf Finkelman, who was tattooed with the number 161073, recalls his liberation from Gunskirchen Lager: "One day the German guards just left the camp. We ran into the kitchen and grabbed whatever we could. I saw many people with a handful of butter or other items, and others attacked them. There were stampedes and people died from being trampled to death. I decided to go to the German barracks, picked up some blankets, and slept through the night. Very early the next morning I walked to the highway, which was about one-half mile from the camp. This is where I first saw American soldiers in jeeps, tanks, and trucks. They threw candy and food at us. Many of the people grabbed whatever they could and started eating. Many died from this because their stomachs could not sustain this type of food. The Army discovered several thousand dead people in the camp."[13]

Gunskirchen Lager was entered by a narrow road. American troops had to dodge the dazed men and women fleeing the camp. The barracks were low-slung wooden buildings with dirt floors that were built for 300, but housed 3,000. The inmates would lie side by side without enough room to turn over. Those too weak to move defecated where they lay. Lice crawled from person to person.

All around the camps, people pleaded pitifully in broken English for food, water, even cigarettes. The liberators had stern faces and tears in their eyes as they walked around, determined to do their utmost to stop the suffering. Results were soon noticed. A German food train was located and brought to within a kilometer of the area. Local farmers with wagons organized and hauled the food into the camps. Inside, a public address system organized the inmates. When the first wagon load arrived, order was thrown to the wind and physical force was used. The recently freed inmates could not believe that more food would come. When the pandemonium ended, a kitchen was organized by the women and a meal was started.

During this period, water was being brought in along with medical supplies. One 71st Infantry Division officer performed first-aid with the help of a German medic. A dressing on a wound that had not been cleaned or redressed in six weeks was invested with vermin. There was a long line that ended only when the first-aid supplies ran out.

After all of the survivors were fed, the stories came out. The inmates were mainly Hungarian Jews sprinkled with a small group of political prisoners from

Gunskirchen, Austria, May 1945: Corpses at one of the camps liberated by the 761st (photograph by Sgt. Samuel Teicher, courtesy of the United States Holocaust Memorial Museum).

Germany, Austria, Czechoslovakia, and Yugoslavia. The stories were similar only in the hardships and terror thrust upon the victims. One story was told about inmates being marched from camp to camp, during which time the SS took random target practice on inmates. Prisoners who ran were automatically shot. The SS seemed to think this was great fun. Another story told of a barracks so crowded that the inmates could not lie down, but had to squat and remain in that position. This was during sub-zero weather in unheated facilities. Many hands and feet froze, for which no medical attention was provided.

It was agreed that the local civilians were kind to these people, helping whenever they could. It was difficult to believe that people within a few kilometers did not know that the death camp existed. Even a German medical officer, stationed at Lambach, denied knowing about the camp when questioned. Without exception the German medical personnel appeared at first shocked, then ashamed. They were then determined to do their utmost to stop the suffering.

After a long, painful day for everyone present, the recently freed survivors were fully fed for the first time in months or years. Even though they had to use the same barracks as before, they fell asleep with smiles on their faces. There was hope in their hearts and a future to look forward to.

21

Advance to the Enns River

The weary tankers advanced closer to the Soviets who advanced from the East. The Panthers and elements of the XII Corps found themselves farther east than any other U.S. Army unit on the Western Front.

When it became apparent that the war would end in a few days, orders came down restricting the issuance of gasoline. No fuel would be issued to the 761st. 2nd Lieutenant Horace Jones from the battalion supply section went outside of the division, where he successfully importuned a black quartermaster outfit for 30,000 gallons of fuel. Jones recalls: "By going out and begging those enlisted men, telling them who we were, and what we wanted, and what had happened; we had come this far and wanted to go all the way. They agreed, helped, and sent me on my way saying 'Just get there first!'"[1]

Able Company reached the Austrian border first. They arrived at 0430 hours on May 2 near the town of Ering, a few kilometers from Braunau, Austria (Hitler's birthplace). They gazed across the Inn River and contemplated crossing it with their Sherman tanks. The river was icy cold, turbulent, and had a width varying from 50 to 150 yards. Their tanks knocked out two machine gun nests across the river, opening the way for the infantry and the smaller vehicles to cross the dam into Austria.

Unable to negotiate a safe crossing, the 761st Tank Battalion advanced up the river to the dam at Egelfing. There, with tracks wider than the road-space on the dam, no guard rails, and no margin for error, the Panthers made their way across. Private Christopher Navarre from Charlie Company recalls this hair-raising experience: "I thought this was the most dangerous thing we ever did. You know something? Some of the tank crews stayed in their tanks with the driver! I stayed in our tank until we got started and then I realized there was no need for more than one man to risk plunging hundreds of feet down the dam with the tank. Our tank commander was the only one to stay in our tank with our tank driver. We walked behind it because we had to man it as soon as it got across. Before we crossed we

197

had to put some indirect fire across the river because we didn't have any artillery following close behind. That is how we made it across but I know that some of those damned fools stayed in their tanks."[2]

On May 4 the last Sherman tank crossed into Austria. This made the sixth country that the Panthers fought in. Charlie Company crossed over first, followed by Able and Baker Companies. They went on the attack immediately.

The Panthers rolled down the Salzburg-Vienna Highway, taking village after village with the infantry before running into a concentrated enemy force in Wels. Surprisingly, the opposition was not stiff and Wels fells after a short battle. Afterwards, a major airstrip on the town's eastern outskirts was taken. The Panthers destroyed Messerschmitts, Junkers, Focke-Wulfs and other types of enemy aircraft, along with their hangers. Planes attempting to take off were blasted from the sky by a deadly stream of accurate .50 caliber machine gun fire. Later, the Panthers discovered a downed Junker transport plane with a full load of mangled and burning enemy soldiers.

The Panthers then headed south in the direction of Steyr, located along the Enns River. They smashed through Bad Hall and Lambach. Able Company captured over a thousand scared and unresisting enemy soldiers there.

Outside of Lambach, Able Company ran into a hot spot, the first stiff opposition encountered in Austria. After a brief but hard-fought battle, the smoke cleared. The enemy lost two Mark IV Panzers, two machine gun nests, and four *panzerfausts* and a large number of soldiers. Three hundred soldiers capitulated.

During this period, the Nazi High Command negotiated for a full-fledged surrender. On May 5, 1945, Admiral Hans von Friedburg, Dönitz's successor as chief of the *Kriegsmarine* (Navy), negotiated for Germany's formal surrender with General Dwight David Eisenhower in Reims, France. The following day General Alfred Jodl, the *Wehrmacht's* Chief of Operations joined the surrender negotiations.

Also on May 5, the 761st Tank Battalion received the historic order: "YOU WILL ADVANCE TO THE ENNS RIVER AND YOU WILL WAIT THERE FOR THE RUSSIANS!" The Panthers proceeded to their appointed rendezvous with the Russians. Late afternoon on May 5, Lieutenant Teddy Weston, Able Company's 2nd Platoon Leader, rolled his tank platoon into Steyr and down to the Enns River. With no Russians in sight, the curious young man crossed the bridge alone into the territory set aside for the Soviets. Still with no Russians in sight, he returned to his appointed position.

At this point the enemy was no longer aggressive but apparently waiting behind the Enns River for an opportunity to surrender. The 71st Infantry Division took approximately 13,000 prisoners, of which 9,000 were German and 4,000 were Hungarian. The captured units represented a motley, disillusioned crew glad that their fighting days were over. They regarded American captivity as a stroke of good fortune. According to several prisoners of war, one of these units was formed in Linz, Austria, in late April 1945. It consisted of convalescents, recruits, and stragglers from the 11th SS Panzer Grenadier Division "Nordland" and the 5th SS Panzer Division "Wiking." This was only the beginning. In a few days the 71st Infantry Division's total prisoner of war count, for this area alone, would exceed 80,000.

Four generals graced the Division prisoner cage. Maj. General Kurt Wagner, commanding general of the 7th Anti-Aircraft Artillery Brigade responsible for the defense of Steyr, stated that he had completely lost contact with his unit after all of its guns were destroyed. Maj. General Gustav Auffenberg, commanding general of Fortress Area South Danube, stated that he was to assume command of *Volkssturm* troops that never showed up. Maj. General Kovacs, a Hungarian, stated that like almost all of his countrymen, he had his fill of the war. Brig. General Lothar von Block stated that he was hard pressed to find a haven for himself and his staff in view of the advance of both Americans and Soviets.

During this period a Soviet heavy tank prowled the U.S.–held territory, looking for these generals and escaping German soldiers. There were a few tense moments when the tank's crew wanted to shoot German prisoners held by the Americans. This tank popped up in a variety of places for a few days and then disappeared east of the Enns River, back into its own territory.

Finally, after 183 days without relief, the 761st Tank Battalion came to the end of the trail. They had traveled 2,197 combat miles and 493 non-combat miles. Along the way the Panthers aided in the capture or liberation of more than 30 major towns, four airfields, three ammunition dumps, several branch concentration camps, and one radio station. In the course of their work they destroyed 461 wheeled vehicles, 34 tanks, 87 antitank guns, 27 big guns, 58 pillboxes, 49 machine gun nests, and an exorbitant number of small arms and crew-served weapons. In combined operations with the infantry, the Panthers inflicted a reported 129,640 casualties on the enemy and captured 15,818. To inflict this lethal pain, they lost 33 tanks to antitank fire, 19 to mines, eight to *Panzerfausts*, seven to artillery, and four to Panzers. The Panthers suffered 201 non-combat casualties and 304 combat casualties, of which 34 were men killed in action.

Trezzvant Anderson describes the historic day of May 6, 1945: "Meanwhile, coming from still another direction down the Steyr flow, from the Alps bordering the area, was Lieutenant Burgess's Assault Gun Platoon, which came over the Steyr River at the dam at Mittereg, and there one big Sherman dropped off into the waters of the river. Without hesitation, the intrepid Chicagoan, whose calm 'Line Up And Follow Me!' had become a byword command in the 761st, dived into the chilling waters, fully clothed, and hooked a steel cable from another tank onto a submerged vehicle, and it was pulled out to safety and further use on that same day. May 6, Lieutenant Burgess and his platoon of 105 howitzers laid eyes on the Russians across the Enns! His was the first 761st element to actually see the Russians, and it was the end of the war for up where Dog Company was located with the 71st Division CP, Captain English had furnished ten tanks from the 'Mosquito Fleet' to act as

Charlie Company's 4th "Cool Stud" tank at the end of the trail. The previous three tanks were destroyed by enemy action. Note that the tank commander, Daniel Cardell, has his wife's name painted on the turret. "Cool Stud" is the name of Charlie Company's rooster mascot (courtesy E. G. McConnell).

'Honor Guards' while General Lothar von Rondulic, commanding general of the German Army Group South, signed the surrender papers ending the hostilities for the thousands of enemy troops in Austria! And the 'Cease Fire' order was given!"[3]

A few hours later, Ole Blood & Guts himself, Lt. General George S. Patton, Jr., rolled by in his star-studded jeep with a look of satisfaction on his face. But behind the facade, Patton was troubled over why he had not been allowed to seize Berlin ahead of the Soviets.

VE Day finally arrived. At 0241 hours on May 7, 1945, General Alfred Jodl and Admiral Hans von Friedburg signed the surrender documents in Reims, France: "We the undersigned, acting by authority of the German High Command, hereby surrender unconditionally to the Supreme Commander, Allied Expeditionary Forces and simultaneously to the Soviet High Command all forces on land, sea, and in the air who are at this date under German control." The German High Command had delayed this capitulation to allow more of its population to escape into British- or American-held territory. General Eisenhower had to threaten to leave the Germans to the tender mercies of the Soviets to get them to sign.

Able Company ends a touch football game after receiving word that the war in Europe had ended. Corporal Floyd Dade, Jr., has his hand raised in jubilation, May 7, 1945 (courtesy Mr. and Mrs. Floyd Dade, Jr.).

Platoon Sergeant Johnnie Stevens, Jr. recalls these final moments: "When the last little pack of Germans gave up, the Russians came up one side of the river, we came up the other. And they had lady tankers! This is what knocked me for a loop! And that's where I learned my first Russian words. The meeting was real friendly, full of joy and understanding. Lot of hugging and kissing and all that stuff. And they brought out the vodka. Yeah, it was nice."[4]

To add to the festivities, the Russians invited the Panthers to a boxing match. They set up a smorgasbord with the finest food and vodka for a party. The 761st had an outstanding boxing team back at Camp Claiborne with fighters like Staff Sergeant George Riley, a fast, clever, hard-hitting former middleweight contender; and Leonard "Chico" Holland. Captain Ivan Harrison remembers Chico: "Chico Holland was a helluva fighter. He never professed to be a boxer. He would stand straight up and hit like thunder. He was a winner and he fought the same way in tanks. He would knock them out. He was fearless, the type of guy you would meet only once in a lifetime. When he got out of the Army he became very wealthy because he had nerve. I could have made money with him but I was scared. He had

Major General Willard G. Wyman, Commanding General, 71st Infantry Division, presents 45 awards to officers and enlisted men of the 761st for gallantry in action, heroic achievement, and meritorious service; May 27, 1945 (National Archives photograph).

a bar, a bowling alley, several apartment houses. He was a great gambler. It was such that Caesar's Palace in Las Vegas would send a plane to pick him up. I know that joker told me one time he had $72,000 when he got there and in about four days in was down to less then $10,000. And guess what? He came back with $200,000."[5]

The Panthers totally outclassed the Russians. Private Harry K. Tyree, one of the fighters, recalls: "We won all but one match out of ten or 12 matches. After the boxing matches were over, here come the girls. It was time to start doing the dancing, beating the knees and stuff like that. This American captain who was in charge of recreation for the 71st Division came by and said: 'Now you boys can go back to your outfits. The boxing matches are over.' This Russian major got up on the table and said: 'If they go, everybody go and party over!' Naturally, we got up there and started beating our knees and enjoying it. It was so funny."[6]

On May 9, as the festivities continued, Lt. Colonel Paul L. Bates sent a letter of commendation to the officers and enlisted men of his battalion:

Battlefield-commissioned officers of the 761st. *Top (left to right):* Moses E. Dade, Leonard "Chico" Holland, Horace A. Jones and William Kitt. *Bottom (left to right):* Joseph A. Tates, Theodore A. Weston, Frank O. Cochrane, and Warren G. H. Crecy. All are 2nd lieutenants except for 1st lieutenant William Kitt, who had been promoted prior to this photo session. All received their battlefield commissions in the first six months of 1945 (McCarter and Carrington, 761st photograph, courtesy E. G. McConnell).

It is with great pride that I review the accomplishments of the 761st Tank Battalion. You have more than lived up to the many indications of battle success recalled in your training in the United States and by the fine commendations received from the many officers who inspected you there. Your conduct in England as you drew your equipment and made final preparations for the fighting ahead was a model of the American soldier.... Equipment shortages and the great variety of equipment you have received have called upon you to continually adapt yourselves and modify your concepts of the ability, limitations, and characteristics of weapons and vehicles.... Fighting in France, Belgium, Luxembourg, Holland, Germany and Austria, with the Third, Seventh, and Ninth Armies, with the 17th Airborne, 26th, 71st, 79th, 87th, 95th and 103rd Infantry Divisions, has required your adjusting yourselves to the requirements of a great number of different units.... The courage you have shown in your tanks has been magnificently matched by the truck drivers as they brought up supplies. The maintenance men have worked tirelessly to keep the armor going. They have gone without food and sleep, and used every means possible to obtain spare parts.... The mess personnel, radio repairmen, clerks, all have performed their work in a superior manner. At times, all have been called upon to lay down their regular work and use their guns.... The medical personnel followed fearlessly and always cared for us regardless of enemy fire. You have met every type of equipment in the German Army, planes, V-bombs, bazookas, panzerfausts, 88s, 75s, artillery, self-propelled guns, tanks, mines. All have hurt you. All have destroyed some of your equipment. But all are behind you, useless, the German soldier defeated, his politician silent and you are victorious! I salute you and look forward to your continued superior work in any assignment received, either as individuals or as a battalion.[7]

On May 15, Maj. General Willard G. Wyman, the commanding general of the 71st Infantry Division, sent a letter of commendation to the commanding officer of the 761st Tank Battalion:

1. Now that the end of this great war in Europe has been reached, it is appropriate that recognition be given to the superior manner in which you and the members of your battalion have performed during the period of 29 March 1945 to 15 May 1945, the time you were closely affiliated with the 71st Infantry Division.

2. The combat missions which were assigned your battalion were performed magnificently, which unquestionably made possible the rapid advance of the entire division, and you share generously in the honors which are ours through the phenomenal progress which was made across Germany and Austria. The splendid way in which you and the members of your command responded to the tasks assigned you is worthy of high praise.

3. The excellent combat record of your unit as veterans has been further sustained while operating closely with this command. Please extend to all members of your battalion my congratulations and my sincere thanks for a job well done.[8]

In an area approximately 40 miles north of the 761st Tank Battalion's position, the infamous Nazi 3rd SS Panzer Division *Totenkopf* (Death's head) found itself surrounded by elements of the 11th Armored Division. This was after they struggled for many miles to reach the American demarcation lines that ran in the vicinity of Freistadt to Pregarten, Austria. Their desperate attempt to avoid capture by the Soviets left them exhausted and dehydrated. For two days the SS

Map by William Kaiser, Jr. (National Archives).

Totenkopfs were kept tightly grouped together without any provisions. Civilians who attempted to deliver water to them were roughly turned away and their buckets emptied on the ground. As thirst became a life or death concern, many attempted to escape and got shot down.

As they were being forced-marched away, the local townspeople began shouting at them: "The Russians want you!" Then at a point approximately one mile out of Pregarten, they found a broadly smiling Russian commissar waiting for them. It was obvious that they would be turned over to the Soviets and they became restless. Soon many of them just lay down on the ground and refused to move. The joint American-Soviet escorts briefly conferred. Then, without warning, they opened fire on the sitting and prone POWs. It was a complete slaughter. The ones standing immediately jumped back in line and continued their forced march. As night fell many of the SS *Totenkopfs* escaped. They are the ones who brought back the story of the "Pregarten Massacre." The rest were sent to Odessa to stand trial as war criminals. Some were executed and the rest were sentenced to 25 years at hard labor. What remained of the infamous Nazi 3rd SS Panzer Division *Totenkopf* disappeared into Siberia.

22

Whatever Happened to the 758th Tank Battalion?

The 758th Tank Battalion (Light), the first of the three "Negro" tank battalions to be activated, landed in Italy on November 17, 1944. They were assigned to the 92nd Infantry Division in the Fifth Army. On December 24, they received orders alerting them for front-line duty.

The 758th Tank Battalion (Light) (light indicating M-5 light tanks), rarely worked together as a combined unit. Companies and platoons were constantly shifted to and from various infantry, tank, and reconnaissance units. Consequently, tactical errors resulted from the battalion's use in combat. Despite this, the tankers performed with distinction.

The 758th was composed of Companies A, B, and C, who conducted operations with 17 light tanks each. They had a Service Company and a Headquarters Company to support them. The light tanks were armed with 37 millimeter cannons, which were extremely accurate for target practice but could not reach enemy positions up in the mountains. Headquarters Company had a platoon of 75 millimeter open turret assault guns that helped to make up for this shortcoming.

Early on, they supported the 370th Infantry Regiment's advance up Italy's eastern coast. They encountered fierce enemy resistance as they pushed forward on the heavily mined roads. Three light tanks fell into deep craters in the bed of a canal during a crossing and drowned out. Sergeant Jefferson Hightower will never forget this incident:

> In my memory it was February 12, 1945, and the Germans were retreating to the north and the 92nd Infantry Division wasn't able to break through. There was a canal that went down to the Mediterranean Sea. 758th, A Company, First Platoon, which I was a part of, was given the job of crossing that canal and picking up the infantry and making an advance up the coast. I was in Tank number 3,

206

Jefferson Hightower during training at Fort Knox, Kentucky, January 12, 1942 (courtesy Jefferson Hightower).

Lieutenant McLain was in tank number 1. When he hit that canal he turned over and all of them jumped out into the cold water and made it back to the beach. Tank number 2 tried to pass him and they turned over too. I'm in Tank number 3 and I'm sure he is going to tell me to turn around and go back. He is lying there in the sand on the beach cursing and waving me to go across. My driver, who was very good, went around those two tanks and kept his foot on the gas long enough to keep water from sucking up into the engine and we made it across. Tank number 4 turned over and Tank number 5 commanded by Sergeant Seymour Miller of New York made it across. As soon as we made it across some officer from the 92nd told us to go back. "We can't go any farther right now and all you guys do is draw fire." He was right, we were drawing fire. We drew fire from those big naval 12- and 14-inch guns. We stayed around and did a little bit of firing and then the officer insisted that we go back because he had infantry out there and he didn't want their positions given away. We made it back across that canal by taking the same route. I will never forget that because the shells were coming so close to us that I could see fire coming out of the tail ends. They came right at us and we had to maneuver through them. If they caught you — you were gone![1]

The M-5 light tanks of the 758th supported the medium tanks of the 760th Tank Battalion by providing screening and reconnaissance. The medium tanks of the 760th provided the main armor support for the 92nd Infantry Division.

On April 5, 1945, elements of the 758th Tank Battalion supported the 370th Infantry Regiment for its final offensive action in Italy. They advanced north to take the mountain town of Massa. Stiff enemy resistance and mountainous terrain slowed the pace. After several weeks of fighting, the regiment reached its objective.

It was during this assault in the predawn darkness of April 5 that 1st. Lieutenant Vernon J. Baker, a platoon leader in Company C, 370th Infantry Regiment, 92nd Division, led his 25-man platoon up Hill X through mortar and artillery fire. The objective was the Aghinolfi Castle near Viareggio, which the Germans had fortified into a mountain stronghold.

This was during the Germans' last desperate stand in Italy, and the fighting was fierce. Baker kept his men moving forward, always mindful of his training at OCS: "Keep going! Keep the men going! Set the example! Complete the mission!" The rest was reflex.

Baker's platoon advanced to about 250 yards from the castle when he noticed a telescope pointing out of a bunker at the edge of the hill. He low-crawled to the opening, stuck his M-1 Garrand into the slit, and fired off his entire clip. He looked inside and saw two dead German soldiers; one was still sitting slumped in his chair.

Baker then stumbled upon a well-concealed machine gun nest and liquidated two more German soldiers. He went back to report on the situation to his company commander, Captain John Runyon, who, like all of Baker's superior officers, was white. Then a German soldier appeared from out of nowhere and tossed a "potato masher" hand grenade that bounced off of Runyon's helmet. Luckily for Baker and Runyon it failed to explode. Baker shot and killed the German soldier as he fled.

By this time Baker's platoon was being ripped apart so he went into the canyon alone. He found a hidden bunker entrance and blasted it open with a grenade. He dropped a German soldier who emerged after the explosion and two more as he dashed inside with his weapon ablaze.

Realizing that reinforcements were not going to show up, Captain Runyon ordered a withdrawal. Baker burned inside because he wanted to finish the fight. He volunteered to draw enemy fire upon himself to effect the evacuation of his wounded men. Only seven of his original 25 men survived the battle. Together they liquidated 26 German soldiers and destroyed six machine gun-nests, two observation posts, and four dugouts.

Runyon told Baker that he was going to get reinforcements. The reinforcements never came and Baker never set eyes on Runyon again. Fifty years later Baker was stunned to find out that Runyon had been put in for the Medal of Honor by the white leadership of the 92nd Infantry Division. Probably nowhere in the Army was prejudice and stereotyping more prevalent than in the 92nd Infantry Division where racism at the highest levels and a perceived lack of leadership totally demoralized the men. Regardless, Baker received the Distinguished Service Cross for his actions on April 5, 1945.

From another direction, the 758th's Assault Gun Platoon provided support to the famous 100th Infantry Battalion of the 442nd Regimental Combat Team (Nisei) in its push on Mt. Belvedere near Seravezza. Orville C. Shirey, the author of *Americans, The Story of the 442d Combat Team*, describes the support: "The 100th Battalion had attacked to the north at 0500, April 5, behind a tremendous demonstration of power by artillery. The 599th and the 329th Field Artillery Battalions, the Regimental Cannon Company, Company B of the 895th Tank Destroyer Battalion, Company B of the 84th Chemical Battalion (4.2 mortar), and the Assault Gun Platoon of the 758th Tank Battalion had all let fly a ten-minute concentration on the enemy position."[2]

In the ensuing assault, Orville C. Shirey describes one of many instances of heroism by the 442nd Regimental Combat Team: "...Private First Class Sadao S. Munemori, an assistant squad leader of Company A, also contributed immeasurably to the success of the attack. When his unit was pinned down by the enemy's grazing fire and his squad leader was wounded, command of the squad developed on him. He made frontal, one-man attacks through direct fire and knocked out two machine guns with grenades. Withdrawing under murderous fire and showers of grenades from other enemy emplacements, he had nearly reached a shell crater occupied by two of his men when an unexploded grenade bounced from his helmet and rolled toward his helpless comrades. He rose into the withering fire, dived for the grenade, and smothered the blast with his own body. By his swift, supremely heroic action, Private First Class Munemori saved two of his men at the cost of his life and did much to clear the path for his company's advance."[3] Sadao S. Munemori was posthumously awarded the Medal of Honor.

A member of the 758th Tank Battalion (Light) recalls the attack through the mountains: "Our biggest problem with the little Japanese-Americans was keeping up with them; they moved like greased lightning. Instead of following the paths which tanks have to do, they went across the mountains like crazy. We worked out a system. As they took out across the mountains, we wound our way along until we received a signal from them. Then we would lay down a barrage as a diversion. Jerry would be concerned about us and the Nisei would move in swiftly from the rear and mop up. I do mean mop; they turned those Germans every way but loose."[4]

As the 92nd Infantry Division increased its pressure, the German lines caved in. On April 24, elements of the 758th Tank Battalion entered the La Spezia Naval Base and took up defensive positions. The Gothic Line had been pierced and the division's objective was reached.

The 758th Tank Battalion held and defended its positions and assisted in

As elements of the 442nd Regimental Combat Team (Nisei) advance up Mount Belvedere, the assault gun platoon of the 758th Tank Battalion (light) fires in support with 75 millimeter howitzers. Seravezza, Italy, April 1945 (National Archives photograph 111-SC-205288).

mopping up bypassed pockets of resistance. Then, on September 25, 1945, the battalion deactivated in Italy.

On June 14, 1946, the 758th Tank Battalion reactivated at Fort Knox, Kentucky, and became a part of the Armored Force School. In 1948, the battalion moved to Fort Bragg, North Carolina, and became a part of the 82nd Airborne Division.

In November 1949, the 758th Tank Battalion was re-designated the 64th Heavy Tank Battalion and was assigned to the 2nd Armored Division at Fort Hood, Texas. In July 1950, the battalion received orders for deployment to Korea and was assigned to the 3rd Infantry Division. They trained in Japan with the new M-48 tank, the best armored and armed vehicle in the Far East.

In November 1950, the 64th Heavy Tank Battalion performed an assault landing on Wonsan, North Korea, where it relieved elements of the 1st Marine Division, the "Frozen Chosin." Together they withdrew under the onslaught of a massive Chinese intervention. They assisted in the evacuation of U.S. Marines and Korean civilians by holding the final line of resistance behind which 105,000 troops, 100,000 civilians, and 17,500 vehicles were evacuated in the largest beachhead evacuation in U.S. military history.

In early 1951, the battalion joined Task Force Bartlett to clear a path for the 25th Infantry Division. They inflicted heavy enemy casualties and accomplished the mission in five days, giving the Allies a needed boost to their confidence.

In March, the 64th Heavy Tank Battalion participated in Operation Tomahawk. They raced north with the 3rd Infantry Division and linked up with the 2nd Ranger Company, the 4th Ranger Company, and the 187th Airborne Regimental Combat Team (The "RAKKASANS"), who had parachuted behind enemy lines. Together they caught the enemy in a crushing vice and continued pushing north. On March 29, the battalion was among the first American units to cross the 38th Parallel in the current Eighth Army advance.

In late April 1951, the Chinese launched another major offensive, this one a two-army attack against the United Nations' front which pushed the Allies south. The 64th Heavy Tank Battalion covered the 3rd Infantry Division's withdrawal to the Seoul area, where the line of resistance stabilized at the 38th Parallel.

From May 1951 to July 1953, the battalion held and defended positions around the 38th Parallel while it underwent a historical change with the integration of white soldiers into its ranks. This came as a result of Executive Order #9981, signed by President Harry S Truman on July 26, 1948: "…It is essential that there be maintained in the Armed Forces of the United States the highest standards of democracy with equality of treatment and opportunity for all in our country's defense."

In its final action of the Korean War, the battalion repelled an enemy penetration into the South Korean lines. In the fierce fighting that ensued, Company A drove into an enemy regimental assembly area, where they fought at point blank range. Finally, they had to call artillery on themselves. When the smoke cleared, 300 enemy soldiers lay dead. For this action, Company A received the Distinguished Unit Citation.

In November 1954, the 64th Heavy Tank Battalion departed Korea with the Distinguished Unit Citation and two Korean Presidential Unit Citations.

In April 1958, the battalion was again deactivated. Then on June 17, 1963, the 64th Armored Regiment with three battalions was activated. On May 1, 1966, a 4th battalion was activated and assigned to the 3rd Infantry Division in Wurzburg, Germany. In August 1983, the 4/64th Armored moved to Fort Stewart, Georgia, and joined the 24th Infantry "Victory" Division.

On August 6, 1990, the 4/64th Armored was alerted for duty in the Persian Gulf. They deployed on August 27 to Saudi Arabia, where they joined Operation Desert Shield and trained with the new M1-A1 Abrams tank.

On January 27, 1991, the start of Operation Desert Storm, the 4/64th Armored jumped off and began routing the Iraqis from Kuwait. On February 19, they began cross-border operations into Iraq and spearheaded in a sandstorm with less than 100-meter visibility. They destroyed dug-in elements of Iraq's 26th Republican Guard Commando Brigade and cut lines of communications to Baghdad.

On March 9, the 4/64th Armored moved back to Saudi Arabia and prepared for redeployment to the United States. On March 23, 1991, they arrived at Fort Stewart, Georgia, and received a hero's welcome.

23

Whatever Happened to the 784th Tank Battalion?

The 784th Tank Battalion, the last of the three "Negro" tank battalions to be activated, landed in France on Christmas Day, 1944. A medium tank battalion, they consisted of six companies; A (Able), B (Baker), C (Charlie), D (Dog), Headquarters and Service. Able, Baker, and Charlie operated with the M-4 Sherman medium tanks; Dog with the M-5 Stuart light tanks; Headquarters with the 105 millimeter Assault Gun Platoon, the Reconnaissance Platoon, and the 81 millimeter Mortar Platoon. Service took charge of maintenance, transportation, administration, and other tasks.

On December 26, 1944, approaching Soissons, France, while enroute to join the 104th Infantry Division, the battalion heard bomb blasts. As the explosions increased in intensity and rapidity, they discovered the source, a flaming ammunition train. An ammunition company officer requested and received their help in saving the undetonated rail cars. Using tanks as recovery vehicles, the tankers worked all afternoon while the explosions continued. They saved 160 of the original 300 rail cars. After this diversion, the 784th Tank Battalion continued its road march and joined the 104th Infantry Division near Eshweiler, Germany, on December 31.

Along the Ruhr River in an area between Durden and Murken, the 784th supported the 104th as they held and defended their positions. The tankers fired alongside the artillery. On February 3, they were released from the 104th and assigned to the 35th Infantry Division.

Staff Sergeant Franklin Garrido from Baker Company recalls an incident during which he fought as an infantryman while on his way to the 35th Infantry Division after his tank broke down:

> One of the things that can happen and usually does happen to
> tankers when spearheading without stopping to lube the bogy wheels
> is that they burn out. That's what happened to me. We were

spearheading, going as fast as we could without stopping when the bogy wheel, at least one, in my tank burned out. We pulled over to the side where an armored division was bivouacked. Two other tanks from the battalion also pulled over because they too had burned out bogy wheels. I was the highest-ranking noncom there so I took charge. The first thing we did was beg the armored division for a couple of cases of ten-in-one rations, which they gave us. The next thing we did was to get preacher, who was a member of another crew, to evacuate the civilians in a house so that we could use it as a command post. He was a preacher, he was always quoting the gospel. He is the one person who could really evict people from their houses. Within minutes he had them flying out the door. While we were there waiting for Service Company to come up and put on our new bogy wheels an infantry lieutenant came up to us and asked if he could borrow one of our machine guns. I was a little bit leery because I might not get it back. I told him, how about us taking it and going with you. I'll ask my gunner if he will go with you. That was okay with him just as long as he had the machine gun. They were notified that on a hill a few kilometers away was a German encampment. He was ordered to capture the hill. The lieutenant had a squad of infantrymen, which we called doughs, from doughboy. When we had to shoot at German infantrymen coming toward us, we referred to them as doughs. Any infantry, we called them doughs.

We loaded up on a weapons carrier and drove to the base of the hill. We spread out and charged. I was in armor, the whole time being in tanks. I was not used to running against the enemy without any protection around me. I felt naked. We were ordered to fall and fire. We fired, I had my grease-gun with me and fired along with the machine gunner I was commanding. I fed ammunition to the machine gunner. We did that about three times before reaching the top of the hill. There were two Germans there. One was intact and the other was wounded. He was lying on the ground groaning. The wounded man was shot by a dough. He just walked up to him and dropped his M-1 on his temple and let go. The other must have been drinking a lot of schnapps because he acted as if he was intoxicated. We left the dead on the top of the hill and took the other German prisoner. On the way back, one of the doughs took his canteen and smelled it and sure enough, he smelled alcohol.[1]

On February 8, the 784th Tank Battalion joined the 35th Infantry Division at Geilenkirchen, Germany. Together they prepared for a major offensive. On February 26, Able Company assisted elements of the 134th Infantry Regiment in the capture of Hilfarth across the Ruhr River. The following day Able Company assisted in the capture of Wassenburg while Baker Company, along with the 137th Infantry Regiment, took Goldrath.

Top: The remains of a German soldier dominate the foreground as the snow thaws. In the background, tankers from the 784th Tank Battalion load shells into their tank outside of Merode, Germany, on February 1, 1945 (courtesy U.S. Army Military History Institute). *Bottom:* A basic Sherman tank fitted with an M1A1 dozer blade was used for clearing rubble, filling craters, and knocking down enemy emplacements in the face of direct fire. Here the tankdozer comes to the rescue of a battalion truck that was snared by a bomb crater underwater near Marode, Germany, February 1, 1945 (courtesy U.S. Army Military History Institute).

On February 28, Task Force Byrne was organized with the mission of liberating the town of Venlo across the border in Holland. The force consisted of the 320th Infantry Regiment, the 784th Tank Battalion less Able Company, the 654th Tank Destroyer Battalion, artillery support, and attached engineer and medical units. Colonel Bernard A. Byrne, commanding officer of the 320th Infantry Regiment, commanded Task Force Byrne. On March 1, the 784th Tank Battalion spearheaded down the road from Widenrath to Venlo, bypassing pockets of resistance except in towns and villages. The task force moved so swiftly that the enemy did not have time to destroy bridges. The coordinated assault of tanks and infantry surprised and quickly wiped out enemy positions. The task force entered Venlo at around 1800 hours on March 1st.

The 134th and 137th Infantry Regiments, along with Able Company, followed Task Force Byrne, mopping up bypassed enemy forces. The task force then set out in the direction of Staelin, Sevelen, and Rhineburg. The battalion had little trouble moving ahead except for scattered resistance and blown bridges. In Staelin a tank was knocked out by *Panzerfaust* fire. The burning tank was pushed out of the way and the task force continued without delay.

A force that consisted of a company of light tanks, a company of medium tanks, an assault gun platoon, and a company of infantry entered Sevelen around midnight on March 2nd. When they reached the middle of town, the enemy blew the bridges behind the tanks and launched a counterattack. Wes Gallagher of *The Los Angeles Times* reported: "With a bridge blown behind them, a Negro tank battalion task force staged a miniature 'Bastogne' in Sevelen today, mauling Nazi parachute units in savage street fighting while cut off for 18 hours."[2]

The following day, March 3, reinforcements entered Sevelen and counterattacked. When the smoke cleared, 53 enemy soldiers lay dead, 27 surrendered, and a large supply of food and ammunition fell to the task force.

Wes Gallagher went on to report:

> The 784th Tank Battalion was fighting its first offensive action beside the 35th Infantry Division. The battalion won a place in the hearts of the men of the battle hardened 35th Division, who fought from St. Lo to Venlo and beyond, by the battle it put up here and the spearhead fighting it did to get here.
>
> Sergeant Walter (Pop) Hale, a 47-year-old veteran of the last war from Little York, Illinois, who came back in this war as the commander of a tank bulldozer, was called out under fire to fill craters in a road. He went on to knock out a German 88 millimeter anti-tank gun.
>
> Sergeant Ambrose Hicks of Mt. Vernon, New York, an artillery mechanic, was sent back to help bring a supply convoy through. He saved three trucks parked near a burning ammunition truck loaded with 2,300 pounds of TNT.

Before moving on to the next objective, the remaining tanks of Task Force Byrne are serviced by their crews. Company D, 784th Tank Battalion, Sevelen, Germany, March 1945 (National Archives photograph 111-SC-336785).

There were Negro tank men who climbed out of the shelter of their tanks under mortar and shell fire to refuel....

I had studied the brilliant history of the outfit, and among the ranks of its enlisted men, I had formed some of my most cherished friendships. But I had not seen the battalion under actual combat conditions, the skill and daring of the battalion's colored tank commanders. There were countless stories of how these Negro sergeants carried on alone in the heat of the battle, even when their white commanding captains and lieutenants had been wounded or lost in action.

Along the lonely German fields and roads that beckoned to the Ruhr, I had a chance to test the truth or falsity of those stories, and I found that the glowing tales of heroism which had been attributed to these brown warriors were only a small part of a much greater truth.[3]

Able Company, still attached to the 134th Infantry Regiment, smashed through light resistance west of Geldern, where they made contact with the King's Royal Rifles of the British 8th Armored Division. Able Company was then released from the 134th Infantry Regiment and received a letter of commendation from the regimental commander through the division commander:

> 1. I desire to commend Company A, 784th Tank Battalion, for a splendid performance of that unit while attached to this organization for the period 25 February to 4 March 1945.
> 2. The Company Commander, Captain Robert L. Groglode, 01017224, and his entire company proved indispensable to the 134th Infantry Regiment in the assaulting of Hilfarth and the Ruhr River and the dash to Wassenburg, Bergenlen, and Geldern.
> 3. Their high morale, aggressiveness, and willingness to fight deserves commendation.[4]

On March 4, 1945, Baker Company, along with the 1st Battalion, 320th Infantry, Regiment assaulted the town of Kamperbruch, Germany. The tanks fired with caution, believing friendly infantry operated in the eastern section of town. Baker Company lost three tanks to anti-tank fire. In one action, tank commander Sergeant Douglas F. Kelly ordered his crew to stay in the tank after it was hit. They returned fire until their ammunition began to explode. Finally they dismounted and Kelly made his way to a forward observer's post under mortar and small-arms fire, where his direction of artillery knocked out four enemy anti-tank guns.

Between March 12 and 25, 1945, the 784th Tank Battalion moved to Tegelen, Holland. There they performed maintenance and trained replacement personnel, who had no previous armored training. Like the 761st, this politically sensitive and unwanted tank battalion was meant only to pacify and quiet Eleanor Roosevelt, and was never intended for combat. Thus, the Armored Force Replacement Training Center turned out no replacements for the 784th.

Staff Sergeant Garrido recalls an incident as he approached a small town along the Rhine River:

> Rhineburg, Germany is where I was wounded. Rhineburg was a little town on the Rhine. We cleared the way to Rhineburg for the infantry under small arms and mortar fire. I was riding uncovered with my hatch open for better vision. We were in a line formation about 50 to 100 yards apart. It was just a platoon of tanks, five or possibly six. We moved in on Rhineburg and captured it. Prior to moving into Rhineburg, my tank was hit by a mortar shell and fragments flew up and hit me in the face. It felt like a baseball bat or something. I fell to

the floor. It hurt and I told my crew that I was hit, I was hit, I was hurt and I was going to kill the first Kraut that I see. That was a trickle down that we heard from General Patton. He admonished all of his troops to not call the German soldiers Jerry because Jerry sounds too friendly. "If you have to call those SOBs anything, call them Krauts." That was the first time I used the word Kraut because I was in pain. I told my crew, just keep going and I'm going to kill the first Kraut I see. We skidded into the town square. On the cobblestones we skidded to a stop where the doughs were rounding up prisoners. As the first prisoner walked past my tank, I climbed up and out of the turret and cocked my submachine gun and I leveled down on the first one I saw. I was going to kill him. The prisoner screamed, he fell down to the ground in the fetal position and started screaming: "*Nein! Nein!* (No! No!) *Bitte! Bitte! Bitte!* (Please! Please! Please!)"

Franklin S. Garrido (courtesy Franklin S. Garrido).

I was concentrating on whether I was going to shoot him in the head or in the belly. I was thinking, if I shoot him in the head, it will kill him instantly. If I shoot him in the belly, his guts will fall all over the place and he'll be screaming even more. I was aiming for his head and he kept saying, "*Nein! Nein!*" He then said, "*Kinder! Kinder!* (Children! Children!)," I turned away. In the meantime my crew was yelling at me, "Don't do it! Don't do it!" The doughs were yelling at me, "Kill him! Kill the SOB! Kill him!" My crew won out. I couldn't shoot the man.[5]

The 784th Tank Battalion continued its push towards the Rhine River with the 35th Infantry Division. On March 26, Able Company attached to the 134th Infantry Regiment as part of Task Force Miltonberger. Under control of the 79th Infantry Division, they crossed the Rhine River to exploit the XVI Corps Rhine bridgehead. The remainder of the battalion, along with the 137th Infantry Regiment, later crossed the Rhine and attacked in the direction of Neukoln. Resistance became more frequent, until the enemy became disorganized and withdrew through the Ruhr towns. Then the Germans began surrendering by the hundreds.

Staff Sergeant Garrido recalls crossing the Rhine River: "We crossed the Rhine at night. They were still bombing and machine gunning, sending artillery into the area. We crossed on a pontoon bridge. Being a Southern Californian, I'm not used to seeing wide, deep, swift rivers and it scared the heck out of me. At midnight with no lights I had to lead my tank across this deep, wide, fast-flowing river under fire. I was scared. I was a good swimmer and I kept telling my crew if the tank goes down or if a shell hits one of the pontoons, just ride with the flow of the current. We made it across the bridge. It was scary."[6]

Staff Sergeant Garrido went on to describe an incident shortly after crossing the Rhine:

> Kamperbruck is where our tanks got knocked out, two light tanks and one medium tank. This was in the afternoon, possibly 1600 hours. We were ordered to make up a platoon of tanks plus two light tanks for reconnaissance. Captain Abernathy ordered the formation of a second platoon, which I was the number five tank, the last tank in the column. The two light tanks were scouting ahead of us. Our orders were to join C Company because they were in trouble. On the way there, we passed a company of doughs from the 35th Infantry Division. We continued on another two miles when the lead tank, a light tank, was hit in the transmission. The four man crew jumped out uninjured. The lead tank blocked the road. In tank warfare, if you're shooting at a column, what you should do is knock out the rear tank first so the other tanks can't turn around and retreat. My tank was the rear tank. I ordered my driver to back up and I guided him around a building. The tank in front of me became the last tank and it was hit and knocked out. The crew ejected safely. That's when I was ordered by Lieutenant Peterson to pick up men who were wounded in a burning building. We put one on a door and carried him back to where our tanks were.[7]

Staff Sergeant Garrido and Technician Dave Adams made their way through mortar and small arms fire, and evacuated three wounded men to safety. Garrido and Adams received the Bonze Star for their intrepidity and devotion to wounded comrades. Garrido went on to say: "Lieutenant Peterson then ordered me to go back to the infantry and tell them that we lost two tanks and needed help. I loaded up with hand grenades and clips for my machine gun and I took off running. I probably broke [miler Roger] Bannister's record before he did. I ran and everything that moved I threw a grenade at or a blast of submachine gun fire. The infantry was eating upon my arrival. I told them essentially what happened. They insisted that I eat with them. I guess that was the first time the 35th Infantry Division was integrated. I had beans, bread, and a cup of coffee. We finished and lined up, I as infantry, and we marched up to where the tanks were. Evidently, the German anti-tank gunners retreated. By that time it was getting dark. The M-5 light tank, the first one hit, its motor was still running. The infantry captain asked me if I knew how to shoot that thing and I said yea. The first thing, I said, the engine is still running, maybe it can move. The M-5 had twin Cadillac engines. The transmission was in the front and there was a neat hole in it. It had been a long time since I fired a 37 millimeter, but you just don't forget those thing. He pointed to a haystack and said knock it out, I did. He then pointed to another target and I knocked it out too. That was it."[8]

The 784th Tank Battalion continued the offensive, supporting various infantry regiments. On April 10, Baker and Charlie Companies attached to the 17th Airborne Division for a brief period for an attack on Oberhausen and Mulheim. On April 13, elements of the battalion reattached to the 35th Infantry Division, where they patrolled the wooded area around Blatz on the west bank of the Elb River. There they mopped up small pockets of resistance and took prisoners.

SS troops evacuating French, Polish, Russian, and Jewish political prisoners from the East discovered American troops advancing in their direction. They herded their evacuees into a hangar on the edge of Gardelegen. They poured gasoline on the structure, set it afire, and waited outside with their machine guns at the ready. Caught between a blazing fire and machine gun bullets, many of the prisoners burned alive as they pressed on the walls. The ones that made it out were cut down by a deadly blanket of machine gun fire. Others died as they emerged from underneath the walls after clawing and digging themselves free. Of the 1,100 prisoners, only 12 survived.

As the war in Europe began grinding to a halt, Staff Sergeant Franklin Garrido was about to become an eyewitness to genocide:

> One of the last large cities that we captured was the medieval city of Hannover. We entered without firing a shot under a plethora of white sheets, pillowcases, towels, underwear, socks, anything white; signs of surrender. When we reached the edge of town we stopped, reloaded, and prepared to jump off at 0600 the next morning. At 0600 we were lined up for what we thought would be Berlin; it was only about 100 kilometers away. We took off in a convoy, traveling along at a clip of about 35 or 40 miles per hour. The sun was out. It was a beautiful spring morning. The sky was clear, dew was on the ground, and I was lulled into daydreaming about Los Angeles and the California girls. And then I saw this large tall spiral of black greasy smoke ascending into the sky. When we rounded the curve, I saw this compound. There was a large hangar like building surrounded by a wire fence. On the nearest corner, there, what I

Genocide at Gardelegen. Of the 1,100 concentration camp evacuees, only 12 survived (U.S. Army Signal Corps Photograph, Harry S Truman Library).

thought was laundry, clothes hanging on the fence. As we got closer, I saw the clothes, to my horror, was human skeletons, alive! Human skeletons who were clinging onto the fence begging us with their eyes to help them. At that time the radio crackled and we heard an urgent message over the air telling the tanks not to run over the bodies.

We hadn't reached the gate yet and the urgent sounding voice said: "Slow down! Don't run over the bodies!" The convoy slowed down from 35 miles per hour to 5 miles per hour. And sure enough, as we came closer to the gates of the camp we had to thread our way through the bodies. When the barn-like structure was set on fire, it was where the inmates were kept, the doors were locked. As the inmates scrambled to escape the fire, they were machine gunned. Some of them made it to the road, but they were machine gunned and their bodies were strewn all over the place. We didn't stop. In fact, the same urgent voice, probably an officer said: "Don't stop! There are people in the rear echelon who can help these people. Your job is to continue to pursue the enemy. It was the SS that did this and we want to catch them. Don't stop!"

Years later I had a librarian at the Holocaust Museum in Los Angeles do some research for me. I told her that the only name I could remember about the area was Gardelegen. The concentration camp was on the outskirts of the town Gardelegen, Germany. Gardelegen was not a concentration camp. It was a satellite camp where they farmed out forced laborers to the various war industry factories in the area. One of the factories was Wolfsburg. Wolfsburg was and still is the home of Volkswagen. After we threaded through the bodies, we continued pursuing the retreating Germans until we reached the Elb.[9]

Franklin Garrido goes on to describe the last days of the war: "The Elb River was approximately 40 or 50 miles from Berlin. I told my crew to get ready for the big one, we are going in to Berlin. But unknown to us the 'Big Three' had already made a decision that the Allies on the west side of the river would halt. That would give the Russians the honor of capturing Berlin which was all right with us. My company, Company B, was held in reserve. Two companies of the 784th were at the Elb River when the Russians swept through Berlin. They swept through Berlin with a vengeance, Hitler committed suicide, and the war ended. The Soviet Army met the American Army at the Elb River. Company B was not there but two other companies were."[10]

On April 26, the battalion moved to Immensen, where it performed occupation and control over Immensen and the surrounding communities. On May 26, the battalion moved to and governed Kelberg and the surrounding communities. With a loss of 140 men in battle, of which 24 were killed in action, the 784th returned to the United States and was deactivated on April 29, 1946, at Camp Kilmer, New Jersey.

24

Occupation and the Fruits of Victory

With the war finally over in Europe, the Panthers of the 761st Tank Battalion wanted to know; would they be sent to the Pacific, held in Europe for occupation or sent to the States to be held in strategic reserve? Orders came down that they would be held in Germany to perform occupation and control over five Bavarian towns. On June 18, 1945, they moved their command post from Austria to Bissengen, Germany, and began occupation. The individuals who wanted to return home had to wait until they accumulated enough points in a point system that awards points for length and type of service. It now became apparent that the battalion would be broken up instead of returning to the states as a combined unit.

During this period Germany was in turmoil, with hunger, disease, and social unrest at critical levels. Many civilians were hundreds of miles from home and others had no homes or families to return to. These civilians, referred to as displaced persons or simply DPs, were of all ages. Many were children and many infirm. Most of the DPs in this area were from Poland.

General Patton had harsh feeling for the DPs, as described in his diary: "Everyone believes that the displaced person is a human being, which he is not, and that applies particularly to the Jews, who are lower than animals. Either the displaced persons never had a sense of decency or else they lost it during their period of internment by the Germans. My personal opinion is that no people could have sunk to the level of degradation these have reached in the short space of four years."[1] Patton was later relieved of his command because of his controversial remarks.

On July 23, the Panthers detached from the 71st Infantry Division and attached to the 6th Armored Group and later to the 7th Armored Group for short periods, before being attached to the "Old Reliables," the 9th Infantry Division, on September 21.

Technician Joseph E. Wilson, Sr., remembers:

The battlefields in Europe fell silent, except for where we stood. For deep in the snow-covered mountains of Bavaria, small pockets of diehard German units laid siege to road junctions and proved to be more than a nuisance to our forces. "Get your weapons and get on the truck," bellowed the platoon sergeant to the troops in the company area. Our weapons were other than M-1 rifles, and I was armed with a submachine gun called a grease gun. Tankers did not carry the Garrand rifle for obvious reasons. Minutes later, five "deuce-and-a-half" trucks loaded with troops headed for the mountains. The summer air was cold and damp and our clothing was clearly inappropriate for the situation we found ourselves in. Equally distressing, we soon learned that the enemy facing us was not a group of individuals, but an organized German Army unit that had been bypassed and was still a capable, well-led, cohesive, and effective killing machine. Here we were poorly equipped, in a state of shock, facing machines guns that spat out green tracer bullets, one of which stuck in the heel of my right boot and fizzled and sputtered like a Fourth of July firework while I was in the prone position behind a tree. We withdrew and returned to the company area and loaded for bear. Ears perked up in the German unit for the faint noise they thought they heard was now a loud rumble. A platoon of Pershing (M-26) tanks each armed with a 90 millimeter cannon, a pair of .30 caliber machine guns, plus a .50 caliber machine gun. These five tanks assumed a tactical formation in front of the German unit and all hell broke loose. As a result some joined their Führer in death and others became POWs.[1]

On July 30, the Panthers traveled approximately 175 miles to their new command post in Teisendorf, Germany, site of the Nazi V-2 rocket laboratory. They conducted occupation and control duties along with tank training near Chiemsee, site of King Ludwig II's Island Castle. The training program emphasized cannon firing of the 75 millimeter, 76 millimeter, 90 millimeter guns, and the 105 millimeter Howitzer. Headquarters Company, Service Company, and the Medical Detachment set up operations in Teisendorf; Able Company in Neukirchen; Baker Company in Siegsdorf; Charlie Company in Petting; and Dog Company in Anger.

The social relationships between the Panthers and the German citizens were agreeable mainly because both groups were treated as less than human. The empathy each felt for the other developed into a rapport that did not exist between the white American soldiers and the defeated, downcast German citizens. The way Platoon Sergeant Johnnie Stevens saw it: "We were treated better by the civilian population than we were treated in America. See, in our own country, we could not buy a hot dog when we were in uniform, had to ride in the back of the bus when we were in uniform — you were nothing in uniform. But over there, you were

Warren G. H. Crecy (*third from right*) enjoys a Coke with officers and senior NCOs from other units at a Rausthaus in Teisendorf, Germany, 1945 (courtesy Margaret Crecy).

treated like a king. We ate together, slept together. After the war was over and the Germans had dances again, we were invited. That's why a lot of black GIs took their discharges in Europe. They said, 'Look, ain't nothing in America for me. I can't get a decent job when I go back, I know that. I'm not gonna have any privileges, I can't even vote. So what the hell do I want to go back there for?!'"[2]

On August 6, the United States dropped the first of two atomic bombs on Japan, and on August 14 Japan surrendered. Throughout the United States, people celebrated the victory over Japan.

Back in Europe, the Panthers celebrated too. On August 23, Paul Robeson, the world renown Negro baritone and actor, visited the 761st Tank Battalion. At the officer's club he praised officers and enlisted men for helping to win the war. He discussed the importance of their victory over Fascism. Afterwards he went on a sightseeing tour to Obersalzberg.

At Obersalzberg, Robeson took time out for posterity with some of the heroes of the Battle of Tillet. The photo session took place in the yard of Hitler's personal property. Johnnie Stevens, who stood next to Paul Robeson, commented: "Hitler had once said that no black or no Jew would ever set foot on his personal property. I had news for him, we had lunch there with Paul Robeson."[3]

Photo taken on Hitler's personal property. *Left to right:* 2nd Lieutenant William Kitt; Staff Sergeant Henry Conway; Mr. Paul Robeson; Staff Sergeant Johnnie Stevens; 2nd Lieutenant Moses Dade; 2nd Lieutenant Warren G. H. Crecy. *Kneeling:* Sergeant Finley and 2nd Lieutenant Frank Cochrane (courtesy Johnnie Stevens, Jr.).

That evening Paul Robeson held an outdoor concert in the Alpine town of Bad Reichenhall. He opened by leading the Panthers in singing "The Star Spangled Banner," where his robust voice cannonaded over the mountains. He followed with songs from his Broadway musicals and then he launched into Negro spirituals. He lifted every heart as his voice bathed the crowd in waves of spectacular sound. He closed his performance with his famous version of "Ole' Man River" from *Showboat.* Then came the climatic wallop when he lifted his voice in an exultant, breathtaking finale.

On November 5, Lt. Colonel Paul L. Bates took leave of the 761st Tank Battalion. He transferred to the 90th Infantry Division bound for the States. Captain Ivan H. Harrison temporarily assumed command and Captain William L. O'Dea became the battalion XO. This inspired Trezzvant Anderson to write the following letter to Truman K. Gibson, Jr., the special aide on Negro affairs to the Secretary of War. The letter, dated November 7, 1945, stated: "The men are enthusiastic

over the assumption of command by one of their own race, and morale has jumped and sentiment everywhere is surging in the hope that no racially discriminatory Army policy in this theater will cause us to lose our capable commander, or otherwise impede his rise to the proper rank of his station in the same sense as any other combat battalion commander. Perhaps you can help us on that?"

Lt. Colonel Bates describes his return to the States: "[My girlfriend] found out where I was, and I got a pilot to fly her to be with me for three weeks. After the war, I stayed in Europe for a few months

The 761st got an up-close view of Obersalzberg and the residences of the Nazi leaders as these photographs from the collection of Joseph E. Wilson, Sr., clearly demonstrate. *Top:* The "Eagle's Nest" (Hitler's Teahouse). *Bottom:* Entrance to Kaserne (Fort) Obersalzberg. *Facing page:* Göring's mountain home.

to try to settle myself down and figure out what I wanted to do, and when my transport landed in Boston, she was waiting at the dock for me. I couldn't get away from her, so three months later I married her. She was always there picking me up and cheering me up. I was a very confused person when the war was over. I couldn't put behind me all the contradictions I'd encountered, and how badly my men had been treated. I didn't drink, or anything like that. I was just very confused. Taffy got me through this very tough time."[4]

Shortly following Bates's departure, Lt. Colonel Frank K. Britton assumed command. On February 1, 1946, the new battalion commander submitted his report of operations for the final quarter of 1945:

Baker Co. Panthers talking about home and their families on Christmas Eve, 1945, Siegsdorf, Germany. This newly arrived M-26 Pershing tank, armed with a 90 millimeter cannon, replaced the battleworn M-4 Sherman tank. Photograph taken by T/4 Joseph E. Wilson, Sr. (courtesy Joseph E. Wilson, Sr.).

During the period 1 October 1945 to 31 December 1945, the 761st Tank Battalion redeployed 432 enlisted men and seven officers. Enlisted replacements received were negligible as they were just below the critical score and in turn were redeployed. Therefore the battalion has exerted every effort toward maintaining the integrity of the unit. One hundred eleven men reenlisted in the Regular Army, all for the battalion. The majority of these reenlistees are tank trained and many are specialists. Thirty officers volunteered to remain on active duty until 30 June 1947....

A composite, emergency tank company was organized within the battalion, utilizing all trained personnel, officers and enlisted men. The purpose of this company was to have a striking force organized in case of armed resistance, riots, or insurrection.

Relations between personnel of the battalion and the German civilians have been agreeable. This might be attributed to the exemplary conduct of the men....

During the period the men of the battalion wrote the battalion history [*Come Out Fighting*] and publication was commenced in

The new post–Nazi Germany in the making. German children on their way to school take time to look into the camera with a Panther. Siegsdorf, Germany, 1945 (courtesy Margaret Crecy).

Salzburg, Austria. The book was paid for by popular subscription and will be mailed to all former members of the battalion. Cost of publication was $1,040 for 2,000 copies....

With the expected arrival of replacements in the near future, plans are being made for training that will comply with existing directives and based on proven past experience. Competent, experienced Regular Army "Tankers" are being groomed to fill key positions; this will expedite the indoctrination and training of the new arrivals. It is felt that with the success of the recruiting program the individuality of the unit will be preserved.[5]

On April 1, 1946, the 761st celebrated its fourth anniversary with a gala field day highlighted and addressed by the battalion commander. The day began with a moment of silence for fallen comrades and then an activation day ceremony that was followed by a track meet in Freilassing. That evening they enjoyed a civilian floor show in Traunstein and some watched *Westward to Bataan* in the headquarters auditorium.

The new Panthers continued to perform occupation and control duties in the same area. Their tank training intensified with the M-26 Pershing tank that replaced the battle-worn Sherman tanks. With the German military disarmed and denazified, the threat now came from the East as the Cold War developed.

On June 1, 1947, the 761st Tank Battalion deactivated in Germany. On November 24, 1947, the 761st reactivated at Fort Knox, Kentucky, as a training battalion. Finally, on March 15, 1955, the 761st deactivated for good.

Back home, African Americans were still being lynched and race riots erupted as race relations grew increasingly violent. As the United States assumed the leadership over the new world order it was unable to resolve the internal contradictions of its own democratic society. Some of the new world changes brought social and economic gains for African Americans but racial discrimination prevailed. Johnnie Stevens recalled:

> We knew that we were coming back to the same prejudice we left. I was waiting at Fort Benning [Georgia] to come home, and I had all those medals and decorations on my chest, all of my stripes and stars. There were eight soldiers at the bus stop from the 26th Division, whom I had spearheaded for. The bus came, and the driver says, "Hey, boy, you got to wait a minute!" I said to myself, here we go again. There was this big tough-looking sergeant, and he says, "Hey, don't you see those gawd damned medals on that man's chest? He was with us in combat. Now he's gonna get on this damn bus, and he is gonna ride up front with us!" Then he says, "Sarge, get on the bus." I got on and sat down beside him. I talked and drank with these guys all the way to Atlanta. And all those people that didn't want me to get on the bus, they didn't open their mouths.

Though we came back to the same identical thing that we had left, in a way World War II was good for the black soldier and the black people, for the simple reason that we really learned a lot. We learned what it was to live without prejudice. And believe it or not, we learned it from other countries. We didn't encounter any prejudice in France, Austria, Holland, Belgium, Luxembourg; none of those places did we encounter prejudice. But we had to come right back to the United States and bump into it again.[6]

Charles "Pop" Gates recalls coming home:

That was one of the major reasons I got out of the service. I didn't bawl anybody out who was my rank. Generally, it was full colonels and brigadier generals. I said to myself, they're gonna think back and say — now, there's a man I'm gonna get. I would have gotten closer to home, but it would have been Leavenworth, not Kansas City....

They wanted to start a Missouri National Guard unit. I was asked for a list of available Negro soldiers in the area. Would I be commander of the unit? I said I can for one year. That was 1949. I retired from the Guard in 1964. The reason I accepted was because a Missouri congressman said that Negroes were incapable of running a military headquarters. I was determined to prove he didn't know what the hell he was talking about. We ended up with one of the most outstanding National Guard units in the fifth Army area.[7]

Jackie Robinson, the sensational running back of the UCLA football teams of 1939 and 1940, had to shoulder one of the toughest postwar responsibilities. On October 23, 1945, Robinson and Negro League pitcher John Wright were signed by Branch Rickey, president of the Brooklyn Dodgers, to play on their farm team, the Montreal Royals of the International League.

Robinson pointed out: "Maybe I should buy a lot of cotton to stuff in my ears. I don't think I'll have to take anything I didn't have to take before but maybe there'll be more people ready to give it to me.[8]

Robinson would have missed this opportunity, had it not been for the ankle he broke while playing football. The injury didn't keep him from being drafted into the Army in 1942. In those days, "they were drafting everybody except the guys whose seeing eye dogs had flat feet." However the injury prevented him from going overseas with the 761st Tank Battalion and he was placed on inactive duty. Afterwards he played professional football in Hawaii with the Honolulu Polar Bears until his ankle gave out on him again. Unable to play football, he tried out as an infielder with the Kansas City Monarchs of the Negro National League. He became their starting shortstop and had a batting average of .300.

Robinson never played much baseball until he got out of the Army. During high school and college he was too busy setting records and winning championships in football, basketball, and track & field.

While playing baseball for the Montreal Royals, Robinson led the International League in batting average. Branch Rickey brought him up to play for the Brooklyn Dodgers. At this news, Robinson responded: "I realize what I'm going into. I realize what it means to me and to my race and to baseball, too. I'm very happy for this chance and I can only say that I'll do my best to make the grade.[9]

Not only did Robinson make the grade, he was an immediate success. He led the National League in stolen bases and was voted Rookie of the Year. In 1949 he won the batting championship with a .342 average and was voted the league's Most Valuable Player. He retired in 1957 with a career batting average of .311 and was elected to the Baseball Hall of Fame in 1962.

Willi Jaehne, the Luftwaffe flight engineer and bridge-crossing guard who was captured near Straubing, explains how he got on with his life after the war: "I tried for years after the war and I finally made it to America. My background was nothing because we didn't have much of an aircraft industry in Germany after the war. If you don't have the right diploma, you won't get the right job, so I tried to get to America. For me it was the land of freedom and finally in 1956 I made it. America was and is very good to me. I got good jobs and finally in 1968 I was hired by Hughes Aircraft in New York. They brought me to California. I spent 16 years with Hughes and had a very good job there. I am grateful!"[10]

2nd Lieutenant Warren G. H. Crecy, "The Baddest Man in the 761st," volunteered to remain in Europe and did so for five years before returning home. He served on a variety of assignments, one as a prison officer during the Nuremberg trials.

In 1952 Crecy found himself in the Korean War over the protest of his wife, Margaret. He had only been there three months when he was hit by mortar fire upon dismounting his tank. The concussion blew off his lower jaw, shattered his ear drums, and inflicted severe internal injuries. Although charred, disfigured, and near death, upon regaining consciousness his first thoughts were of his men. He had to be restrained from going through enemy fire to see about them.

Flat on his back, suffering excruciating pain with recurrent fever, Crecy spent the following five years in recovery. His doctors didn't think he would make it but his survival attempts were so innovative that they benefited future medical technology. Caught between the finality of death and the uncertainty of survival, he remained courageous. When he heard of other patients who were despondent, he visited them and encouraged them to resume the fight. Crecy eventually underwent plastic surgery and had an artificial jaw put in place, but he still suffered.

Crecy worked vigorously on any assignment given to him. He became officer in charge of the supply store at the hospital and received a commendation for employing recovering patients and helping with their rehabilitation. On his better

Author Joseph E. Wilson, Jr., received this photograph from Willi Jaehne, the Luftwaffe flight engineer and bridge-crossing guard who was captured near Straubing. Pictured is Jaehne's brother, Armin, who was killed in Russia on December 23, 1942. "What a waste of human lives this terrible war gave us," Jaehne wrote to the author. "Will we ever learn?"

days he would don his uniform and return to the post. He prayed that one day he would get back to his tanks. In 1965, he was heartbroken when the Army finally retired him at the rank of major with full disability. At his retirement he received the Army Commendation Medal and a citation for meritorious service.

Crecy spent his remaining years in and out of hospitals, courageous to the end. His children practically grew up there. In 1976 his son, Warren G. H. Crecy, Jr., gave him a proud moment when he graduated from West Point. That same year, Crecy attended a reunion of the 761st Tank Battalion. He didn't attend any of the previous reunions because he didn't want his fellow Panthers to feel sorry for him. On October 26, 1976, due to complications of his war wounds, the "Baddest Man" finally lay down to rest. Crecy was interred in Arlington National Cemetery with military honors.

A teary-eyed Margaret Crecy affectionately reflected on her husband's contributions:

My husband, as you all know, was a true soldier. When we came back from Germany in 1950, Harding was assigned to Fort Benning. I was pregnant with our second child and went back home to Texas. We had the baby but unfortunately the baby was killed in a terrible accident that I was badly hurt in.

At Fort Benning when the Army was desegregated, my husband was part of a desegregated unit. He was the only black soldier, he was the commanding officer of an all-white unit. He got orders to go to Korea and I rejected the idea of him going into battle again. I needed him, our children needed him. He told me in no uncertain terms, "This is my job, I'm a soldier!" Oh, how I wished that I could have been successful in keeping him home. He left from Fort Lewis near Seattle on July 12 and October 13 was the end of our world as we knew it. I sent him away that morning and watched him march up on the plane, proud as always, uniform immaculate, back straight. I got back a completely torn body. He had massive head wounds.

A mortar shell hit his tank as he was coming out to get to one of his disabled tanks. He received massive head wounds. The impact severed the lower part of his face and he lost 60 percent of his hearing. His heart was practically shattered.

My first word of this was that he was dead. It was corrected by a telegram telling me that he wasn't dead and they evacuated him to a hospital in Japan, but there was no hope.

I called the Red Cross and I never failed to thank Red Cross for this because they had me in contact with the hospital within four hours. They told me, "No!" I couldn't talk to him because he couldn't talk. He had no speech but he was awake. I asked the doctor to put the phone near him and see if he can hear my voice and let me know if he moves his eyes or whatever. They did that and the doctor said he blinked. My life, it looked like a glow of light came over me because I knew he was strong and I knew he would fight. I began to feel better immediately.

They transferred him to Letterman Hospital at the Presidio of San Francisco. I was in San Diego at the time and they were going to alert me when he was coming in. On his way in he had a relapse and they had to stop in Hawaii. Finally, upon arrival at Letterman Hospital, again his physical condition was so bad that they really couldn't do anything but try to stabilize him.

To keep his face from collapsing they had inserted a plastic block. He had a permanent tracheotomy that had been done on the battlefield in Korea. It was a matter of keeping him still so there would be no further injuries so they had him padded and blocked. He had no control and they had to use gauze pads and a pump to control his saliva.

This was for years because his body was so badly shattered. Finally they began building him up with high proteins. It was five

236

Warren G. H. Crecy, Sr., after extensive plastic surgery, receiving his promotion to Major in 1961. He holds the Silver Star, the Bronze Star, two Vs for valor, and the Purple Heart with three Oak Leaf Clusters for heroism in World War II and the Korean War. He was recommended for the Medal of Honor by Lt. Colonel Philip W. Latimer, USAR (Ret.), with a supporting statement by CW3 Christopher P. Navarre, Sr., USA (Ret.) in 1997 (courtesy Margaret Crecy).

years before they could start reconstructive work on him. It was the intent that they would rebuild his face.

Within a few years after the reconstructive surgery, they actually put him on active duty. He worked actively as one of the commanding officers at the Presidio because of the Bay of Pigs, the Cuban Crisis. I nearly died. He continued on a patient/active status. At night he would still rock back and forth in pain and froth at the mouth. He wanted this opportunity. He said, "I'm a soldier. I can't lay down." Even though he was hurt he still maintained the same concern for his men that he showed in World War II.

In the life that he led after his Korean interlude, he would sit and review his *Come Out Fighting* book, the story of the 761st Tank Battalion, and cry. He would talk about his fallen friends and his surviving friends. He would trace the battles throughout Europe. He remarked about their heroism. He said that our future lived with the memory of these men, that this was the greatest contribution that our people could make.[11]

When asked why no African American received the Medal of Honor in World War II, Margaret Crecy replied:

It was simply because they were black. Listen, nobody was for them. Suppose you were to go out by yourself into a vast jungle. You know that everything in that jungle is against you. This is what the 761st faced. Patton didn't want them and he said "I don't care who you are." All he wanted was someone to fight good. Nobody was coming up with the kudos afterwards. That tells you, you don't have to be right, you don't have to be great, all you have to be is black to be kicked in the behind by everyone. No matter what you do, when they are finished using you, they throw you away like a tissue.

To me it would really make me proud and our family would be proud too. Harding would say, "Give it to everyone because we fought as a unit."

For the honor of having black men receive this so many years late, we can still approach our young people and say to them, you do have strong role models. You don't have to look at any other black entertainer or sports star. You have real men, ordinary men, who work hard like your mothers and fathers for their family, who are strong enough and concerned about their country despite all of the hate and indignities that they received, they still went on and did their job. This is what the young black people need to know. No matter who downs you, go on and do the right thing. Do your job and hopefully this will be the beginning.

I'm not asking for the Congressional Medal of Honor for anyone but I am asking that all the people in the world, especially America, to stop looking at us as ignorant, cowardly savages. We are indeed human beings. Some of us are intelligent and some of us are more intelligent. We love, we marry, we create families and we hope for the best.[12]

25

The Presidential Unit Citation

The quest for the Presidential Unit Citation began on July 25, 1945, when the 761st Tank Battalion submitted to General Eisenhower's Headquarters, United States Forces Europe, over the signature of Captain Ivan H. Harrison, a recommendation that it be awarded the Distinguished Unit Citation. Also known as the Presidential Unit Citation, it is the highest honor that can be bestowed upon a military unit.

Ivan Harrison remembers: "Everyone else was doing it for themselves but no one was doing it for us. Frankly, I just love those men, like father to son. I was much older than them. I made Jimmy Lightfoot my adjutant when I was acting battalion commander. His father was a professor at Howard University and Jimmy Lightfoot became a lawyer when he was about 22 years old. He and I got together and he wrote most of this draft and we sent it in. We sent it through the commander of a regiment to the Commanding General U.S. Forces European Theater. Bates was on leave then in Holland and I was acting battalion commander. Bates would have signed it if he was there, he would have."[1]

The recommendation consisted of a four-page narration, four exhibits, a report of damage to the enemy, remarks by Under Secretary of War Robert L. Patterson, and a Chart of Path of Origin. The exhibits are letters of commendation from the commanding general of XII Corps along with the commanding generals of the 26th, 103rd, and 71st Infantry Divisions.

The recommendation stated: "This unit has distinguished itself by extraordinary heroism in battle and has exhibited great gallantry, determination, and esprit-de-corps in operations against the enemy, overcoming such hazardous conditions as adverse weather, mountainous terrain, and heavily fortified enemy positions."[2]

General Eisenhower's office sent the recommendation to Third Army Headquarters for an evaluation. The reply, dated August 18, 1945, stated: "1. Not favorably considered. 2. After a careful study of the 761st Tank Battalion described in basic communication, it is considered that the action, while commendable, was not sufficiently outstanding to meet the requirements for a unit citation as set forth in Section IV, Circular 333, War Department, dated 22 December 1943." The letter was signed; "For the Commanding General; R. W. Hartman, Lt. Col., Assistant Adjutant General."[3]

After having fought and died in Northern France, the Ardennes, the Rhineland and Central Europe, the Panthers asked nothing, but hoped that their sacrifices would not go unnoticed by history. Trezzvant Anderson notes, "The going was not always smooth, and the tempo was not always pleasant to the Negroes, for the fact remained that they were Negroes, and there were occasions when they were brutally reminded of that fact, after the battle had ended. The problem of *race*, which had *not existed* on the field of battle, raised its ugly head after the din of battle had subsided, and *it hurt, it really hurt!* To think that while the enemy shells were falling, and death was a matter of but moments, yea, seconds, and every man was a brother when safety could save a life, that all that could be so easily forgotten after the risks and perils of the battlefield had vanished. But it was a ghastly truth, and it hurt to the very core! But these grim warriors, who had faced the enemy's 'finest troops' took it with quiet solicitude, and realized in their hearts, that they were men of quality, men of character and of caliber! That had been proved in the crucible of war, where one mistake is the last mistake."[4]

On February 12, 1946, the final decision from General Eisenhower's office regarding the Distinguished Unit Citation came down to the commander of the 761st Tank Battalion. "1. Disapproved 2. While the operations of the 761st Tank Battalion were commendable, it is not felt that they meet the requirements for a Distinguished Unit Citation." It was signed; "By Command of General McNarney: L. S. Ostrander, Brigadier General, USA, Adjutant General."[5]

The Panthers reacted with anger and disappointment. Able Company's Walter Lewis, after hearing the bad news, stated, "This was an unfortunate occurrence and something must be done to rectify it. It does not reflect the democratic principles on which this country is founded. I will not be at rest until the day of adjustment for this fiasco comes."[6]

During 1947 and 1948 a formal board took into consideration the compiled facts of this case and concluded with disapproval. Since that time numerous requests for reconsideration have been denied as no new evidence was uncovered that could substantially affect the initial denial of the citation.

In 1967, Congressman Frank Anunsio from Illinois introduced a bill into Congress after this matter was brought to his attention by a member of his district. The bill would enable the President of the United States to award the Presidential Unit Citation to the 761st Tank Battalion.

In 1977, Congressman Anunsio brought this matter to the attention of his colleague, Congressman John Conyers of Michigan. Congressman Conyers sent a letter to the Secretary of the Army, Clifford Alexander. This resulted in the reopening of this case to see if after 32 years of continuous correspondence that the 761st Tank Battalion and Allied Veterans Association could be assured that their case had been given every opportunity for fair and just consideration.

The summary of consideration partially stated:

Col. Paul L. Bates, former commander of the 761st (courtesy Paul L. Bates, USA [Ret.– Dec.]).

> After seven months of intensive research covering the National Archives, the Army Library, the Library of Congress, Office of the Chief of Military History, and the Eisenhower Library in Abilene, Kansas, extensive documentary materials were compiled which taken together, are credible evidence and have not been viewed in total context with previous evidence; that there are clear indications that racial discrimination and inadvertent neglect on the part of those in authority, at the time the recommendations were originally considered, may have been a factor in the disapprovals; that the climate created by the Army commanders could only have made it difficult to provide proper recognition for a "Negro" unit during the period 1944-1947; that the accomplishments of the unit are quite impressive and the high enemy casualties and equipment losses were achieved despite documented adverse weather conditions and problems in resupply peculiar only to a dispersed "Negro" unit attached to several other units in a segregated Army; that under the configuration the 761st operated in, with no controlling headquarters element, it would have been very difficult for the unit to compile timely statistical information necessary to prepare well documented and timely recommendations; thus resulting in submission of recommendations after the close of hostilities.[7]

Retired Lt. Colonel Charles "Pop" Gates, president of the 761st Tank Battalion and Allied Veterans Association at the time, wrote a letter to President Jimmy Carter dated March 16, 1977:

DEPARTMENT OF THE ARMY

THIS IS TO CERTIFY THAT
THE PRESIDENT
OF THE UNITED STATES OF AMERICA

HAS AWARDED THE

PRESIDENTIAL UNIT CITATION

TO THE

761ST TANK BATTALION

UNITED STATES ARMY

FOR
EXTRAORDINARY HEROISM IN MILITARY
OPERATIONS AGAINST AN ARMED ENEMY.

IN THE EUROPEAN THEATER OF OPERATIONS DURING THE PERIOD

31 OCTOBER 1944 TO 6 MAY 1945

GIVEN UNDER MY HAND IN THE CITY OF WASHINGTON
THIS   24TH   DAY OF   JANUARY   19 78

SECRETARY OF THE ARMY

Unit recognition at last: Note the date, more than 30 years after the war.

Secretary of the Army Clifford Alexander, fastens the P.U.C. streamer to the colors of the 761st as Lt. Colonel Charles "Pop" Gates, USNG (Ret.), president of the 761st Tank Battalion and Allied Veterans Association, looks on (courtesy Col. Paul L. Bates, USA [Ret.–Dec.]).

Sir, would the President consider aiding a small group of World War II Veterans in their quest to secure two citations which, we feel, should be included to the outstanding combat record of the 761st Tank Battalion? The citations we are interested in being granted and added to our record are the Presidential Unit Citation and the French Croix de Guerre…. Enclosed is a novel written by Mr. David J. Williams, one of our unit commanders during World War II, which truthfully, brutally, and dramatically describes some of our ordeals and achievements during the combat phase of World War II in a fictitious manner. The novel is entitled *Eleanor Roosevelt's Niggers* and this title is explained in the preface of the book…. Members of our Washington, D.C. Chapter, Mr. David Williams, or I would be most honored to meet with you or your appropriate staff representatives for a few minutes to discuss the worthiness of the battalion to receive these citations. This quest has been a 32-year effort and will be continued. Thank you, Mr. President, for your consideration.[8]

The 761st Tank Battalion & Allied Veterans Association received a great deal of attention with the release of David Williams's book *Eleanor Roosevelt's Niggers*. The unit received this label in the 1940s, meant as a slur and a reminder that FDR's First Lady insisted that black soldiers receive a chance to fight in the Great War.

"The book's shocking title and contents caught the attention of Senator Richard Stone from Florida, who after reading the book decided to launch an inquiry from his office. He later decided to push for the citation: "I had more than a slight hunch that the reason why the battalion never got the citation was because it was black. It was unfair and unjust that it did not receive the citation when it accomplished so much and more than other units that were highly decorated."[9]

On January 11, 1978, the Secretary of Defense, Harold Brown, sent a memorandum to the President of the United States proposing the award of the Presidential Unit Citation. A handwritten correspondence on the memorandum was returned: "Presume that in comparison with other tank battalions the 761st exhibited 'extraordinary' heroism. Therefore, am signing. J.C."[10]

On January 24, 1978, after years of lobbying by 761st Veterans and friends, the long-awaited day arrived: "By virtue of the authority vested in me as President of the United States and as Commander in Chief of the Armed Forces of the United States, I have today awarded the Presidential Unit Citation (Army) for Extraordinary Heroism to the 761st Tank Battalion, United States Army. Jimmy Carter."[11]

Upon learning the good news, David Williams said: "I'm terribly happy and yet sad because a lot of our men are dead and won't be here to see this." He went on to say: "It's taken a long time for the Army to become aware of what it is like to be a black soldier in the 1940s…the special kind of courage it took for the black soldiers to shrug off the second class treatment he got and then go fight and die."[12]

The presentation of the Presidential Unit Citation took place on April 20, 1978, at Sommerall Field, Fort Myer, Virginia. Secretary of the Army Clifford Alexander fastened the PUC Streamer to the colors of the 761st Tank Battalion and stated: "The adverse conditions to which I refer were not restricted to the natural elements. In addition to rain and snow and cold, the 761st had to endure a climate of racial discrimination which, for millions of Americans, blemished the accomplishments of our nation in that war against Nazi oppression. In a war where enemy prisoners were frequently granted more respect than black American soldiers, these men and hundreds of thousands of other blacks answered their country's call, as had been the case in every other American war but one."[13]

26

A Dream No Longer Deferred

There are several lasting monuments to the World War II Panthers. In Mannheim, Germany, a *Kaserne* (fort) has been posthumously renamed in honor of 1st Sergeant Samuel J. Turley. In Gelnhausen, a *Kaserne* has been posthumously renamed for 2nd Lieutenant Kenneth W. Coleman, and in Giessen there is one for Staff Sergeant Ruben Rivers.

There are 14 permanent World War II cemeteries erected on foreign soil. The 761st Tank Battalion has fallen comrades in three of them; 22 at the Saint Avold–Lorraine American Cemetery in France, one at the Margraten American Cemetery in Holland, and one at the Luxembourg American Cemetery, very close to where the men fell. I believe that the others were sent home for interment.

Saint Avold is located near the western edge of the Sarre mining region of France and covers 114 acres of rolling landscape. It lies 28 miles east of Metz and 17 miles southwest of Saarbrücken. It is the largest American cemetery in Europe. Its monument memorial stands at the crest of a hill and is flanked by the Walls of the Missing on either side. An American flag is flown daily in front of each wall. The monument memorial proudly stands 67 feet tall, is rectangular in shape and is made from Euville limestone with bold vertical figures carved into it. Sitting high on the tower are three superimposed Angels of Victory each bearing a laurel wreath. Above the entrance stands a 26-foot-tall sculpture of Saint Nabor (another name for Saint Avold) extending his blessings upon those interred here or those commemorated on the Walls of the Missing.

Inside the monument memorial is a chapel and on the walls are large maps in colored glazed ceramics portraying military operations in Europe from D-Day to the end of the war. High on the walls above the maps are the flags of the different components of the military services. To the right of the entrance is the inscription: "IN PROUD REMEMBRANCE OF THE ACHIEVEMENTS OF HER SONS AND IN HUMBLE TRIBUTE TO THEIR SACRIFICES THIS MEMORIAL HAS BEEN ERECTED BY THE UNITED STATES OF AMERICA."

Netherlands U.S. Cemetery–Margraten (courtesy Pierre Ackermans).

Mr. Floyd Dade, Jr., visits his fallen comrades at St. Avold, France, for the 50th Anniversary of World War II (courtesy Mr. and Mrs. Floyd Dade, Jr.).

The graves area is reached by descending a broad flight of steps from the front of the monument memorial. The headstones are set in perfectly straight lines. Stars of David mark the graves of those who professed the Jewish faith and Latin crosses mark all others. There are 10,489 dead buried here. They came from every state in the Union and the District of Columbia, as well as Puerto Rico, Canada, the United Kingdom, and Mexico. There are three Medal of Honor recipients, whose headstones are inscribed in gold leaf. Ruben Rivers would become the fourth.

Approximately 40 miles northwest of Saint Avold stands the Luxembourg American Cemetery. It began as a temporary burial site during the "Bulge" and now extends 51 acres. It is entered through a tall wrought iron gate. Each section of the gate weighs more than a ton and bears gilded laurel wreaths, the ancient award for valor. The massive stone pillars are surmounted by gilded bronze eagles and each pillar is engraved with a cluster of 13 stars representing the original 13 colonies.

This uniquely shaped monument memorial is a tall, columnar, square chapel that rises 50 feet above its podium. It is made from white valor stone from the Jura Mountains of France. The pylons are faced with operations maps on one side and on the other, stone tablets with the names of 371 Missing in Action, whose remains were either never recovered or positively identified.

The graves area contains the remains of 5,076 American military dead, including a woman Army nurse. In 22 instances, two brothers rest side by side. General George S. Patton, Jr., who died as a result of an automobile accident shortly following the war, is interred here with his men.

Mr. David J. Williams II took a trip to Europe for the 49th Anniversary of the Battle of the Bulge. He recalls:

> When I went to France, I went to all of our old battle sites. I went to where Rivers was killed. Things have changed, the towns have grown up. Incidentally, the French have no monuments, the cemeteries are the only monuments to us. When you get into Belgium every little town has a museum. The French, I found them hostile. I went into Chateau Salins with my son to get a cup of coffee. My company took that town. The old lady knew who I was obviously when I told her in French [we liberated that town]. She glared. She pointed at the church. The church was new and I remembered that we shelled it mercilessly because the Germans had an OP up in the tower. So I got out and my son said, "My God, these people don't like us." I said no they don't. They took an awful beating but the Belgians and Hollanders were wonderful. At the reunion there were more Germans there — there with their medals on. My son said that I should wear my medals. Some of the Germans even wore their helmets. I thought we were going to have a fistfight. Imagine, old men punching each other?[1]

In the town of Gunskirchen, Austria, stands a monument to the victims of the Holocaust, whom the 761st helped to liberate. The inscription translated from German states: "From March 12 until May 5, 1945, during the final days of the National Socialist Rule, Gunskirchen Concentration Camp was located in the woods directly opposite this monument. It was an annex of Mauthausen Concentration Camp. About 15,000 people were imprisoned here during those few weeks. They were mostly Hungarian and Polish members of the Jewish faith, of which many died; 1,227, which were buried in a number of mass graves in these woods. They were transferred in 1979 to the Cemetery of Honor at Mauthausen." There are no remnants of this death camp. The barracks were torn down and trees were planted on the site.

Back home, several streets have been renamed in honor of members of the 761st Tank Battalion. At the Corpus Christi Naval Air Station in Texas, Third Street has been renamed Crecy Avenue in honor of the "Baddest Man in The 761st," the late Major Warren G. H. Crecy, Sr. At Camp Clark, Missouri, Gates Avenue was named in recognition of Retired Lt. Colonel Charles "Pop" Gates for outstanding National Guard service.

In 1992 Captain Thomas O'Sullivan from Fort Knox happened to sit next to "Pop" Gates at a Fort Leavenworth military banquet. "Pop" Gates said he told O'Sullivan "some lies" about his exploits with the 761st. Later, O'Sullivan looked up Gates in Studs Terkel's 1984 book, *The Good War*. He realized Gates's comments "were understatements." Captain O'Sullivan then contacted Mr. and Mrs. Zachary Fischer from New York. They agreed to finance a memorial obelisk at Fort Knox. It was decided that it would have four sides and each side would tell the history of the 761st from activation to the Presidential Unit Citation.

The obelisk was dedicated in October 1993 at a Fort Knox Memorial Park. A modest number of people, about 25 men and women, attended a brief unveiling ceremony. Maj. General Larry R. Jordan, Jr., addressed the group of well wishers and noted that Patton wrote in his personal papers that the 761st "looked impressive but I have no confidence in the inherent fighting ability of the race." Jordan responded: "From your record you certainly exceeded Patton's expectations."

In Texas the determination of one woman will soon lead to the construction of a monument at Fort Hood, formerly Camp Hood, where the 761st trained from September 1943 to August 1944. Beverly Taylor obtained permission from the post commander, Lt. General H. G. Taylor, to have it located near the main gate.

On November 11, 1992, Bill Miles and Nina Rosenblum's Academy Award–nominated documentary, *Liberators Fighting on Two Fronts*, aired nationwide on PBS-TV. The film focused on the 761st Tank Battalion and the 183rd Engineer Combat Battalion, who fought racism on one front and the Nazis on the other.

The documentary sparked Beverly Taylor's interest in African American participation in World War II. She paid a visit to Fort Hood's military museums and found no trace of the 761st's involvement. This is when she decided to push for the monument. In her first major step she had a temporary monument to the 761st dedicated near Fort Hood's main gate on September 15, 1993. The ceremony was addressed by the Fort Hood Chief of Staff, Brig. General Leon J. LaPorte. Former Panthers Philip W. Latimer and Charles "Pop" Gates were the guest speakers. At the end of the ceremony, the three-foot marker that bears the 761st crest with its motto, "Come Out Fighting," was unveiled before a small but appreciative crowd. Philip W. Latimer, president of the 761st Tank Battalion & Allied Veterans Association at the time, wrote a poem to commemorate the event entitled "Back to Killeen in Ninety Three." Latimer proudly penned:

> We came to Killeen in forty-three.
> Not much there for us to see.
> Camp Hood sprawled all over the place.
> And our men searched hard for a friendly face.
>
> To colored clubs they all must go.
> Once a week only to the picture show.
> Step very carefully when you're on the town.
> That's where the "no colored" signs abound.
>
> We're coming again in ninety-three.
> Many great changes we all will see.
> We fought with valor in the ETO
> And our PUC we can gladly show.
>
> They're glad we trained at old Fort Hood.
> And we succeeded as we knew we would.
> They want to honor us one and all.
> And build a monument strong and tall.
>
> As a native Texan I swell with pride.
> That the people now are on our side.
> Fifty years is a long time to wait.
> But just the same it sure feels great.

On October 16, 1994, Fort Hood's Headquarters Avenue was renamed 761st Tank Battalion Avenue. The ceremony was addressed by the new III Corps and Fort Hood Commander, Lt. General Paul E. Funk, who said, "It is about time those brave soldiers were justly honored. As you know, they were embroiled on two fronts, in the battle at home against segregation and racism, and abroad against the Germans.

The history of this elite unit is not well known, but it is becoming more well known. Everyone knows that our services in those days were rigidly segregated, and most of the books have neglected or ignored the services of black servicemen. And more importantly, their sacrifices. Courage is color blind. The acts of courage of the 761st were frequent, and certainly possessed uncommon valor."[2]

During the ceremony the Fort Hood Deputy Commander, Maj. General Frank Miller, discussed Beverly Taylor's determination: "Sometimes a single person can make a difference. Mrs. Taylor's drive and determination set her on a mission to have the efforts of the 761st Tank Battalion recognized and honored."[3]

After the ceremony E. G. McConnell commented: "I just asked someone to pinch me. This is unbelievable. After having served here over 50 years ago and to see the reception, when we couldn't even walk the streets here. There has been quite a change."[4]

McConnell's former company commander, Retired Lt. Colonel Ivan H. Harrison, was on hand. McConnell remembers him: "We called him 'Court-Martial Slim.'" When asked why they called him "Court-Martial Slim," Harrison broke out into laughter and explained: "I was trial judge advocate, this is like the county prosecutor in the Army. Any man who had a charge referred against him by anyone in the organization, it was my responsibility to check the case out and to try or not to try. A case was only referred to me if they were pretty sure that they were guilty, something like AWOL and I used to get them all. And since most of them had been investigated by the judge advocate general's office, they would try them. So I had to try them and they were guilty. So I became 'Court-Martial Slim.' [Laughs] But they had the idea that I'm trying and accusing them and all that. I'm not! I'm just an administrative man in the chain of command. That's all. They know it. In fact, McConnell, he was in my company. [Laughs] He's a good man now. He's over all of that stuff. I put McConnell in jail when we were getting on the boat to go overseas. He was overseas fighting in the war for three months before he got any damn pay. He will tell you six months but it was only three. In a case like that I could recommend remission and get him a little money or something or stop taking his money away from him. I did that! He's not bitter about it. He's a good guy, looking out for himself, that's all."[5]

Most of the Veterans of the 761st Tank Battalion had vowed never to return to this post or its surrounding communities. Although racism is not defunct, times have changed. Killeen's mayor, retired colonel Raul Villaranga, is the first and only Puerto Rican American mayor in the state of Texas. His town is rich in its diversity, with over 47 recognized ethnic groups and an approximate 50 percent minority population, of which 31 percent are African American and 14 percent are Hispanic. Mayor Villaranga invited the 761st Tank Battalion & Allied Veterans Association to have their next reunion in Killeen: "I understand the bitterness that may cloud your memories of Killeen, but I ask you to provide Killeen the opportunity to welcome you back to our community as we honor the contributions of this magnificent fighting organization to our nation's freedom. Please contact me if I can be of assistance in making the triumphant return of the 761st Tank Battalion to Fort Hood and Killeen one of the greatest moments in the battalion's postwar history."[6]

The general membership of the 761st Tank Battalion & Allied Veterans Association accepted the Killeen invitation, for August, 1996.

On June 30, 1995, the main processing center at Fort Hood was named in honor of Staff Sergeant Ruben Rivers. The ceremony was addressed and highlighted by Colonel Charles M. Burke, the III Corps Chief of Staff, along with Philip W. Latimer and Beverly Taylor. The theme of the event was "A Grateful Nation Remembers." The ceremony was co-sponsored by the 50th Anniversary of World War II Commemoration Committee headed by Master Sergeant Richard Jung.

The honor for Ruben Rivers dated from June 6, 1990, when Congressman James Inhofe (R-OK) introduced House Resolution #4976 to the second session of the 101st Congress:

> Mr. Speaker, today I am introducing a resolution to award a fellow Oklahoman with a much deserved Congressional Medal of Honor for heroic actions during World War II. The efforts of Staff Sergeant Ruben Rivers were brought to my attention by one of my constituents who had the pleasure of being aquatinted with this brave American.
>
> Staff Sergeant Rivers committed acts of bravery above and beyond the call of duty during a tank battle that occurred in the Alsace-Lorraine region of France. On the first day of battle, his leg was torn apart by shrapnel from an anti-tank mine, he fought on for his country. His commanding officer and the company medic urged that he be evacuated for medical attention, but Rivers thought only of his fellow soldiers, who would surely need his support.
>
> Staff Sergeant Rivers took control of his tank again early the next morning, helping to turn back another round of advancing German tanks. The next day his tank was once again hit — this time with a final, fatal blow. In all, Rivers fought for two long days and nights while in dire need of emergency attention....
>
> If anyone is interested in becoming a co-sponsor to this resolution, please contact my office.

In March of 1993 the following article appeared in the *Daily Breeze* newspaper:

> RECHECKS OF WWII BLACKS SET FOR MEDALS OF HONOR. Washington — Amid suggestions that racism tainted the process of choosing Medal of Honor recipients, the Pentagon is re-examining whether any black Army Veterans of World War II should receive the nation's

highest decoration for heroism.... Now the Army is asking any black colleges and other minority institutions to bid on a contract to re-examine whether "recommendations for the Medal of Honor for black soldiers were processed in accordance with public law...."

"'If there is a problem, we need to fix it,' Shari Lawrence, spokesperson for the U.S. Total Army Personnel Command in Alexandria, Virginia, said last week. "No one told us you have to do this, but we're saying, if no one received it in World War II, let's make sure that was justified."[7]

After the awarding of the Presidential Unit Citation in 1978, David Williams went all out to have Ruben Rivers awarded the Medal of Honor. He claimed that the struggle for the PUC was so intense that he didn't want to bring up two issues simultaneously. On April 2, 1993, Congressman George Miller (D-CA) introduced House Resolution #1681, a bill to waive the time limitations applicable to award-ing the Medal of Honor to Ruben Rivers:

> Mr. Speaker, I rise today to introduce a bill to enable the President to award the Medal of Honor posthumously to Ruben Rivers, of Tecumseh, Oklahoma, for acts performed at risk of his life and beyond the call of duty while serving as a staff sergeant during World War II.
>
> The time is long overdue for Sergeant Rivers to be awarded the Medal of Honor for his acts of bravery. He was injured severely enough in battle for his commander to order his evacuation for treat-ment of a leg torn to the bone by shrapnel. Sergeant Rivers not only refused to abandon his battalion, but also refused morphine to kill the pain because he wanted to remain alert. He fought for two days in an intense battle and was killed in the line of duty on November 19, 1944, in Guebling, France, trying to destroy German antitank positions that were firing on his company.
>
> To this date, no black serviceman has been awarded the Medal of Honor for his acts during World War II, despite the fact that 1.2 million blacks served in that war. This bill would waive the 1952 time limitation of awarding Medals of Honor for World War II, in order that Sergeant Rivers can be justly recognized for his outstanding ser-vice to our country.
>
> Mr. Speaker ... the time has come to pay tribute to this war hero. I hope that my colleagues join with me authorizing the Presi-dent to award the Medal of Honor posthumously to Ruben Rivers.

At this news petitions began to be sent to Congressman Ronald V. Dellums, Chair-man of the Armed Services Subcommittee. The petition echoed the statements of Congressman Miller and expounded that the petition signer strongly and patriotically supports the above. Friends and Veterans from around the country and overseas took time to get signatures from their friends, families, churches, and organizations. Ms. Diane Bowman from Congressman Dellums's office said that they got the message loud and clear.

Los Angeles County Supervisor Yvonne Brathwaite Burke responded to the petition in a letter dated July 6, 1993:

> Dear Mr. Wilson, Thank you very much for your letter and for the petition to finally pay proper homage to Sgt. Ruben Rivers. I have forwarded my signed petition to Congressman Dellums.
>
> It is difficult to comprehend that, out of 1.2 million black soldiers who served our country during World War II, not one was awarded the Congressional Medal of Honor. Hopefully, this situation will now be rectified.
>
> On behalf of Sgt. Ruben Rivers, his family, and the residents of the Second District in Los Angeles County, we thank and applaud your efforts.

Then on July 9, 1993, the Chairman of the Joint Chiefs of Staff, General Colin L. Powell, responded: "Dear Mr. Wilson, Thank you for the information about Staff Sergeant Ruben Rivers. I am aware of Sergeant Rivers's heroic actions in November, 1944 while assigned to the 761st Tank Battalion. I wish you and all those involved the best of luck in your efforts to initiate a formal review to re-evaluate those actions."

After the issue was pushed a little further, General Powell's special assistant, Colonel Lawrence B. Wilkerson, responded in a letter dated September 2, 1993: "Dear Mr. Wilson, General Powell is extremely busy right now as he brings his chairmanship to a close and prepares to retire from the Army. So he asked that I answer your questions.

"The Pentagon does not become involved in the matter of awarding the Medal of Honor to Staff Sergeant Rivers until an appropriate request is made by competent authority. So far, no such request has been made. I understand that there is a bill in the House of Representative which seeks to reopen the Rivers case. You might want to write to the bill's sponsor, Congressman George Miller of California, and ask about the details."

The Pentagon awarded Shaw University in North Carolina the contract of researching whether recommendations for the Medal of Honor for black World War II soldiers were processed in accordance with public law. This author and others immediately contacted Shaw University and sent documents relating to Crecy, Rivers, and Turley.

Pursuant to his request, the West Coast Chapter of the 761st Tank Battalion and Allied Veterans Association invited Shaw University's Dr. Daniel K. Gibran to

Los Angeles to speak publicly and to interview comrades and family members of the MOH candidates from the 761st. A conference was held on Sunday, February 27, 1994, at the California Afro-American Museum in Exposition Park, Los Angeles.

Sergeant Lonnie Johnson (USAF-Reserve) opened the conference by making the introductions and reading a welcome prepared by Mr. Joseph E. Wilson, Sr.: "It is indeed a privilege and a joy to welcome you here to honor three of America's unsung heroes of that Great Second International War. Each war has its outstanding participants who are singled out and great honors are bestowed upon them. But Warren G. H. Crecy, Ruben Rivers, and Samuel Turley, through no fault of their own, did not receive their just due. The recognition that should have been theirs 50 years ago is still the focus of our efforts today, and we say with a loud voice: 'We are determined to right this wrong, no matter how long it takes.' For this voice is as old as yesterday, but as young as tomorrow."

At this point the World War II reenactors of the California Historical Group paraded in the colors. Harlan Glenn, looking like a young Captain David Williams, led Mark Tellinghuissen, Robert Lisby, and Brian Grafton of the 2nd Armored Division in a historical color guard ceremony.

After the playing of the National Anthem, Chaplain John Brewster, a Lt. Colonel in the California State Military Reserve, gave the opening prayer. Then Mr. Warren F. Taylor, Sr., a former officer in the 761st, gave a brief slide presentation. Lt. Colonel Guy J.C. Coulombe from the California State Military Reserve began the remarks. He was followed by Mr. Roger "Bill" Terry, National President of the Tuskegee Airmen, Inc. He was followed by West Point graduate, Major Warren G. H. Crecy, Jr., son of the late Major Warren G. H. Crecy, Sr.

Shortly before the intermission, Supervisor Yvonne Brathwaite Burke's chief deputy, Mr. Michael Davis, gave a short speech. He alluded to Crispus Attucks throwing the first stone at the Boston massacre that symbolized the beginning of America's struggle for independence. He said another first stone has been thrown here today. He concluded by presenting the surviving family members of the men being honored with the County of Los Angeles Commendation in their memory. Supervisor Burke recalls: "It was a moving honor for our heroes — on an extremely warm day."

During the intermission a small crowd gathered around the World War II exhibit put together by the 100th/442nd Veterans Association, Sons & Daughters Associate Chapter of Los Angeles. Dr. Takeo Susuki, a former first sergeant with the 442nd's 522nd Field Artillery Battalion, talked of his participation in the liberation of Dachau while his son Mark, in a recreative effort, interpreted the artifacts and photos. In the program booklet the 100th/442nd Sons & Daughters expressed: "We thank you for allowing us to be asked to witness this most important redress in America's military history."

When the conference resumed Mr. David J. Williams II spoke in detail of the heroics of Ruben Rivers. He was followed by Mrs. Anese Rivers Woodfork, the younger sister of Rivers. Shaw University's Dr. Daniel Gibran, representing the Department of Defense, closed out the conference with final remarks before answering questions.

At the conclusion, Lt. Colonel John Brewster gave the closing prayer and the California Historical Group retrieved the colors. The approximately 100 attendees slowly left the auditorium. Major Warren G. H. Crecy, Jr., was surprised and elated to be reunited with one of his former West Point instructors, retired Sergeant Major William Lawrence.

The conference received worldwide coverage from the multi-media communications vehicle for veteran-related activities, opportunities, and events — BRAVO, the Brotherhood Rally of All Veterans Organization. In the April/May 1994 issue of *BRAVO Veterans Outlook*, Mr. Tony Diamond and Mr. Vaughn Binzer reported on the conference:

> At a Medal of Honor conference held at the California Afro-American Museum in Los Angeles Exposition Park on February 27, 1994, the 761st Tank Battalion & Allied Veterans Association called for support in their quest to have the Medal of Honor awarded to three men that fought with the 761st Tank Battalion in Europe during WWII. The three men, Ruben Rivers, Warren G. H. Crecy, and Samuel Turley had been recommended for the nation's highest award for valor during World War II, but they were awarded lesser medals such as the Bronze or Silver Stars. Why?
>
> Many soldiers who served during America's segregated military during World War II were recommended for the Medal of Honor, but none were awarded to "colored troops." Why?
>
> Those veterans who served in the military after the integration of the services by President Harry S Truman, know that the color of a man's skin does not indicate whether he is a coward or a hero. Many black servicemen received the Medal of Honor during Korea, Vietnam, and World War I. Black soldiers received the Medal of Honor during our Civil War. Then why not during World War II?
>
> According to some people, the answer is the racism against black soldiers during World War II, "the big one," when many officers and NCOs were from the American South and still harbored ideologies that included the view that black people are not equal and are to be subjugated by the white race. Whatever the reason, no man of African descent received the Medal of Honor from that war.

Mr. Diamond and Mr. Binzer concluded: "While the U.S. military, through its regulations and decorations, tries to make the honors program uniform throughout the services, the qualitative aspects in the judgment of one who makes such recommendations for the Medal of Honor and other awards is based upon that person's experiences and values. A commander's knowledge of military history comes into play and he weighs the act of the person being recommended against the citations of previous recipients to judge if the recommended person's deeds measure up to those who received it before....

"But to discriminate against a recommendation for the Medal of Honor because of the color of the proposed recipient's skin is unconstitutional, un-American, and unwarranted. We look forward to learning of the results of this study."

As a result of this coverage, the Jewish War Veterans of the USA joined our campaign. Mr. Howard Metzger, JWV's Assistant National Director of Communications, sent a letter expressing the organization's support: "Enclosed please find our press release and letter of support to Army Secretary Togo West in your campaign to award the Congressional Medal of Honor to Ruben Rivers, Warren G. H. Crecy, and Samuel Turley.

"The Jewish War Veterans of the USA supports you in this endeavor."

JWV Commander Edward D. Blatt sent the following letter to the Secretary of the Army:

> Dear Mr. Secretary, The Jewish War Veterans of the USA (JWV), this nation's oldest, active national veterans organization, joins with and supports the campaign of the 761st Tank Battalion & Allied Veterans Association to have the Congressional Medal of Honor awarded to three African American World War II Veterans — Ruben Rivers, Warren G. H. Crecy, and Samuel Turley — who served in the European theater.
>
> In November of 1944, these three men performed acts of heroism which qualified them for the Medal of Honor.
>
> Unfortunately, prejudice, anti–Semitism and specious reasoning has played a role in denying worthy soldiers the Congressional Medal of Honor. As a matter of fact, one of our members, Tibor Rubin, whose meritorious and heroic acts in a prisoner-of-war camp during the Korean conflict were worthy of this high honor, has been denied because of the misguided attitudes of his commanding officers. Some of this nation's heroes have been denied combat medals due to prejudice or other actions, separate from their heroism in battle.
>
> JWV hopes that you will look into this matter, and work to ensure that those heroes recommended for battlefield commendations are reviewed based on performance, and not the capricious whims of superiors or others.

Lt. Colonel Patricia A. Sigle, Chief of the Military Awards Branch, responded to the JWV with the following letter, dated July 11, 1994:

Dear Mr. Blatt, This replies to your letter to Secretary West concerning award of the Medals of Honor to Mr. Ruben Rivers, Mr. Warren G. H. Crecy and Mr. Samuel Turley for their actions during World War II.

Your desire to honor the heroic deeds of these Veterans in understood. Unfortunately, there are no provisions under existing law whereby your request may be honored.

As stipulated in Title 10 of the United States Code, recommendations for award of the MH based upon actions during World War II had to be submitted into military channels for considerations by May 1951, and the award had to be approved by the President by May 1952. The only exception to this time limit for which the law provides is when it can be conclusively established that a recommendation was submitted in a timely manner and when no award was made, either due to loss of the recommendation or through inadvertence.

In this case, the above exception does not apply. There is no evidence available to show that award recommendations for the MH were submitted within the time limit prescribed by law.

I regret that my reply could not be more encouraging. The fact that the Army cannot now support an award of the MH for Mr. Rivers, Mr. Crecy, and Mr. Turley in no way detracts from their courageous and meritorious service to the Army and our nation during World War II.

The JWV, mindful of the injustices that they too suffered, would not give up. On July 20, 1994, they responded with the following letter:

Dear Mr. Secretary, I wish to respond to the letter of July 11, on your behalf from Lieutenant Colonel Patricia A. Sigle, Chief of the Military Awards Branch, concerning the awarding of the Congressional Medal of Honor to Ruben Rivers, Warren G. H. Crecy, and Samuel Turley for their actions during World War II.

The letter stated that Title 10 of the US Code stipulates that in order for recommendations for awarding the Medal of Honor to be considered, they had to be submitted into military channels by May 1951, and the award had to be approved by the President by May 1952. The only exception to this time limit was when it can be established that this recommendation was submitted, yet no action was taken "due to loss of the recommendation or through inadvertence." It was concluded that the exception did not apply in this case.

The Jewish War Veterans of the USA (JWV) disputes this unyielding approach on the grounds that prejudice may have played a key role in denying these three African American soldiers the Medal of Honor. Unfortunately, prejudice, anti–Semitism, racism and other specious reasons have in the past played a role in denying worthy soldiers this high award. The actions of these men saved the lives of their fellow soldiers, and in fact, Mr. Turley made the ultimate sacrifice for his actions. An investigation was undertaken to see if these recommendations were lost, or if other factors contributed to these men not being awarded the Medal of Honor.

The Congressional Medal of Honor should be awarded for heroism, above and beyond the call of duty, on the field of battle without there being any time constraint. Those deserving must not be denied because of skin color, religion or creed. JWV asks that you continue your investigation into this matter. If the failure is based solely on a statute of limitations issue, may we respectfully suggest that in your capacity as the Secretary of the Army, that consideration be given by you to submit an amendment to Title 10 for tolling provisions in special circumstances for congressional action.

In their 99th national convention held on August 21–27, 1994, the JWV adopted the resolution to support the campaign for the "Medal of Honor for African American Veterans." The formal resolution concluded: "JWV calls on the Department of the Army to review the files of these brave men to see if they were denied the Medal of Honor because of color or prejudice. If the failure to award the Medal of Honor was based solely on a statute of limitations issue, JWV suggests to the Secretary of the Army, Togo D. West, Jr., that consideration be given to submit an amendment to Title 10 to provide for tolling provisions in special circumstances for congressional action."[8]

Shortly after the convention we heard back from the office of U.S. Senator Barbara Boxer (D–CA). A member of her staff called to tell us that the senator signed and forwarded the petition to Congressman Dellums and will support this bill.

Finally, on Sunday April 28, 1996, *Los Angeles Times* announced:

Seven black World War II heroes are in line to get the Medal of Honor. Their names have been sent to President Clinton, who says the honors are long overdue. *U.S. News & World Report* says the combat records of the nominees met the standards of a special Army awards board. They are: 1st Lt. Vernon J. Baker, 76 of Idaho, the only one still alive; Staff Sgt. Edward A. Carter, Jr. of Los Angeles; 1st Lt. Charles L. Thomas of Michigan; Pvt. George Watson of Alabama; 1st Lt. John R. Fox of Massachusetts; PFC Willy F. James, Jr. of Kansas; and Staff Sgt. Ruben Rivers of Oklahoma.

This list will now be sent to Congress, which must waive the 1952 time limitation for awarding Medals of Honor for World War II. The waivers are included in the 1997 defense-authorization bill.

White House Deputy Press Secretary Ginny Terzano disclosed: "The President believes these are honors that should have been bestowed a long time ago. It's doing the right thing to give the Medal of Honor to them now."[9]

The first proposed recipient, Vernon J. Baker, whose heroic exploits are summarized in Chapter 22, is delighted about this long-awaited recognition but his heart desires that the other six could have been honored in their lifetimes; "It's been late, but it's never too late to say it was a job well done. I'm so very, very sorry that they're not here."[10]

The second proposed recipient, Edward A. Carter, Jr., was born in Los Angeles, California, on May 26, 1916. His mother was a native of India and he received his early education there. Traveling around the world with his Christian missionary parents, he attended a military academy in Shanghai, China. Upon graduation he joined the Chinese Army that had already been engaged in battle with the Japanese since 1931. After six months on the front he was discharged because of his youth.

He then returned to Los Angeles, where he got right back into the wars. He was recruited around 1936 at the age of 20 to become a soldier of fortune for the Abraham Lincoln Brigade of the Spanish Loyalist Army in the Spanish Civil War. This was the bloodiest of the smaller wars leading up to World War II.

General Francisco Franco and a handful of well-financed, right-wing Spanish generals led a revolt against the weaker Loyalist Army. Fascist and conservative groups from around the world supported General Franco's revolt. The Germans sent tanks, aircraft, and about 10,000 troops; the Italians sent another 75,000 troops. This is where the Nazi Luftwaffe revolutionized modern warfare by testing and perfecting mass bombings from the air. The grim aftermath inspired what is probably Pablo Picasso's greatest painting, the heart-wrenching masterpiece entitled *Guernica.*

The Loyalists, with the support of Communist and liberal groups from around the world, held out until 1939. Edward A. Carter, Jr., was a corporal when what was left of his unit fell back into France, where he escaped and made his way back to the United States.

Back in Los Angeles, the handsome young "Eddie" became popular throughout the Central Avenue section of town known as Little Harlem. He enjoyed the jazz scene and spent a great deal of time at the Club Alabam inside the Dunbar Hotel, at the Lincoln Theater, and at other night spots along Central Avenue. He also took pleasure in taking the street car (U-Line) over to J-Town, known today as Little Tokyo, or to Chinatown to enjoy an authentic Asian meal.

In 1941 Carter enlisted in the United States Army and headed for Camp Wolters, Texas, for basic training. He amazed his drill sergeants with his marksmanship with the Springfield 1903 Rifle. On October 25, 1941, the following article appeared in the Bugle, 67th Battalion, Company C newsletter: "Edward A. Carter, 1st Platoon, of Los Angeles, California was the high scorer in rapid firing. He amassed a total of 87 out of a possible 100, which is to say the least, very good for the small amount of training he received so far. I will commit myself by predicting that this man will become one of the area's, if not one of the camp's best shots."[11] Despite his extensive prior military training, combat experience, and proven skills with small arms, the segregated Army made Carter a cook. Not until the closing months of the war did he get an opportunity to fight again.

During the Battle of the Bulge, shortages of infantry replacements in the European Theater mounted sharply. This made it necessary for the Army to begin accepting and training "Negro" volunteers. The training began in early 1945 and the volunteers approached their work with a will. When they finally made it to battle they were eager to close with the enemy. Their strict attention to duty, aggressiveness, common sense, and judgment under fire won them the admiration of most of their comrades.

Edward A. Carter, Jr., now a staff sergeant, took a reduction in rank for this opportunity. He was assigned first to the 69th Infantry Division and then to the 12th "Hell Cat" Armored Division. He was placed in charge of a rifle squad in Company D, 56th Armored Infantry Battalion.

Carter had been with the "Hell Cats" for less than two weeks when he and his squad were on a tank advancing toward the Rhine River near Speyer, Germany. There they ran into a blanket of heavy *Panzerfaust* and small-arms fire from a large warehouse. Carter, armed with a "Tommy" gun and five hand-grenades, volunteered to lead a patrol across 150 yards of open field to check out the warehouse. As Carter's squad dashed across the open field the enemy opened up with heavy machine gun fire, killing one of his men. Carter then ordered the other two to pull back as he provided covering fire. One was killed and the other wounded before they could reach cover. This was before Carter realized that the tanks were not following him. Now there was no turning back and Carter pressed on alone.

Before he could hit the dirt, three bullets from a "burp" gun went through his left arm and knocked him over. Lying there with thoughts of how his entire squad had been wiped out and the sight of his own blood, he became boiling mad. The Germans had convinced him that he was only a few moments away from dying and he decided to take a few of them with him. He jumped up and charged the machine gun nest that had wounded him. One grenade silenced them forever. From there he never stopped. Two more grenades snuffed out a mortar squad lobbing shells into the American lines. Still running, Carter was knocked down again by bullets number four and five. This time he was thrown five feet by the force and when he landed, bullets spattered around him like rain. Before he could see from which direction the fire was coming, bullet number six ripped through his shoulder. As he lay in a narrow slope he attempted to take some of the wound pills he had carried. As he raised his canteen to wash down the medicine, bullet number seven smashed through his left hand. This really made him mad but there was nothing he could do about it. Carter could only squeeze his badly wounded body into the ground.

Several hours later he looked up and saw eight German soldiers coming toward him in a skirmish line. With his "Tommy" gun he fired off three clips of ammunition killing all of the Germans but two, whom he captured. Because Carter had learned German years ago from his German stepmother, he obtained valuable information from his prisoners on the disposition of enemy troops. He then used his prisoners, one officer and one enlisted man, as a human shield to get back to his own lines.

This worked well until the Germans opened up with artillery. Carter immediately sought cover with his prisoners. Just as they jumped behind a gutted building, a German 88 millimeter shell blew the hell out of it. Splinters stuck into Carter's leg for wound number eight. However, the smoke and dust from the explosion gave him a smoke screen, which he took full advantage of.

Carter hobbled through the smoke. When he was about 50 yards from his own lines, and when escape seemed near, the Germans made one last attempt to stop him. His "Tommy" gun barked again and three more Germans fell. The "Hell Cats" could not believe their eyes when from of a cloud of black smoke, Carter emerged with his two prisoners.[12]

Although wounded eight times and armed only with a Thompson sub-machine gun and five hand-grenades, Carter killed a large number of German soldiers. He maintained that he had no exact figure because he did not have time to count. He also gained valuable information by reconnoitering enemy positions and interrogating his prisoners. This information proved vital in breaking the Germans' valiant efforts to prevent the Allies from reaching the Rhine River. His company commander, 1st Lieutenant Russ Blair would see to it that his man would receive the Distinguished Service Cross.

When Eddie returned home, the black community fleetingly hailed him as a conquering war hero. People gathered around this warm and colorful man to hear his combat exploits and to take pictures with him. On October 4, 1945, the Army finally approved his Distinguished Service Cross and had it presented to him a short time later at Patriotic Hall on Figueroa Street in downtown Los Angeles. The American Legion made the presentation. State Senator Jack Tenny from Los Angeles County pinned the DSC on Carter's chest as County Council Commander Mel W. Horn looked on.

In 1946 Carter re-enlisted in the Army. At the rank of Sergeant First Class, he was honorably discharged months before his unit, the 3rd Battalion, 9th Infantry Regiment of the 2nd Division, deployed to Korea. One of the first American units to reach Korea, their ranks were badly depleted early on. Carter was forced out of his beloved Army due to his involvement in the Spanish Civil War, a victim of the McCarthy era communist witch hunt. With his spirit broken he found work as a vulcanizer with Anderson Tire in Los Angeles. Then on January 30, 1963, Edward A. Carter, Jr., one of America's unsung heroes, died in obscurity at the young age of 46. He was buried with military honors in the West Los Angeles VA Cemetery.

Edward A. Carter, Jr. (courtesy the Carter family).

263

The third proposed recipient, Charles L. Thomas, the former commanding officer of Company C, 614th Tank Destroyer Battalion, volunteered to spearhead a tank and infantry task force behind a platoon of his towed tank destroyers. On December 14, 1944 the force started out to take the strategic town of Climbach located only five miles from the German border. On that cold and foggy morning with visibility of less than 300 yards, 1st Lieutenant Thomas slowly ascended the steep, winding road to Climbach in an armored M20 scout car. The enemy had the road zeroed in and opened up with heavy artillery, mortar, and automatic weapons. The tanks and infantry immediately deployed to the sides of the road. Thomas, on the road within a thousand yards of Climbach, had his armored car blown out from under him by a mine. He then took mortar fire that shattered the windshield spraying him in the face with glass and metal. Although wounded, Thomas dismounted from his burning vehicle and helped his crew, including a wounded man, to dismount. He then scrambled on top of the vehicle, secured the .50 caliber machine gun, and placed a deadly stream of fire into the advancing enemy infantry. In the ensuing firefight he was hit several more times in the chest, arms, and legs. He refused to be evacuated.

Thomas's swift action kept the enemy at bay long enough for the tank destroyer crews to dismount their half-tracks, detach and swing their guns around, and return fire. Thomas directed the displacement of two of his tank destroyers. His platoon acted as a base of fire, taking the brunt of the enemy's fire while the remainder of the task force attempted to flank the enemy positions. Exposed on a hillside, the ten-man tank destroyer crews, loaded, aimed, and fired continuously. When the enemy infantry came near, they ran back to their half-tracks and fired the vehicle's .50 caliber machine guns. Gun crews reduced in size to only two men continued in action for four hours. When Thomas felt certain that the survivors were well positioned and the platoon leader was in full control of the situation, he finally permitted himself to be evacuated.

The performance of the 3rd Platoon, Company C, 614th Tank Destroyer Battalion enabled the task force to capture Climbach and forced the enemy to withdraw to the Siegfried Line. This platoon received the Presidential Unit Citation, the first black unit to do so. The men won four Silver Stars, two of them awarded posthumously, and nine Bronze Stars. 1st Lieutenant Thomas received the Distinguished Service Cross.

In March 1945, 1st Lieutenant Thomas, still recuperating from his wounds, came home to Detroit. He was hailed as a conquering hero by the "Negro" press and depicted in comic books. He remained humble: "I know I hung on to one thought — deploy the guns and start firing or we're dead.... I was sent out to locate and draw enemy fire, but I didn't mean to draw that much."[13]

Charles L. Thomas remained in the Army and retired with the rank of major. Despite all of the publicity he received in the "Negro" press, when he died in 1980, his local newspapers in his area failed to print his obituary.

Top: January 11, 1997: The coffin of Edward A. Carter, Jr., leaves Los Angeles bound for Arlington National Cemetery. The Jackie Robinson Post 252 of the American Legion performs the honors (courtesy V. Commander Gene Ivory, JRP #252). *Bottom:* The coffin of Edward A. Carter, Jr., arrives at Arlington National Cemetery, January 14, 1997 (courtesy the Carter family).

Gravestone of Edward A. Carter, Jr. (courtesy the Carter family). Note the error by Arlington Cemetery: Carter's rank was SFG, not SSG.

The fourth proposed recipient, George Watson of Birmingham, Alabama, had been drafted into the Army and assigned to the 29th Quartermaster Regiment. On March 8, 1943, the ship he was on took direct hits from Japanese dive-bombers near Porloch Harbor, New Guinea. The damage was so severe that everyone was ordered overboard. Watson remained in the water, helping those who couldn't swim to reach the life rafts. The 28-year-old Watson made continuous trips back and forth. When the ship finally went down, Watson was too exhausted to swim clear of the suction. The men whose lives he saved could only watch helplessly as he disappeared beneath the waves. His body was never recovered.

Private George Watson was posthumously awarded the Distinguished Service Cross, the first black soldier to receive it during World War II. He has a memorial at the Manila American Cemetery in the Philippines, and at Fort Benning, Georgia, the George Watson Memorial Field is named in his honor.

The fifth proposed recipient, John R. Fox of Boston, Massachusetts, by way of Cincinnati, Ohio, served as a forward observer for Cannon Company, 366th Infantry Regiment, a separate regiment in the Fifth Army assigned to the 92nd Division at the time. In the early morning of December 26, 1944, 1st Lieutenant Fox and his men found themselves overrun by German soldiers trying to break into their observation post (OP), a two-story house near the Italian village of Sommocolonia.

Fox reasoned that the only way to stop the enemy was to call artillery fire on his own position. First he called for a smoke screen to cover the escape of the remaining troops in the area. He remained behind and adjusted Cannon Company's 105 millimeter guns to "walk" high-explosive shells to his OP. The radio at the fire command post crackled as Fox's voice came over the air: "There are hundreds of them coming. Put everything you've got on my OP."[14] He continued: "That round was just where I wanted it. Bring it in 60 more yards." "Fire it! There's more of them than there are of us. Give them hell!"[15] No further communications came from Fox. The shattered bodies of Fox and his men were found in the rubble when the position

"The Negro tank battalion attached to my command fought bravely in the critical Battle of Bastogne . . . the Negro soldiers were damn good soldiers, of which the Nation could be mighty proud."—General George S. Patton Jr., commander of the Third U. S. Army on the Western Front.

Gen. Patton

From *Stars and Stripes,* the daily newspaper of the U.S. Armed Forces in the ETO (1945) (courtesy Christopher P. Navarre, Sr.).

was taken a few days later. This action by Fox and his men, at the cost of their own lives, inflicted heavy casualties on the enemy, killing approximately 100 German soldiers. This swift and selfless action delayed the enemy's assault and gave his unit time to regroup in order to meet this assault.

Fox was recommended for the Distinguished Service Cross at the time but the paperwork was either lost or destroyed. It was not until April 15, 1992, that the medal was posthumously awarded. Painful memories are still stirred up when his widow, Mrs. Arlene Fox and their daughter Sandra, speak of him 50-plus years later.

The sixth proposed recipient, Willy F. James, Jr., was a volunteer infantry replacement assigned to Company G, 413th Infantry Regiment, 104th Division. On the foggy morning of April 7, 1945, Private First Class James volunteered to scout ahead and draw fire to point out enemy positions. His regiment had just established a bridgehead across Germany's Weser River and the capture of the town of Lippoldsberg was vital to holding it. As the fog began to lift, a German vehicle drove out of Lippoldsberg and right to James's position. When James opened fire all hell broke loose. He then scouted ahead under fire another 200 yards, observed the enemy positions, then returned to report. In the ensuing assault he took the point. When his platoon leader fell, James dashed to his aid while firing at enemy positions. As he attempted to drag 1st Lieutenant Armand J. Serrabella to safety, a burst of enemy automatic weapons fire nearly decapitated James. He was posthumously awarded the Distinguished Service Cross.

William S. Harden, who covered James's point position with his Browning automatic rifle remembers James as, "a flamboyant guy, fearless under fire, the kind of guy who gave us all spirit."[16]

The heroic actions of the seventh and final proposed recipient, Ruben Rivers, are detailed in Chapter 10. Rivers's older sister, Grace Rivers Woodfork, mindful that the families and comrades of these World War II heroes have grown old and many have died waiting for their government to pay this debt of honor, looked forward to the day when her younger brother would be finally honored: "Oh, I just pray that they will hurry up so that I live to see it."[17]

During the investigation, no documents could be found showing any nominations for the Medal of Honor, only oral statements from company commanders and a clerk typist. The focus then shifted from re-examining whether "recommendations for the Medal of Honor for black soldiers were processed in accordance with public law," to upgrading the few Distinguished Service Crosses that had been awarded to African Americans. This was the same standard used for white soldiers when the War Department wanted to increase the number of Medal of Honor recipients.

The Medal of Honor investigation focused on the nine African American soldiers who received the Distinguished Service Cross. The three DSC recipients who were excluded are: 1st Lieutenant Robert Peagler of New Milford, Connecticut, who died on Okinawa on June 25, 1945; Private First Class Jack Thomas, of Albany, Georgia, who received the Distinguished Service Cross on April 9, 1945, in Germany; and Staff Sergeant Leonard Dowden, of New Orleans, Louisiana, killed in the Pacific on July 17, 1945. Sources indicate that the "Army Senior Officer Awards Board" and the Joint Chiefs of Staff removed them from consideration.

Ruben Rivers, whose highest award was the Silver Star, was an exception for several reasons. Despite the fact that senior officers and some of the investigators argued against him, his commanding officer, David J. Williams II, never abandoned his commitment to Rivers or to his men of Able Company. Williams said. "God is keeping me alive for this, I know it." There were also two House resolutions in Congress to support Rivers. In addition, substantial support came from the general public. The Congressional Armed Services Committee received a substantial number of petitions and the Secretary of the Army also received his share. Individuals throughout the country wrote to their local representatives in Congress, who took immediate action. In short, Ruben Rivers had too much support to be denied.

Major Warren G. H. Crecy and 1st Sergeant Samuel Turley received only brief mention in the closed-door meetings. Sources indicate that their denials resulted from their not receiving the Distinguished Service Cross and/or none of their commanders standing up for them. The investigators acknowledged: "Clearly, those associated with the 761st Tank Battalion believed that the bravery of Turley and Crecy was not sufficiently recognized or rewarded. Though their bravery was given some measure of recognition, as evidenced by the Silver Star, the adequacy of that recognition remains a contentious issue."[18]

Medal of Honor historian Lou Varrone made the following comments in his monthly column: "We are all aware that for every Medal of Honor recommendation approved there are countless others which for various reasons went unrewarded. These due to lack of proper documentation, eyewitnesses, recommendations poorly written — if at all — or buried in administrative bungling. 'Despite the statute of time limitation,' said General Maxwell Taylor in later defense of one of his Screaming Eagles, 'every recommendation should be properly reviewed whether on our first or last battlefield'.... Over these 20 years past some 240 officially documented CMH recipients have been published in the Static Line column. In addition your own military experience should well qualify you to judge the merits of the enclosed nominee. The tribute is for the recommendation of Major (then sergeant) Warren G. H. Crecy."[19]

During World War II the War Department reserved the exclusive right to award or disapprove all recommendations for the Medal of Honor. According to procedures, all recommendations had to be forwarded even if field commanders recommended disapproval. A War Department Decorations Board was set up to evaluate recommendations before submission to the Chief of Staff and the Secretary of War for final action.

Meanwhile, on August 21–25, 1996, the 761st Tank Battalion & Allied Veterans Association held their 48th annual reunion in Killeen and at Fort Hood, Texas. Their national president, Jefferson Hightower, gave a unique welcome:

> "AMAZING GRACE!"
>
> What a wonderful song, especially the third verse. Amazing Grace brought us through the Great Depression years — the blatant discrimination, the segregation we went through while in the service of our country — and also to the recognition we finally achieved. Amazing Grace brought most of us home safely after World War II — to what we hoped would be a better United States. Some of us even came home safely from Korea and Vietnam. We came home, married (before we started living together), raised a family and, when we were able to, attended reunions of the 761st Tank Battalion & Allied Veterans Association. This past year, His Grace called home Horace "Big" Jones, our chaplain, Cleophus Naylor, and maybe others whose names I do not have at this time. For those of us here in Killeen, His Grace has brought us together for the 48th time and, as the third verse says, "safe so far." And we hope His Grace will see us safely home and allow all of us to reunite next year in Seattle. Now let's party![20]

The festivities opened on Thursday morning, August 22, at the Killeen City Hall, where the former national president of the 761st Tank Battalion & Allied Veterans Association, Philip W. Latimer, read his poem entitled "Back to Killeen in 93." He had no clue when he wrote it three years earlier that he would be at City Hall reading it to the mayor, the city council, the Secretary of the Army, high-ranking officers from Fort Hood, and a large crowd of well wishers. Harsh memories of a hate-filled, segregated Killeen started to fade with warm images of a much-changed city that has opened its arms to the 761st Tank Battalion & Allied Veterans Association. Latimer commented: "The 761st fought and died not just for black people, but for all Americans. We will never take a back seat again. Thank you, Killeen, for honoring us."[21]

Kenneth Hamm was so moved that he sent the following correspondence to Philip Latimer:

> Dear Colonel Latimer,
>
> The greatest moment of our forty-eighth reunion was the street-naming ceremony. Every speech on that occasion was meaningful and eloquently delivered. I enjoyed them all. But, your extemporaneous talk describing your family's values and lifestyle affected me (and probably everyone) the most. It was very poignant and honest. I believe there was not a dry eye in the audience when you finished. I was so moved that I had to compose the following poem to thank you for it. This is only my second attempt at poetry. I hope it is OK.
>
> Sincerely yours,
> Kenneth Hamm (Co. A)

> I want to tell you about the family Latimer.
> Great Americans, the kind that I prefer.
> They live in Texas a southern state.
> Where racial tolerance is not so great.
> But they believed from way way back.
> That we are one.
> Whether white, brown, yellow or black.
> This lesson they learned from the words of the Lord.
> And they teach it to their kids with full accord.
> Now Colonel Latimer or Brother Phil,
> I met in the Army, I remember still.
> He was an officer and I an E.M.,
> We did not socialize or speak then.
> A "Honky" then he was to me,
> But now a Buddy I long to see.
> At reunions we meet as man to man,
> And I respect him more for his racial stand.
> The views of the Latimers the World should adopt,
> To create Peace, Love and Harmony in every spot.
> And so my friends by unanimous decree.
> Three cheers to that Super Family Tree.
> Let's wish them health and everything good.
> I pray there's a Latimer in your neighborhood.[22]

Following the poem, a new street sign was unveiled. Avenue E had 761st Tank Battalion Avenue added to it. Killeen resident and former Panther James Williams unveiled the street sign with City Councilwoman Rosa Hereford and Secretary of the Army Togo D. West, Jr., standing by his side. Mr. Williams then wiped away tears as his son, James R. Williams, Jr., put his arm around him: "It makes me feel so gratified to see this," said Mr. Williams, who fought in World War II, Korea, and Vietnam, and then retired at Fort Hood. "It took a long time to get this recognition. This makes up for a lot of things. Most of us swore we'd never come back here, but the Killeen people are so great now. We never imagined they'd name a street after us."[23]

The address of Secretary of the Army Togo D. West, Jr., was a highlight of the ceremony. West remarked that Ruben Rivers was expected to be among those to be honored by the president soon with the Medal of Honor.

In the rain on Friday, a ground-breaking ceremony was held at the main gate area of Fort Hood. The now-retired Lt. General H. G. Taylor, who granted Beverly Taylor permission to erect the monument near the main gate, was the guest speaker. It rained hard and everyone headed for the Officer's Club for a luncheon. There, Mr. Wolf Finkelman, who was liberated from the concentration camp at Gunskirchen Lager by elements of the 761st Tank Battalion and the 71st Infantry Division, spoke to the rain-soaked crowd.

On Saturday morning a prayer breakfast and memorial service took place at the Killeen Plaza Hotel, where the 761st bivouacked for the reunion. The acting chaplain of the association, Reverend Clarence Copeland, Sr., officiated. He was assisted by an outstanding and inspirational chaplain from Fort Hood whom he allowed to give the invocation. The memorial service ended with the signing of the Post Everlasting Book and the singing of the song, "My Buddy."

That evening a farewell banquet was held at the main ballroom of the Killeen Plaza Hotel. Eloquent speakers included Jesse Brown, Secretary of Veterans Affairs; Congressman Chet Edwards (D-TX); Killeen mayor Raul Villaranga; Baron Bates; Ronald Cornish, Killeen NAACP; Beverly Taylor; Philip W. Latimer; Reverend Clarence Copeland, Sr.; Jefferson Hightower; William McBurney; and Flossie Nelson. Baron Bates, the son of the late Paul L. Bates, spoke of his father's life. He concluded by remarking that when his father was on his deathbed he stated that his purpose in life was to lead the 761st Tank Battalion.

The 4th Infantry Division Band played old and familiar tunes. They also played the "Black Tankers March" written by Philip and Louise Latimer. At the conclusion, the large crowd of approximately 300 danced and socialized. Jefferson Hightower commented that this was by far the best reunion the association ever had and gave credit to Beverly Taylor for doing an outstanding job.

At the reunion this author met Christopher P. Navarre, Sr., a retired U.S. Army warrant officer. He was the Charlie Company gunner who took a reduction in rank from first sergeant to private to fight with the 761st. He received the Bronze Star for his actions during Task Force Rhine. He was originally recommended for the

Silver Star but the Bronze Star was all he received. We worked together and took care of this. Six months later, on February 23, 1997, he received his long-awaited Silver Star in a formal ceremony held at Fort Lewis, Washington, during the fort's annual Massing of the Colors. The award was presented by Lt. General George A. Crocker, Commanding General of I Corps and Fort Lewis. Crocker spoke as follows:

> To Chief Warrant Officer Christopher Navarre, Sir, let me tell you publicly what an honor it is to have you here today. Today, we have demonstrated that the responsibility of the chain of command never ends. Your World War II Company Commander [Captain Charles "Pop" Gates] never gave up the fight to obtain for you the recognition you so richly deserve. As a young private, you performed with valor in the face of the enemy. Today, over 50 years late, we, on behalf of a grateful nation and your company commander recognize your contribution to our Freedom.

In January 1997 the remains of Sergeant First Class Edward A. Carter, Jr., were exhumed from the VA Cemetery in West Los Angeles for shipment to Washington, D.C. He was memorialized on January 11, in a heartfelt ceremony held at the Angelus Funeral Home in Los Angeles, California. The ceremony attracted veterans of all branches, ages, gender, races; active-duty and retired, and from as far away as Washington, D.C. They came to pay homage to this unsung hero and to acknowledge that although the honor came late, it is never *too* late.

The Medal of Honor candidate from Los Angeles had a long and impressive list of honorary pallbearers in attendance. The list included The 555th "Triple Nickel" Parachute Infantry Association; The 761st Tank Battalion & Allied Veterans Association; The American Legion — Chappie James Post #578; The Buffalo Soldiers — 9th & 10th (Horse) Cavalry Association; The Hispanic American Airborne Association; The RAKKASANS—187th Airborne Regimental Combat Team Association; The Rudy Hernandez MOH Chapter of the 11th Airborne Division Association; The Tuskegee Airmen, Inc.; The Veterans of Foreign Wars — Inglewood Post #2122; and the WIMS — Women In the Military Service.

The Jackie Robinson Post #252 of the American Legion performed the ceremony with pride and distinction. Under the command of Vice Commander Paul J. Madison (USMC-Ret), they served as active pallbearers and performed the honor and color guard duties. Past Commander Bill "Chief" Johnson (USN-Ret) stood at the right side of the flag draped coffin as Adjutant Barbara Henry stood at the left. They maintained the position of parade rest during the duration.

Pastor Ed Smith of the Zoe Christian Fellowship Church opened the service. Chaplain Lt. Colonel Michael DeRenzo of the Los Angeles Air Force Base began the remarks with an inspiring invocation that set the tone for the event. Bob Archuleta, the Los Angeles County Commissioner of Veterans Affairs, made an

THE UNITED STATES OF AMERICA

TO ALL WHO SHALL SEE THESE PRESENTS, GREETING:

THIS IS TO CERTIFY THAT
THE PRESIDENT OF THE UNITED STATES OF AMERICA
AUTHORIZED BY ACT OF CONGRESS JULY 9, 1918
HAS AWARDED

THE SILVER STAR

TO
CHRISTOPHER P. NAVARRE
(THEN PRIVATE, UNITED STATES ARMY)
FOR
GALLANTRY IN ACTION
in the European Theater of Operations between 15-23 March 1945

GIVEN UNDER MY HAND IN THE CITY OF WASHINGTON
THIS   22d   DAY OF   January   19 97

EARL M. SIMMS
BG, USA, THE ADJUTANT GENERAL

SECRETARY OF THE ARMY

Top: Mr. Christopher P. Navarre, Sr., accepting his long-awaited (52 years) Silver Star from Lt. General George A. Crocker as CSM Leon Guerro looks on (courtesy Christopher P. Navarre, Sr.). *Bottom:* Christopher P. Navarre's Silver Star Citation.

emotional speech. He said that he had to meet this exceptional man, if only at his grave: "Sergeant Carter, Sergeant Carter, sir. I'm here to meet you.... When you get back home be sure to tell those who went before you that they have been given the long overdue recognition ... and because of them, the upside-down nation has righted itself. And by the way, when you see Private Eugene Obregon, tell him a monument in tribute to all Hispanic Medal of Honor recipients will soon be dedicated in their honor. Thank you, Sergeant Carter."[24]

Juanita Scott, the WIMS chairperson, in an informative speech, spoke of the women's role in the military. She then introduced Lt. Colonel Patricia Jackson, the women veteran's coordinator for the West Los Angeles VA Medical Center. Both ladies credited the deeds of men like Edward Carter who paved the way for their success in the military. Rudy Garcia, the president of the Rudy Hernandez MOH Chapter of the 11th Airborne Division Association, followed. He concluded: "Through all of our divisions, the one thing that unites us is the Red, White and Blue! Carter and his compatriots, through their deeds, continue to remind us of the significance of those colors."[27] Former Tuskegee Airman Celes King III made the final remarks. He said that this honor is late, but it is never too late and that we must see to it that this kind of neglect never happens again.

Veronica Brooks and Ray Woodard lifted every spirit with their solos of the old and new "Negro" spirituals. Then everyone joined in and sang the Negro National Anthem — "Lift Ev'ry Voice and Sing:"

> Lift ev'ry voice and sing, til earth and heaven ring.
> Ring with the harmonies of liberty;
> Let our rejoicing rise, high as the list'ning skies,
> Let it resound loud as the rolling sea.
>
> Sing a song full of the faith that the dark past has taught us.
> Sing a song full of the hope that the present has brought us;
> Facing the rising sun of our new day begun,
> Let us march on till victory is won.
>
> Stony the road we trod, bitter the chast'ning rod,
> Felt in the days when hope unborn had died;
> Yet with a steady beat, have not our weary feet,
> Come to the place for which our fathers sighed.
>
> We have come over a way that with tears have been watered,
> We have come, treading our path thro' the blood of the slaughter.
> Out from the gloomy past, till now we stand at last,
> Where the white gleam of our bright star is cast.
>
> God of our weary years, God of our silent tears,

Thou who has brought us thus far on the way;
Thou who has by thy might, led us into the light,
Keep us forever in the path, we pray.

Lest our feet stray from the places, our God, where we met thee,
Let our hearts, drunk with the wine of the world, we forget thee;
Shadowed beneath thy hand, may we forever stand,
True to our God, true to our native land.

Michael Tinsley read the obituary and the acknowledgments and then introduced Allene Carter, the daughter-in-law of the late Edward A. Carter, Jr., and also the Carter family historian and spokesperson. She introduced the members of the Carter family and gave us a glimpse of the "man who was ahead of his time." She also told us of his role in creating the 1401 and 1402 Combat Engineer Battalions, the segregated California National Guard units. She concluded by cordially inviting everyone present to observe a moment of silence on Monday around 1100 hours for all of the unsung heroes. This was the expected time that the Medal of Honor would be presented by President Clinton.

California State Senator Diane Watson made an unexpected appearance. She congratulated the Carter family and invited them to the state capital where they would be "given the floor." She also proposed an Edward A. Carter, Jr., Day. Pastor Ed Smith followed and gave the closing prayer.

The large crowd filed out to the south side of the funeral home where the hearse waited. Chaplain Nazimova Primeaux solemnly led the procession of pallbearers. She had also served in World War II as a master sergeant in the 6888th Postal Battalion serving in the European Theater of Operations.

Taps sounded before the honor guard fired a 21-gun salute — three rounds for each of the seven Medal of Honor candidates. It was a sight to see — veterans of all branches, ages, gender, races, both active-duty and retired — all dressed in their regalia standing at attention and rendering a final hand salute to Sergeant First Class Edward A. Carter, Jr., before sending him to his final resting place at Arlington National Cemetery.

John F. Kennedy once said: "In the long history of the world, only a few generations have been granted the role of defending freedom in its hour of maximum danger." In telling the story of this terrible war, we honor those who fought and died for freedom during our nation's hour of maximum danger. This book's purpose is to remind America of the courage and sacrifice made by all Americans, and in this case, by African Americans who seemed to have been left out of history. They fought under the "Double V" that called for victory abroad against the forces of global domination and they also faced an additional enemy. They had to fight at home for the *right* to fight. There is no secret about the way African Americans lived and were treated throughout World War II, and how they defended a way of life that didn't include full partnership. Faced with hardships, abuse, humiliation, and in many cases death, they persevered. The wounds received in this battle were as deep as any honored by a Purple Heart.

This well-established pattern of racist thinking received support from several presidents. President Woodrow Wilson once said: "The colored people of this nation have no right to expect special treatment. It is my policy that no individual of color should expect a free ride." This comes as a surprise because Wilson received a majority of the black vote when he was elected president. President Teddy Roosevelt once remarked: "Colored soldiers will not fight. It is just a fact of life that they are yellow-hearted and will not fight in battle." This comes as even more of a surprise because Roosevelt became a hero at San Juan Hill largely due to black Buffalo Soldiers.

With freedom at stake both abroad and at home in the 1940s, an estimated 1.2 million African Americans set out to win this freedom with their selfless devotion to freedom in a country where people of color were not free. They exposed the extreme stupidity of the institution of discrimination, segregation and racism. They proved that discrimination, segregation, and racism should be eliminated because to do so is right and also because it is wise. Out of the ashes of World War II came a renewed, proud, and assertive race of people who would henceforth demand their equal share of the American dream. Change was in the atmosphere and America trembled in anticipation of the coming storm.

We ask that the new generation learn from the exploits of the 761st Tank Battalion. They were the first African Americans to fight in armor but not the last. They established that courage is an act of refusing to give up, and by such refusal they paved a way for future generations to serve in a better military and live in a better world. I wish to extend to the men of the 761st my appreciation and a warm farewell. God bless you, and God bless America!

We now will go to January 13, 1997 — the White House — to the long awaited Medal of Honor presentations. The President of the United States of America will have the final word.

The event unfolded in the East Room of the White House with President Bill Clinton presiding over the ceremony. Thanks to the Carter family, this author was in attendance. I can never thank them enough for giving me the opportunity to witness this most important redress in America's military history.

I found a seat right up front with Anese Rivers Woodfork and her 10-year-old granddaughter Milese Tittle to my right, and Maj. General Larry Jordan to my left. The Carter family sat a few seats over to my right. We were asked to stand and the ceremony opened with the band playing "God Bless America." Then the Medal of Honor recipients were escorted to the stage by a military officer. Vernon Baker came up first. He was followed by Sandra Johnson, niece of Charles L. Thomas;

Arlene Fox, widow of John R. Fox; Edward A. Carter III, son of Edward A. Carter, Jr.; Grace Rivers Woodfork, sister of Ruben Rivers; Valcenie James, widow of Willy F. James, Jr.; and Sergeant Major of the Army Gene McKinney, accepting for George Watson, who has no known relatives.

The band changed its tune to "Hail to the Chief" and President Clinton entered. He made the following remarks:

> Secretary Perry, Secretary Brown, other members of the administration, General Shalikashvili and the members of the Joint Chiefs, General Powell, Senator Craig, Senator Kempthorne, Congressman Miller, the members of the families and friends of the Medal recipients, and Mr. Vernon Baker, I'd like to begin by thanking Shaw University, its President, Talbert Shaw, and the authors of the Shaw study on the nomination of outstanding African American soldiers for the Medal of Honor in the United States Army during World War II.
>
> I also want to commend the Department of the Army officials, former and present, who commissioned this study and saw it through. Together, your support and painstaking research made this day possible. Without it, we would not be able to meet our obligation as a people to an extraordinary group of soldiers to whom we owe the greatest debt. Because of the hard work you have done history has been made whole today, and our nation is bestowing honor on those who have long deserved it.
>
> Fifty-two years ago on an August day, Harry Truman stood where I stand now and awarded 28 Medals of Honor to Veterans of World War II in the largest such ceremony ever held. President Truman described those Medal recipients as a great cross-section of the United States. "These men love peace but are able to adjust themselves to the necessity of war," he said.
>
> I believe Harry Truman was one of our greatest presidents. He had not a shred of discrimination in his bones. He integrated the armed forces. But that day, something was missing from his cross-section of America. No African American who deserved the Medal of Honor for his service in World War II received it. Today we fill the gap in that picture and give a group of heroes who also love peace but adapted themselves to war the tribute that has always been their due. Now and forever, the truth will be known about these African Americans who gave so much that the rest of us might be free.
>
> Today we recognize seven men as being among the bravest of the brave. Each of them distinguished himself with extraordinary valor, in the famous words, "at the risk of his life, above and beyond the call of duty." In the greatest struggle in human history they helped to lead the forces of freedom to victory. Their deeds remind us of the indomitable power of the human spirit. And they always will be remembered by men and women who cherish liberty.

Top: Grace Rivers Woodfork and her son, George Livingston, leave the White House with Ruben Rivers's Medal of Honor. They are being followed by two men who were instrumental in making this possible — E. G. McConnell and David J. Williams II. *Bottom:* After years of petitioning Congress, Anese Rivers Woodfork finally holds her brother's Medal of Honor at the Pentagon's Hall of Heroes induction ceremony (both photographs are by the author).

Top left: Staff Sergeant Ruben Rivers. *Top right:* 1st Lieutenant Charles L. Thomas. *Bottom left:* Private George Watson. *Bottom right:* 1st Lieutenant John R. Fox (courtesy Lou Varrone).

1st Lieutenant Vernon J. Baker.

As recipients of the Medal of Honor, their names join the roles of America's heroes, along with Sergeant York, Eddie Rickenbacker, Jimmy Doolittle, Audie Murphy, General Robert Foley, and Senator Bob Kerrey, and only some 3,400 Americans in the entire history of the United States.

For these men, heroism was a habit. Ruben Rivers of Oklahoma was awarded a Silver Star while fighting in France in late 1944. A week later he was terribly wounded when his tank hit a mine. Refusing an order to withdraw, Sergeant Rivers took command of another tank. He radioed in, "I see them. We'll fight them." And he kept on fighting until his second tank was hit and he was killed.

Edward Carter, the son of missionaries, was crossing an open field in Germany when he was wounded five times. But Staff Sergeant Carter continued to advance, and when eight of the enemy tried to capture him, he killed six, took two prisoner, and brought them back for interrogation. In the face of overwhelming danger, they never wavered.

As he led a task force in France, Lieutenant Charles Thomas was wounded by intense fire. While helping others to find cover, he was wounded again and again and again. But he refused evacuation until he had made sure that his forces could return fire effectively.

While scouting a forward position, Private First Class Willy James was pinned down for an hour. But he made his way back to his platoon, planned a counterattack, and volunteered to lead the assault, and then was killed going to the aid of his wounded platoon leader. They were selfless.

When Private George Watson's ship was attacked by enemy bombers, over and over and over again, he helped others to make it to life rafts so that they might live, until he himself was so exhausted, he was pulled down by the tow of the sinking ship.

When the enemy surged into a town in Italy and drove out our forces, Lieutenant John Fox volunteered to remain behind in an observation post. He directed defensive artillery fire, and eventually he insisted that artillery fire be aimed at his own position. He said, there are more of them than there are of us. The barrage he so bravely ordered killed him. And when our forces recovered the position, they found his riddled body among that of 100 German soldiers.

One of these heroes is here today. In an assault on a mountain stronghold in Italy, Lieutenant Vernon Baker wiped out three enemy machine gun nests, an observer post and a dugout. I must say that Mr. Baker has not quite abandoned doing the impossible. I learned before this ceremony that he is now 77 years young, but last year he got the better of a mountain lion that was stalking him. [Laughter] I was also very moved, as I'm sure many of you were, by the comments quoted in today's *Washington Post*, or last weekend, about Mr. Baker's creed in life. He was asked how he bore up under the lack of respect and dignity and honor after all these years. And he said, "Give respect before you expect it, treat people the way you want to be treated, remember the mission, set the example, keep going." Those are words for all of us.

When Vernon Baker's commanding officer first wrote his award recommendation, he observed that Lieutenant Baker "desperately wanted the men of his company to hold their ground, and was willing to sacrifice his own life in an effort to win our battle." That passage was never forwarded. When Ruben Rivers died, no award recommendation was made for the deeds we remember today. It was felt that the Silver Star he had already been given was reward enough for a black man.

But when victory was complete in World War II, our government made a pledge to correct cases in which Medals of Honor were deserved but not awarded. Today, America honors that pledge. ON BEHALF OF THE UNITED STATES CONGRESS, I AWARD THE MEDAL OF HONOR, OUR NATION'S HIGHEST MILITARY AWARD, TO VERNON BAKER; EDWARD CARTER, JR.; JOHN FOX; WILLY F. JAMES, JR.; RUBEN RIVERS; CHARLES THOMAS; AND GEORGE WATSON.

A soldier who receives the Medal of Honor usually needs no further description. But we must remember something else here today; these heroes distinguish themselves in another almost unique way. In the tradition of African Americans who have fought for our nation as far back as Bunker Hill, they were prepared to sacrifice everything for freedom even though freedom's fullness was denied to them.

We remember Edward Carter, who unsuccessfully requested combat duty for three years, because until 1944 African Americans were not allowed into action. When his request was finally granted it was at the cost of his sergeant's stripes, because an African American was not allowed to command white troops. Now those injustices are past.

Our military is among the most integrated institutions in America, a beacon to society, and among the most successful, for America is stronger than ever. In the service of General Colin Powell, General Benjamin Davis, General Chappie James, and countless other

The Medal of Honor (courtesy Department of Defense).

outstanding African Americans, we see the enormous strength that America's diversity has given us. The men we honor here today helped to make their historic progress possible. They were denied their nation's highest honor, but their deeds could not be denied, and they cleared the way to a better world.

Today, America is profoundly thankful for the patriotism and the nobility of these men, and for the example they set, which helped us to find the way to become a more just, more free nation. They helped America to become more worthy of them and more true to its ideals.

To the families of the recipients who are gone, may you take comfort in the honor that has finally been done to your loved ones. And may God embrace their souls. And God bless you, Vernon Baker, and God bless America. Commander, post the orders!

When the President placed the Medal of Honor around the neck of Vernon Baker, Baker had heavy tears in his eyes. At that moment I looked around and didn't

Top: Edward A. Carter III proudly displays his father's long-awaited Medal of Honor. *Bottom:* Valcencie James, widow of Willy F. James, Jr., accepts his long-awaited Medal of Honor from President Bill Clinton (both photographs are by the author).

see a dry eye in the East Room. With the orders posted and the Medals of Honor presented, the President continued: "I think it might be an appropriate way to close to say that when I gave Mr. Watson's medal to the Sergeant Major of the Army, he looked at it and smiled and he said, 'This is indicative of the type of soldiers we have today,' a group of people in our military, men and women, that really do reflect the vast and rich texture of our nation.

"As we adjourn, I would like to pay special respect to the other African Americans who are here who are now or have been in uniform, to the other Medal of Honor winners who are here, and to all of you who have worked so that this day might become a reality. And to all of you again, I say your nation thanks you and God bless you. Thank you."

Afterword

by Joseph E. Wilson, Sr.
First Sergeant, United States Army (Retired)

The United States Army has come a long way since its inception in 1775, making it the nation's senior service. Drifting on a memory, I recall being inside an American tank called the General Sherman. We, as tankers, knew it as the M-4A1, and a later model, the M-4A3-E8. Those of you who have never experienced combat in a Sherman tank, listen to this: The interior is painted a cold, non-color white, but what gets your attention immediately is the frigid atmosphere. It's cold, cold as a winter night on the Lincoln Sea. I think this is what my son had in mind with the working title to this book *Wrapped in Cold Steel*.

Later in the war two new tanks were issued to us: the M-24 light tank, the Chaffee and the M-26 medium tank, the General Pershing. These two new tanks introduced welcomed improvements, but the single improvement that pleased us all was that they had heaters.

Some leopards are chosen by nature to lose their spots and turn black in their mother's wombs. Why Mother Nature does this remains a mystery that can be explained by some. But what is not a mystery is the fact that a black panther is a source of intimidation, whether by hearing the words, seeing the beast, or knowing it is in the vicinity of your comfort zone. Realizing that the black panther is the most efficient and ferocious of the predators, the U.S. Army seized upon this principle during World War II and sent the 761st Medium Tank Battalion to fight and support white infantry units in the European Theater. This separate battalion fought with distinction, earning a reputation that lives today but is unknown to black youth who will be proud of their forebears once they learn of the 761st. To that end, this literary effort is dedicated to the memory of those brave black men who helped win the war by piercing enemy lines with the ferocity of a pouncing black panther.

"Come Out Fighting" was the call to battle that energized the 761st Tanker to a high-level of intensity that enabled him to perform in an above-average manner. Despite his heroism, he was denied his rightful place in history. It seems that if he was walking on water, they would say, "See, he can't swim."

Before coming to the 761st I was a member of the 2nd Gun Section, Battery C, 686th Field Artillery Battalion, and had not yet developed into a mature, job-sophisticated cannoneer. There were times when my mouth was agape as I watched older black artillery men perform their duties with an unimaginable sophistication in handling this 155 millimeter howitzer. This medium artillery piece threw a 95-pound explosive shell nine miles, and when it hit, white American infantrymen would jump and shout: "Fickle Charlie is adjusting!" Fickle was the code name for the 686th Field Artillery Battalion, and Charlie stood for Battery C, and its four guns. My section chief was a heavyset black man who answered to the name of Joe Willie, and when he told me to jump, my only response was: "How high, Sarge?" When I first heard this name, I assumed it was a sobriquet, but later I learned that he was so mean, his friends were afraid to give him a nickname. Joe Willie was his real name. He was from Oklahoma.

These were African American soldiers who did their utmost to accomplish their mission. They were dedicated and loyal despite the rigors imposed by white supremacy and segregation, which were more pronounced in those days. Today "Jim Crow" has taken on a subtlety designed to perpetuate its existence.

Looking back in history, we find many whites who swore that the races must be kept apart. Look at the late, great General George Smith Patton, Jr., who often said that the Negro soldier couldn't think fast enough to fight in armor. How ridiculous, especially for an educated man in a high leadership position. However, this deep-seated nescience was canceled prior to his untimely death in Room 101, 130th Station Hospital in Heidelberg, Germany, in 1945. Before he died, Patton recognized the 761st Tank Battalion in glowing terms. There were other generals who held the Negro back until they too were compelled to revise their thinking. What a waste of time and humanity.

Many of these generals were educated at the United States Military Academy at West Point, New York, an institution where racism was practiced as a matter of routine. I agonize over the treatment black cadets received at this institution. When I read of the abuse meted out to Cadet Henry O. Flipper, graduating class of 1877, my pain was similar but could never equal his. Later, other cadets suffered the same fate. There was Charles Young and others but the one who stands out in my lifetime is Lt. General (Retired) Benjamin O. Davis, Jr., U.S. Air Force, class of 1936. Cadet Davis, like black cadets before him, was given the silent treatment — no one spoke to him for four years. On Sundays, Cadet Davis was forced to go to each dinner table and ask permission to be seated. During the week he ate at a separate table using disposable plates and utensils. What inhumane treatment.

Despite living through this painful period, blacks had to fight for the right to

First Sergeant Joseph E. Wilson, Sr., Augsburg, Germany, 1969.

fight, and we fought without the accolades bestowed upon others, even though deserving such recognition. During World War II, not one African American was awarded the nation's highest medal for bravery, even though commanders submitted the proper and necessary recommendations.

World War II, the war that saved humanity from the greatest menace imaginable, found black America fully involved in our national effort. The 686th Field Artillery Battalion landed at Southampton, England, on a foggy morning in October, 1944. From there we embarked on trains and disembarked at Pontypool, Wales. Here we occupied Quonset huts on the Polo Grounds. During the day and often at night, we made ready for combat. Our off-duty hours were spent doing the same thing, but there was time for socializing with the citizens of Pontypool. In fraternizing, we were astounded to learn of some of the beliefs of these British subjects, such as: "Do you colored blokes have tails?"

It was January 19, 1945, early in the A.M., a day so dismal that the sun threatened to take the day off, the 686th loaded its weapons and equipment on amphibious vessels and set sail from Weymouth, England, for Le Havre, France, located on the opposite shore of the English Channel. From Le Harve, our battalion joined with other American units in a line of vehicles, a convoy stretching over the horizon.

During this introduction into the combat phase of the ground war, the shock that I believed would never happen to me happened. Two Stuka dive-bombers strafed our section of the column in the vicinity of Nancy, France. One of our men, Private Fingers, was killed. This casualty, one of ours, created an atmosphere of sadness and gloom that fell over us and hardened us to face the daily air attacks that followed.

I always thought that a dogfight referred to the snarling, biting entanglement of two canines. Later I learned of another definition listed in the lingo of fighter pilots. Combat artillery men sought protection in slit trenches while the infantry dug foxholes, which lowered the body below the surface of the ground while being strafed by German fighter planes such as the ME-262, the first jet fighter plane. I recall bullets from a strafing German plane striking the front edge of my slit trench, then the other edge without hitting me in the middle. Thanks and thanks again, Father God. While trying to find a level lower than the bottom of my slit trench, I noticed that the strafing had ceased but the sound of gunfire had not. Climbing out of our slit trenches we looked skyward and saw the source of the continued firing, American planes had arrived on the scene. Up to this point we had only seen P-47 Thunderbolts and P-38 Lightnings, but here was an American fighter plane that we were completely unfamiliar with. It was the P-51 Mustang, a new plane. We watched in spellbound fascination as a single P-51 knocked two German fighters out of the sky. The remaining Luftwaffe pilots fled in terror. While watching this deadly display of aerial combat, we were oblivious to the bullets falling to the ground around our feet. This, we learned, was the other definition of a dogfight.

Oftentimes, those with an anti–Jewish slant deny that the Holocaust ever happened. Well, Dachau unfolded before my eyes after our guns blew away the gates and permitted the infantry to enter this concentration camp. Here was one of Hitler's most notorious death factories where the extermination of human life was carried out in assembly-line fashion. During these days in combat, the American Red Cross would give each of us a small bar of chocolate, a bar of soap, and a four-pack of cigarettes. Not being much of smoker, I saved the Red Cross gifts and when we entered Dachau, the death camp, I had a barracks bag full of these goodies. We were so moved by what we saw that we began to hand out chocolate and cigarettes to these emaciated survivors until a sharp command filled the air: "Don't give them candy! It will kill them!" This was easily understood but we gave them cigarettes. Over the years I have been jolted back to the days of Dachau, which happens every time I see a thin Caucasian.

Getting back to the convoy, even though we had come under attack and suffered fatalities, we were not officially in combat — this I learned half a century later because of my son's research into this literary effort, but the 686th Field Artillery Battalion was a part of a vast armada that would bring death and suffering to the German Army, the force that would apply the coup de grâce.

In this area of France, the staging area camps set up were named after American cigarettes. Our camp was named "20 Grand," a cigarette that has gone the way of others like Old Gold, Wings, and a number of other brands. Cigarettes were part of the soldiering experience and some brands will forever be associated with World War II. (Lucky Strike adopted the slogan "Lucky Strike has gone to war" and changed its green package for the white uniform it still wears today.)

I can remember that after we crossed the English Channel, I was missing my gas mask. This disturbed me so much that my only concern was to find the bastard who stole my mask. My father was in Germany during World War I and it is common knowledge that poison gas was used as a weapon against them. The thought of going into combat without a mask terrified me so much that I strolled through an empty pyramidal tent and picked up a mask that belonged to someone else. I have confessed this sin and have been forgiven, but this transgression hung over my head, though my comrades and I agreed that a good soldier never loses in this man's Army. Days later, our battalion entered combat inflicting full-fledged devastation on the *Wehrmacht*.

What has the foregoing to do with the 761st Tank Battalion? Well, there were many other black fighting units that were ignored and are absent from recorded history. Why? Because they were manned by African Americans. There was the 92nd Infantry Division in Italy; the 93rd Infantry Division in Bougainville, South Pacific; there was the 349th Field Artillery Battalion — a sister battalion to the 686th; there was the 969th and the 999th Field Artillery Battalions; the 614th, the 679th Tank Destroyer Battalions; there was the 758th and the 784th Tank Battalions; and there were the volunteer infantry replacements. There were all kinds of Negro (as we were called then) combats units in the war, engineers, transportation units, quartermaster battalions. I could go on and on, but I am especially proud of the 99th Pursuit Squadron, commanded by Lt. Colonel Benjamin O. Davis, Jr. His father, B. O. Davis, Sr., was the first black to attain the rank of brigadier general in the U.S. Army. The 99th Pursuit Squadron became the 332nd Fighter Group when it added other squadrons, and their claim to fame is that they never lost a bomber while escorting American heavy bombers.

It was the fear of death that gave combat a special fascination to me. To listen to a man who says that death doesn't get his spellbound attention is to listen to a liar. This was pronounced as we made tactical moves in advancing on the enemy. Daily we would see dead German soldiers lying all around and in ditches along the road. This we took in stride but to see American infantrymen lying dead among them was quite another experience and we handled it badly. There were occasions when rigor mortis put on morbid and unnerving demonstrations. One that refuses to relinquish a spot in my memory is when we turned over the body of a lieutenant who had been killed as he crawled out of a ditch. His legs were frozen in a grotesque configuration.

I can remember my Battery taking up firing positions in an apple orchard, which provided concealment from the air. There were German dead lying all about, which was to be expected, but to see German women from nearby homes come out without fear, remove these corpses, and scowl at us as though we were the American infantrymen who killed them was unforgettable. Our feelings were soothed somewhat when darkness fell and these same females returned and offered us sex.

The war was rapidly approaching its end and the weather was the worst one could expect. Those days were complete misery, but the events of other days more than compensated, such as the food we combat soldiers ate. A-rations was the normal food prepared by our cooks, B-rations was a small can of meat or cheese with crackers that were the strongest form of bread that I have ever known. C-rations had a more favorable acceptance than B-rations. D-rations was a solid bar of dark chocolate that was difficult to bite or cut and if you ate too much of it, liquid consumed later would cause your stomach to swell to an uncomfortable degree. Because of our disgust with field rations, we would scrounge the villages for food. Top on our lists were live chickens, potatoes, and eggs. The feasts that followed were often interrupted by Stukas and ME-109s, who found many of us in one place, providing a tempting strafing target. Despite this, our morale remained high.

Army officers enjoyed a privilege that we enlisted men (peons) were denied. We watched with envy as officers enjoyed what is known Army-wide as: "Rank Has Its Privileges." This was a whiskey ration for each officer. "Alcohol and enlisted men don't mix and must be avoided" was the widespread belief, but it is common knowledge that the men will get alcohol, especially when it's available in the destroyed villages we passed through. One day when there was a lull, a long break in firing missions, I wandered off to a nearby house that had been destroyed by artillery fire. With my carbine slung over my right shoulder, I entered the basement of this house and received one of the greatest shocks of my life: four fully armed Germans, who surrendered to me. They could have killed me easily, but decided the hands-up posture was the wisest, a "Hobson's Choice."

Thinking back on this incident, I now understand why it turned out this way. In one of my mother's letters she told me not to worry about dying because as she put it: "You're not going to get killed, because I won't let God let you die." My mother was the prayingest woman I have ever known before and since.

The end of World War II approached ahead of schedule. The German Army was defeated, the Jews were freed, and the world celebrated. We in the field also celebrated by firing our weapons in the air, only to have eight men killed as these same bullets came crashing to the ground. What goes up must come down, gravity demands it.

So, my son, that is how I spent my days during World War II. Following the cessation of hostilities in Europe, the 686th Field Artillery Battalion sent many of its men to units that had to be brought up to full strength because of their missions. I became a tanker in Company B, 761st Tank Battalion, located in Siegsdorf, Germany, not far from the Bavarian city of Traunstein. Later I joined Headquarters Company in Teisendorf, Germany. From there I rotated to the States in March 1946.

Thanks for the privilege of telling my story, which gives vent to the pent-up emotions that have weighed heavily on my mind and shoulders all these years. I am elated to see that by accomplishing this rare literary task, you have helped all who peruse these words to face the future with a greater understanding of what really happened.

Requiem of the Buffalo Soldier

The battlefield may be different
The uniforms may have changed —
But one thing that's certain,
Our fight is still the same.

Your cavalry freed our people,
Your tanks and bombers helped end a war.
Vietnam taught us a lesson —
Pride and dignity is worth so much more.

Bravery and courage were the trademarks of,
A history left unwritten —
Of all the battles that were won, and all
The truths that were hidden.

But, we know you as our heroes,

Your sacrifices cannot be erased.
Although, the battlefront may be different,
Our fight is still the same.

Reprinted with permission from Debra Donald Goree — Daughter of former Sergeant Edward Donald, Co. B. 761st Tank Battalion.

Chapter Notes

Chapter 1

1. Department of Defense, 50th Anniversary of World War II Publication (1991–1995) referencing a letter dated November 17, 1942.
2. From the records of the Dorie Miller American Legion Post # 639, Department of California.
3. Quoted in the program for the 1977 Reunion of the 761st Tank Battalion & Allied Veterans Association.
4. Wilson, Dale E. *A Recipe for Failure*. 1993.
5. Reynolds, Clark G. *America at War: The Home Front*. 1990.
6. King, Celes III. Interview. January 1995.
7. Potter, Lou; Miles, Bill; and Rosenblum, Nina. *Liberators Fighting on Two Fronts*. 1992.
8. McConnell, E.G. Interview. May 26, 1994.
9. Garrido, Franklin S. Interview. September 14, 1994.
10. Navarre, Christopher P., Sr. Speech given at the Black History Month Reception. Fort Lewis, Washington. 1989.

Chapter 2

1. Simpson, William M. *A Tale Untold: The Alexandria, Louisiana Lee Street Riot*. 1994.
2. Ibid.
3. Williams, David J. II. Speech given at the MOH Conference in Los Angeles. February 27, 1994.
4. Ibid.
5. Anderson, L.Z. Interview. September 23, 1994.
6. Ibid.
7. Garrido, Franklin S. Interview. September 14, 1994.
8. Williams, David J. II. Speech given at the MOH Conference in Los Angeles. February 27, 1994.
9. Garrido, Franklin S. Interview. September 14, 1994.
10. Potter, Lou; Miles, Bill; and Rosenblum, Nina. *Liberators Fighting on Two Fronts*. 1992.
11. Ibid.

12. Ibid.

13. Garrido, Franklin S. Interview. September 14, 1994.

14. Terkel, Studs. *The Good War*. 1984.

15. Ibid.

16. Anderson, L.Z. Interview. September 23, 1994.

17. Ibid.

18. *Camp Claiborne News*. 1943.

19. Potter, Lou; Miles, Bill; and Rosenblum, Nina. *Liberators Fighting on Two Fronts*. 1992.

20. Bates, Paul L. Fort Hood 761st Tank Battalion Monument Banquet. February 11, 1994.

21. Armbruster, Bob. Western Maryland College. *Alumni Profile of Paul Bates (Class of 31)*. 1994.

22. Ibid.

23. Potter, Lou; Miles, Bill; and Rosenblum, Nina. *Liberators Fighting on Two Fronts*. 1992.

Chapter 3

1. Bates, Paul L. Speech given at the Fort Hood 761st Tank Battalion Monument Banquet. February 11, 1994.

2. Harrison, Ivan H. Interview. August 23, 1996.

3. Ibid.

4. Latimer, Philip W. Letter to the author. 1993.

5. Harrison, Ivan H. Interview. August 23, 1996.

6. Robinson, Jackie. "Jackie Tells Own Story." *Washington Post*. August 23, 1949.

7. Bates, Paul L. Speech given at the Fort Hood 761st Tank Battalion Monument Banquet. February 11, 1994.

8. Ibid.

9. Stone, Bob. Interview with Jackie Robinson. *Yank* Magazine. November 23, 1945.

Chapter 4

1. Anderson, Trezzvant W. *Come Out Fighting*. 1945.

2. *The Dallas Morning News*. July 17, 1994.

3. Anderson, Trezzvant W. *Come Out Fighting*. 1945.

4. Wilson, Joseph E., Sr. Letter to the author. 1993.

Chapter 5

1. McConnell, E.G. Interview. May 26, 1994.

2. Garrido, Franklin S. Interview. September 14, 1994.

3. Potter, Lou; Miles, Bill; and Rosenblum, Nina. *Liberators Fighting on Two Fronts*. 1992.

4. War Department. Bureau of Public Relations News Release. March 26, 1945.

5. Motley, Mary P. *The Invisible Soldier*. 1975.

6. Williams, David J. II. *Hit Hard*. 1983.

7. McConnell, E.G. Interview. May 26, 1994.

8. Blumensen, Martin. *The Patton Papers, Volume II*. 1945.

Chapter 6

1. Bates, Paul L. Speech given at the Fort Hood 761st Tank Battalion Monument Banquet. February 11, 1994.
2. Motley, Mary P. *The Invisible Soldier*. 1975.
3. McConnell, E.G. Interview. May 26, 1994.
4. Dade, Floyd, Jr. Letter to the author. April 6, 1994.
5. Motley, Mary P. *The Invisible Soldier*. 1975.
6. Anderson, Trezzvant W. *Come Out Fighting*. 1945.
7. General Order # 47. 26th Infantry Division. June 18, 1945.
8. Tyree, Harry K. Interview. June 1994.
9. McConnell, E.G. Interview. May 26, 1994.

Chapter 7

1. Anderson, Trezzvant W. *Come Out Fighting*. 1945.
2. Tyree, Harry K. Interview. June 1994.
3. Bates, Paul L. Speech given at the Fort Hood 761st Tank Battalion Monument Banquet. February 11, 1994.
4. Tyree, Harry K. Interview. June 1994.
5. Bates, Paul L. Speech given at the Fort Hood 761st Tank Battalion Monument Banquet. February 11, 1994.
6. Hill, Raleigh. Interview. January 19, 1998.
7. Anderson, Trezzvant W. *Come Out Fighting*. 1945.
8. Bates, Paul L. Speech given at the Fort Hood 761st Tank Battalion Monument Banquet. February 11, 1994.
9. Harrison, Ivan H. Interview. August 23, 1996.
10. War Department. Bureau of Public Relations News Release. March 26, 1945.
11. Anderson, Trezzvant W. *Come Out Fighting*. 1945.

Chapter 8

1. Stevens, Johnnie. Interview. July 4, 1994.
2. Mellenthin, F.W. von. *Panzer Battles*. 1956.
3. Stevens, Johnnie. Interview. July 4, 1994.

Chapter 9

1. Anderson, Trezzvant W. *Come Out Fighting*. 1945.
2. Crecy, Margaret. Interview. August 13, 1994.
3. Anderson, Trezzvant W. *Come Out Fighting*. 1945.
4. Stevens, Johnnie. Interview. July 4, 1994.
5. Tyree, Harry K. Interview. June 1994.
6. Latimer, Philip W. Letter to the author. 1996.
7. Williams, David J. II. *Hit Hard*. 1983.
8. Bates, Paul L. Letter to the author. March 4, 1994.
9. Terkel, Studs. *The Good War*. 1984.
10. Crecy, Margaret. Interview. August 13, 1994.

Chapter 10

1. Anderson, Trezzvant W. *Come Out Fighting*. 1945.
2. War Department. Bureau of Public Relations News release. March 26, 1945.
3. Williams, David J. II. Speech given at the MOH Conference. February 27, 1994.
4. Ibid.
5. Dade, Floyd, Jr. Letter to the author. April 6, 1994.
6. Williams, David J. II. Speech given at the MOH Conference. February 27, 1994.
7. Martindale, Rob. *The Tulsa World*. July 1993.
8. Williams, David J. II. Speech given at the MOH Conference. February 27, 1994.
9. Anderson, Trezzvant W. *Come Out Fighting*. 1945
10. Dade, Floyd, Jr. Letter to the author. April 6, 1994.
11. Williams, David J. II. Speech given at the MOH Conference. February 27, 1994.
12. Ibid.
13. Copy of letter provided by Anese Rivers Woodfork.
14. Woodfork, Anese Rivers. Speech given at the MOH Conference. February 27, 1994.
15. Williams, David J. II. *Hit Hard*. 1983.

Chapter 11

1. Anderson, Trezzvant W. *Come Out Fighting*. 1945.
2. McConnell, E.G. Interview. May 26, 1994.
3. Ibid.
4. Hopton, Leon. Interview. September 7, 1994.
5. McConnell, E.G. Interview. May 26, 1994.
6. Anderson, Trezzvant W. *Come Out Fighting*. 1945.
7. Terkel, Studs. *The Good War*. 1984.
8. Ibid.
9. McConnell, E.G. Interview. May 26, 1994.

Chapter 12

1. Potter, Lou; Miles, Bill; and Rosenblum, Nina. *Liberators Fighting on Two Fronts*. 1992.
2. Stevens, Johnnie. Interview. July 4, 1994.
3. Anderson, Trezzvant W. *Come Out Fighting*. 1945.
4. Ibid.

Chapter 13

1. Sulzberger, C.L. *The American Heritage Picture History of WWII*. 1966.
2. Lee, Ulysses. *The Employment of the Negro Troops*. 1966.
3. 87th Infantry Division Association. *Stalwart and Strong*. 1993.
4. Williams, David J. II. Speech given at the MOH Conference. February 27, 1994.
5. Potter, Lou; Miles, Bill; and Rosenblum, Nina. *Liberators Fighting on Two Fronts*. 1992.
6. Anderson, Trezzvant W. *Come Out Fighting*. 1945.

Chapter 14

    1. Anderson, Trezzvant W. *Come Out Fighting*. 1945.

    2. Ibid.

    3. Bates, Paul L. Fort Hood 761st Tank Battalion Monument Banquet. February 11, 1994.

    4. 87th Infantry Division Association. *Stalwart and Strong*. 1993.

    5. Anderson, Trezzvant W. *Come Out Fighting*. 1945.

Chapter 15

    1. Hagerman, Bart. *17th Airborne History*. 1986.

    2. Dade, Floyd, Jr. Letter to the author. April 6, 1994.

    3. Hagerman, Bart. *17th Airborne History*. 1986.

    4. Motley, Mary P. *The Invisible Soldier*. 1975.

    5. Hungerford, Lauren. Letter to the author. August 21, 1993.

    6. Hagerman, Bart. *17th Airborne History*. 1986.

    7. Hall, Floyd. *17th Airborne, The Bulge to the Rhine*. 1990.

    8. Hagerman, Bart. *17th Airborne History*. 1986.

    9. Latimer, Philip W. Letter from General W.M. Miley. June 7, 1981.

    10. Anderson, Trezzvant W. *Come Out Fighting*. 1945.

Chapter 16

    1. Wilson, Joseph E., Sr. Letter to the author. 1993.

    2. Dade, Floyd, Jr. Letter to the author. April 6, 1994.

    3. Navarre, Christopher P., Sr. Interview. September 24, 1996.

    4. Bates, Paul L. Fort Hood 761st Tank Battalion Monument Banquet. February 11, 1994

Chapter 17

    1. Mueller, R. & Turk, J. Report After Action. 103rd Infantry Division. 1945.

    2. Stevens, Johnnie. Interview. July 4, 1994.

    3. East, W. & Gleason, W. *The 409th Infantry in WWII*. 1986.

    4. Navarre, Christopher P., Sr. Interview. September 24, 1996.

    5. East, W. & Gleason, W. *The 409th Infantry in WWII*. 1986.

    6. 761st Tank Battalion. After Action report. March 1945.

    7. Bates, Paul L. Letter to the author. March 4, 1994.

    8. Latimer, Philip W. Letter to the author. 1993.

    9. Hill, Karen Scott. Letter from M/Sgt. Ernest D. Hill, Sr., to his wife Mrs. Hope Hill. 1945.

    10. Navarre, Christopher P., Sr. Interview. September 24, 1996.

    11. Anderson, Trezzvant W. *Come Out Fighting*. 1945.

Chapter 18

    1. Anderson, Trezzvant W. *Come Out Fighting*. 1945.

2. Dade, Floyd, Jr. Letter to the author. April 6, 1994.

3. McMahon, Gerald. *The Siegfried and Beyond.* 1993.

4. Terkel, Studs. *The Good War.* 1984.

Chapter 19

1. Anderson, Trezzvant W. *Come Out Fighting.* 1945.

2. Stevens, Johnnie. Interview. July 4, 1994.

3. Navarre, Christopher P., Sr. Interview. September 24, 1996.

4. Harrison, Ivan H. Interview. August 23, 1996.

5. Motely, Mary P. *The Invisible Soldier.* 1975.

6. McMahon, Gerald. *The Siegfried and Beyond.* 1993.

7. Jaehne, Willi H. Luftwaffe Flight Engineer 1944–1945. Interview. 1996.

8. Potter. Lou; Miles, Bill; and Rosenblum, Nina. *Liberators Fighting on Two Fronts.* 1992.

Chapter 20

1. Neuhausler, Johannes. *What Was It Like in the Concentration Camp of Dachau.* 1973.

2. Potter, Lou; Miles, Bill; and Rosenblum, Nina. *Liberators Fighting on Two Fronts.* 1992.

3. Ibid.

4. Neuhausler, Johannes. *What Was It Like in the Concentration Camp of Dachau.* 1973.

5. Potter, Lou; Miles, Bill; and Rosenblum, Nina. *Liberators Fighting on Two Fronts.* 1992.

6. Ibid.

7. McMahon, Gerald. *The Siegfried and Beyond.* 1993.

8. Motley, Mary P. *The Invisible Soldier.* 1975.

9. Finkelman, Wolf. *The Story of My Survival During The Holocaust.* 1995.

10. Potter, Lou; Miles, Bill; and Rosenblum, Nina. *Liberators Fighting on Two Fronts.* 1992.

11. Atkinson, Nicole. "A Black Woman's Experience in Hitler's Germany." 1996.

12. Navarre, Christopher P., Sr. Interview. September 24, 1996.

13. Finkelman, Wolf. *The Story of My Survival During the Holocaust.* 1995.

Chapter 21

1. Motley, Mary P. *The Invisible Soldier.* 1975.

2. Navarre, Christopher P., Sr. Interview. September 24, 1996.

3. Anderson, Trezzvant W. *Come Out Fighting.* 1945.

4. Stevens, Johnnie. Interview. July 4, 1994.

5. Harrison, Ivan H. Interview. August 23, 1996.

6. Tyree, Harry K. Interview. June 1994.

7. Anderson, Trezzvant W. *Come Out Fighting.* 1945.

8. Ibid.

Chapter 22

1. Hightower, Jefferson. Interview. August 25, 1996.
2. Shirey, Orville C. *Americans, the Story of the 442d Combat Team.* 1946.
3. Ibid.
4. Matheny, Michael R. *The History of the 64ᵗʰ Armored.* 761ˢᵗ Tank Battalion & Allied Veterans Association reunion program. 1983.

Chapter 23

1. Garrido, Franklin S. Interview. September 14, 1996.
2. Gallagher, Wes. Los Angeles Times. April 1945.
3. Ibid.
4. Lee, Ulysses P. *The Employment of Negro Troops.* 1966.
5. Garrido, Franklin S. Interview. September 14, 1994.
6. Ibid.
7. Ibid.
8. Ibid.
9. Ibid.

Chapter 24

1. Wilson, Joseph E.., Sr. Letter to the author. 1993.
2. Stevens, Johnnie. Interview. July 4, 1994.
3. Ibid.
4. Armbruster, Bob. Western Maryland College *Alumni Profile of Paul Bates (31).* 1994.
5. 761ˢᵗ Tank Battalion. Report of Operations. 1945.
6. Stevens, Johnnie. Interview. July 4, 1994.
7. Terkel, Studs. *The Good War.* 1984.
8. Robinson, Jackie. "Jackie Tells Own Story." *Washington Post.* August 26, 1949.
9. Ibid.
10. Jaehne, Willi H. Luftwaffe Flight Engineer 1944–1945. Interview. 1996.
11. Crecy, Margaret M. Speech given at the MOH Conference. February 27, 1994.
12. Ibid.

Chapter 25

1. Harrison, Ivan H. Interview. August 23, 1996.
2. White House Central File. Jimmy Carter Presidential Library.
3. Ibid.
4. Anderson, Trezzvant W. *Come Out Fighting.* 1945.
5. White House Central File. Jimmy Carter Presidential Library.
6. Potter, Lou; Miles, Bill; and Rosenblum, Nina. *Liberators Fighting on Two Fronts.* 1992.
7. White House Central File. Jimmy Carter Presidential Library.
8. Ibid.

9. Marshall, S.L.A. *The Pacific Stars and Stripes*. January 27, 1978.
10. White House Central File. Jimmy Carter Presidential Library.
11. Ibid.
12. Marshall, S.L.A. *The Pacific Stars and Stripes*. January 27, 1978.
13. White House Central File. Jimmy Carter Presidential Library.

Chapter 26

1. Williams, David J. II. Speech given at the MOH Conference. February 27, 1994.
2. Clark, John. *The Temple Daily Telegram*. October 15, 1994.
3. Hutto, Elke. *The Killeen Daily Herald*. October 15, 1994.
4. Ibid.
5. Harrison, Ivan H. Interview. August 23, 1996.
6. Villaronga, Raul G. Letter to Philip W. Latimer. February 6, 1994.
7. *The Daily Breeze*. March 1993.
8. Jewish War Veterans of the USA. Adopted Resolutions. 1994.
9. The Assciated Press. April 28, 1996.
10. Ibid.
11. Carter Family Archives.
12. Carter, Edward A. III. Interview with the family of the late Edward A. Carter, Jr. June 15, 1996.
13. Galloway, Joseph. "Military Injustice." *U.S. News and World Report*. May 6, 1996.
14. Ibid.
15. Lee, Ulysses P. *The Employment of Negro Troops*. 1966.
16. Galloway, Joseph. "Military Injustice." *U.S. News and World Report*. May 6, 1996.
17. Ibid.
18. Converse, Gibran, Cash, Griffith, and Koln. *The Exclusion of Black Soldiers from the Medal of Honor in WWII*. 1997.
19. Varrone, Lou. *The Static Line*. December 1996
20. 761st Tank Battalion & Allied Veterans Association. Reunion Program. 1996.
21. Latimer, Philip W. Speech given at the street naming ceremony in Killeen, Texas. August 22, 1996.
22. Hamm, Kenneth. Poem sent to Philip W. Latimer. 1996.
23. Hutto, Elke. *The Killeen Daily Herald*. October 15, 1994.
24. Short, Larry & Stevens, Grace. *BRAVO Veterans Outlook* Volume XIII. 1997.

Bibliography

Armbruster, Bob. Western Maryland College Alumni Profile of Paul Bates, Westminster, MD. (31), 1994.

Anderson, L.Z. Interview by telephone from San Francisco, September 23, 1994.

Anderson, Trezzvant W. *Come Out Fighting*. Salzburger Druckerei und Verlag, 1945.

Ashby, Charles P. Interview in New York, N.Y., May 10, 1994.

Atkinson, Nicole. "A Black Woman's Experience in Hitler's Germany." From *The Archives*. The African-American Museum and Library, Oakland, Calif., Fall 1995/Winter 1996.

Bates, Paul L. 761st Tank Bn. Monument Banquet. Fort Hood, Texas, February 11, 1994.

_____. Letter to the author, March 4, 1994.

Baxter, Marion M. *The Chicago Sun*, 1945.

Berder, Roger James, and Warren W. Odegard. *Uniforms, Organization and History of the Panzertruppe*, Calif: Bender, 1980.

Bernstein, Richard. "Comrades and Family Fighting to Honor a Hero." *The New York Times*, March 28, 1993.

Blumensen, Martin. *The Patton Papers, Vol. II*, page 567. U.S. Army Military History Institute, Carlisle Barracks, Pa., 1945.

Bracy, Homer A. Affidavit provided to Congressman James Inhofe, June 20, 1990.

BRAVO, Brotherhood Rally of All Veterans Organization. *BRAVO Veterans Outlook*, April/May 1994.

_____. *BRAVO Veterans Outlook*, Vol. XIII, 1997.

Brisbane, Thomas. Interview in New York, May 10, 1994.

Burke, Yvonne Brathwaite. Letters to the author, July 6, 1993 and August 21, 1995.

Camp Claiborne News. 1943: U.S. Army Military History Institute Library, Carlisle Barracks, Pa.

Carruthers, Robert, and Chris Campbell. *The History of the 64th Armored Regiment*. Fort Stewart, Georgia, 64th/758th Armored Association, 1992.

Carter, Edward A. III. Interview with family of the late Sergeant First Class Edward A. Carter, Jr., June 15, 1996.

Citation for the Bronze Star Awarded to Franklin Garrido. General Order #27, H.Q. 35th Inf. Div., April 21, 1945.

Clark, John. The *Temple Daily Telegram*, October 15, 1994.

Colbert, Osborne. Interview. Inglewood, Calif., September 15, 1995.

Converse, Elliot V. III, Daniel K. Gibran, John A. Cash, Robert K. Griffith, Jr., and Richard H. Kohn. *The Exclusion of Black Soldiers from the Medal of Honor in World War II*. Jefferson, N.C.: McFarland, 1997.

Crecy, Margaret. MOH Conference Dinner, Inglewood, Calif., February 25, 1994.
_____. Interview in Valejo, Calif., August 13, 1994.
Cywinska, Janina. *The New Yorker*, November 1991.
Dade, Floyd, Jr. Letter to the author. San Francisco, April 6, 1994.
Daily Breeze newspaper. Article by Mark W. Wright regarding the MOH, March 1993.
Department of Defense. Military Awards Branch. Letter from Lt. Col. Patricia Sigle to the JWV, July 11, 1994.
_____. 50th Anniversary of WWII Commemoration Booklet.
Dorie Miller Post 639 of the American Legion. Annual Dorie Miller Pearl Harbor Day Dinner Dance Program, December 6, 1973.
Donald, Ed. Letter to the author. Oak Park, Mich., December 20, 1994.
East, William, and William Gleason. *The 409th Infantry in World War II*. Nashville, Tenn.: The Battery Press, 1986.
82nd Airborne Division Association. Information Sheet. Date Unknown.
87th Infantry Division Association. *Stalwart and Strong: The Story of the 87th Infantry Division*. Flourtown, Pa., 1993.
Finkelman, Wolf. Letter to the author. Houston, October 23, 1995.
The 555th Parachute Infantry Association. *50th Anniversary Commemorative Book*. Vol. I. Columbus, Ga., 1994.
Gallagher, Wes. "Negro Tank Battalion Fights Miniature Bastogne All Alone." *Los Angeles Times*, April 1945.
Galloway, Joseph. "Military Injustice." *U.S. News & World Report*, May 6, 1996.
Garrido, Franklin. Interview in Los Angeles, September 14, 1994.
Gibran, Daniel. Shaw University/Department of Defense. Letter to the author, November 23, 1993.
_____. Shaw University/Department of Defense. Executive Summary. *Justice Delayed*, 1996.
Inhofe, James. House Resolution #4976, June 6, 1990.
Jaehne, Willi Horst. Luftwaffe Engineer 1944-1945. Interviews in Inglewood, Calif., 1996.
Jewish War Veterans of the USA. Letters to the author, June 20 and July 20, 1994.
H.Q. 71st Infantry Division. G-2 Period Report, May 5-6, 1945.
Hagerman, Bart. *17th Airborne History*. Paducah, Ky.: Turner, 1986.
Hall, Floyd. *17th Airborne, The Bulge to the Rhine*. Plymouth, Minn.: Kenwood Productions, 1990.
Harrison, Ivan H. Interview in Killeen, Texas, August 23, 1996.
Hideo, Nakamine. 522nd F.A. Bn. Dachau Research Committee, May 16, 1986.
Hightower, Jefferson. Interview in Killeen, Texas, August 25, 1996.
Hill, Ernest, Sr. Letter to his wife, Mrs. Hope Hill. Chicago, 1945.
Hill, Raleigh. Interview, January 19, 1998.
Hirshberg, Charles, Lucy Schulte, and Rafael Yglesias. "Pear Harbor Collectors Edition." *Life* magazine, Fall 1991.
Holmes, Johnny. *The Dallas Morning News*, July 17, 1994.
Hopton, Leon. Interview by telephone from Fresno, Calif., September 7, 1994.
Hungerford, Lauren. Letter to the author, August 21, 1993.
Hutto, Elke. *The Killeen Daily Herald*, October 15, 1994, and August 23, 1996.
King, Celes III, Brig. Gen., SMR. Interview in Los Angeles, January 1995.
Landwehr, Richard. *Pregarten Massacre Update*. Brookings, OR Siegrunen, 1993.
Latimer, Philip W. Letters to the author 1993–1998.
Lee, Ulysses P. *The Employment of Negro Troops*. Washington, D.C., Center of Military History, United States Army, 1966.
Lindsay, Ana. *Inside the Turret* newspaper. Fort Hood, Texas, 1993.

Laughridge, Paul R. "At War, Home and Abroad." *Observer Dispatch*, December 16, 1994.

Los Angeles Sentinel, May 16, 1996.

Los Angeles Times. April 28, 1996, article regarding the MOH from the Associated Press.

Magagnini, Stephen. *The Sacramento Bee*, September 11, 1994.

Marshall, S.L.A. "Gallant Black Unit Finally Wins Citation." San Francisco. *The Pacific Stars and Stripes*, April 27, 1978.

Martindale, Rob. "Black Tank Veterans Fighting Battle to Get Medal for Buddy." Tulsa, Ok., *The Tulsa World*, July 1993.

McBurney, William. Interview in New York, May 11, 1994.

McConnell, E.G. Interview in New York, May 26, 1994.

McDonald, Charles B. *A Time for Trumpets*. New York: William Morrow, 1985.

McMahon, Gerald. *The Siegfried and Beyond*. Cleveland. The 71st Infantry Division Association, 1993.

Mellenthin, F.W. von. *Panzer Battles: The Classic German Account of Tank Warfare in World War II*. New York, Ballantine Books, 1956.

Miley, William M. Letter to Philip W. Latimer, June 7, 1981.

Miller, George. House Resolution #1681, April 2, 1993.

Mitcham, Samuel W., Jr. *Hitler's Legions: The German Army Order of Battle, World War II*, 1985.

Morrison, Allan. "Negro Tankers Cut Path for Third Army." New York, *The Stars and Stripes*, November 27, 1944.

Motley, Mary Penick. *The Invisible Soldier*. Detroit: Wayne State University Press, 1975.

Mueller, Ralph, and Jerry Turk. *Report After Action: The Story of the 103rd Infantry Division*. Innsbruck, Austria: Wagner'sche Universitats-Buchdruckerei, 1945.

Navarre, Christopher P. Black History Month Reception. Fort Lewis, Wash., February 14, 1989.

_____. Interview by telephone from Dupont, Wash., September 24, 1996.

Neuhausler, Johannes. *What Was It Like in the Concentration Camp of Dachau*. Munich: Manz A.G., 1973.

Norcio, Tom. Fort MacArthur Military Museum, San Pedro, Calif. Letter to the author, 1993.

Patton, George S., Jr. *War As I Knew It*. Boston: Houghton Mifflin, 1947.

Pisar, Samuel. *Blood and Hope*. New York: Macmillan, 1982.

Potter, Lou, Bill Miles and Nina Rosenblum. *Liberators Fighting on Two Fronts in World War II*. Orlando, Fla.: Harcourt Brace Jovanovich, 1992.

Powell, Casey A. *Encyclopedia of Forts, Posts, Named Camps, and Other Military Installations in Louisiana, 1700-1981*. Baton Rouge: Claitor's Publishing, 1981.

Powell, Colin L. Letter to the author, July 9, 1993.

Reynolds, Clark G. *America at War: The Home Front*. New York: Gallery Books, 1990.

761st Tank Battalion. *After Action Report of Operations, 1944, 1945 and 1946*. Record Group 407, ARBN-761-0.3. National Archives, Suitland Records Branch, Suitland, Md.

_____ and Allied Veterans Association. Reunion Program. Los Angeles, 1977.

_____. _____. Killeen, Texas, 1996.

Shirer, William L. *The Rise and Fall of the Third Reich*. London: Mandarin Paperbacks, 1991.

Shirey, Orville C. *Americans: The Story of the 442d Combat Team*. Washington, D.C.: Infantry Journal Press, 1946.

Sickinger, Ted. *The Kansas City Star*, April 28, 1996.

Simpson, William A. "A Tale Untold, The Alexandria, La., Lee Street Riot of Jan. 10, 1942." *Louisiana History*, Spring 1994.

Stern, Kenneth G. *Liberators, A Background Report*, February 10, 1993.

Stevens, Johnnie. Interview in Carteret, N.J., July 4, 1994.

Sulzberger, C.L. *The American Heritage Picture History of World War II*. American Heritage Pub. Co., 1966.

Susuki, Takeo, and Mark. 100th/442nd Veterans Association. Interview, Los Angeles, 1994.

Terkel, Studs. *The Good War: An Oral History of World War II*. New York: Ballantine, 1984.

Tyree, Harry K. Interview by telephone from Knoxville, Tenn., June 1994.

United States War Department. Bureau of Public Relations. News Release, March 26, 1945.

Varrone. Lou. *The Static Line*, December, 1996.

Villaronga, Raul G. Letter to Philip W. Latimer, February 6, 1994.

Walker, Kenneth G. "World War II Buffalo Soldiers of 761st Win Again." Washington, D.C., *Washington Star*, January 26, 1978.

Weston, Theodore. Affidavit provided to Congressman James Inhofe, June 20, 1990.

White House. Medal of Honor Program, January 13, 1997.

White House Central File (Gates, C.; Medals and Awards; and "Sev."), Atlanta. The Jimmy Carter Presidential Library.

Wilkerson, Lawrence B. Special Aid to General Powell. Letter to the author, September 2, 1993.

Williams, David J., II. Affidavit provided to Congressman James Inhofe, June 20, 1990.

_____. *Hit Hard*. New York: Bantam Books, 1983.

_____. Interview in Killeen, Texas, August 23, 1996.

_____. MOH Conference in Los Angeles, February 27, 1994.

Wilson, Dale E. "A Time to Live; A Time to Die: The Sad Saga of Staff Sergeant Ruben Rivers." Washington, D.C., *Negro History Bulletin*, Volumes 51–57, December 1993.

Wilson, Dale E. *A Recipe for Failure*. Movato, Calif.: Presidio Press, 1993.

Wilson, Joseph E., Sr. Letter to the author, 1993.

Woodfork, Anese Rivers. MOH Conference in Los Angeles, February 27, 1994.

Index